Rebellious Bodies

Rebellious Bodies

STARDOM, CITIZENSHIP,
AND THE NEW BODY POLITICS

Russell Meeuf

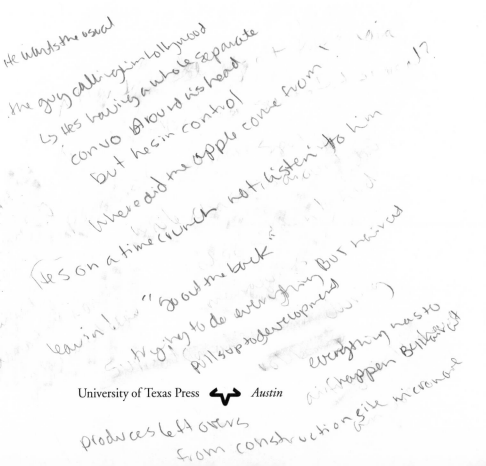

University of Texas Press   *Austin*

Requests for permission to reproduce material from this
work should be sent to:
    Permissions
    University of Texas Press
    P.O. Box 7819
    Austin, TX 78713-7819
    http://utpress.utexas.edu/index.php/rp-form

♾ The paper used in this book meets the minimum requirements of
ANSI/NISO Z39.48-1992 (R1997) (Permanence of Paper).

LIBRARY OF CONGRESS CATALOGING-IN-PUBLICATION DATA
Names: Meeuf, Russell, 1981– author.
Title: Rebellious bodies : stardom, citizenship, and the new body politics /
Russell Meeuf.
Description: First edition. | Austin : University of Texas Press, 2017. |
Includes bibliographical references and index.
Identifiers: LCCN 2016027781| ISBN 978-1-4773-1180-6 (cloth : alk. paper) |
ISBN 978-1-4773-1181-3 (pbk. : alk. paper) | ISBN 978-1-4773-1182-0
(library e-book) | ISBN 978-1-4773-1183-7 (nonlibrary e-book)
Subjects: LCSH: Human body in popular culture. | Human body—Social
aspects. | Human body in mass media. | Body image in motion pictures. |
Celebrities in mass media. | Mass media and race relations—United States. |
Identity (Psychology)
Classification: LCC HM636 .M44 2017 | DDC 155.2—dc23
LC record available at https://lccn.loc.gov/2016027781

doi:10.7560/311806

Contents

Acknowledgments

THIS PROJECT IS INSPIRED BY WHAT I HAVE BEEN IN-
formally calling "the bodies books," a series of groundbreaking
books exploring the relationship between stardom, bodies, and cultural politics, namely Richard Dyer's *Heavenly Bodies* (1986), Yvonne Tasker's *Spectacular Bodies* (1993), and Chris Holmlund's *Impossible Bodies* (2002). This list also
includes several other books exploring bodies and culture more generally,
such as Rosemarie Garland-Thomson's *Extraordinary Bodies* (1997), Kathleen
LeBesco's *Revolting Bodies?* (2003), and Niall Richardson's *Transgressive Bodies*
(2010). By echoing these titles in the title of my own work, I hope to acknowledge how foundational this work has been to my own thinking about bodies,
citizenship, and stardom today.

In writing *Rebellious Bodies*, I am also deeply indebted to the work of my
friend, teacher, and mentor Kathleen Rowe Karlyn, whose insights into gender and popular culture—as well as her engaging prose—I can only aspire
to. Kathleen's work on unruly women informs much of my thinking on stardom and culture, and she provided very useful feedback as this manuscript
took shape.

Portions of chapter 1 appeared as "Class, Corpulence, and Neoliberal Citizenship: Melissa McCarthy on *Saturday Night Live*" in *Celebrity Studies* in
2015, and portions of chapter 3 appeared as "The Nonnormative Celebrity
Body and the Meritocracy of the Star System: Constructing Peter Dinklage
in Entertainment Journalism" in the *Journal of Communication Inquiry* in
2014. Thanks to the anonymous reviewers at those journals for their feedback
at the early stages of this project. I also presented a version of chapter 3 at the
annual conference for the Association for Education in Journalism and Mass
Communications in San Francisco in 2015 and then again at the Malcolm
Renfrew Interdisciplinary Colloquium at the University of Idaho that same

year. Thanks to all those who listened to my presentations and asked good questions about this project.

This book provided an opportunity to explore a number of issues that I don't often write about, from research on the "obesity epidemic" to contemporary race relations to issues of transgender identity. As a cis-gendered, straight, thin (for now), relatively young (for now), able-bodied (for now) white man, I owe a deep gratitude to the scholars who helped me learn more about the key debates in a variety of different fields, both those who I cite in this book and those who helped review my work. Thanks to all my friends and colleagues who have contributed in this way and provided helpful feedback, especially Pat Hart, Becky Tallent, Anna Cooper, Carter Soles, Sarah Cribbs, and Lori Celaya. Additionally, I'd like to thank my circle of friends and colleagues who have patiently listened to me explain my research, asked good questions, and prodded me along the way: Ben James, Erin James, Jenn Ladino, Doug Heckman, Jon Hegglund, Rochelle Smith, Maggie Rehm, Justin Barnes, Kenton Bird, and Annie Petersen. And a big thanks to Jim at the University of Texas Press for seeing me through another project.

Additional thanks go to Alden, Will, and Fern for keeping me grounded and reminding me why creating a future based on justice and inclusion matters.

Finally, I couldn't have done this without the most amazing partner in the world, Ryanne Pilgeram, who provided emotional, logistical, and intellectual support at every stage in this venture. Getting to share my life and my work with you is a tremendous privilege, and I literally couldn't be the scholar I am without you.

Rebellious Bodies

His argument:

rebellious bodies challenge the cultural centrality
of white, able-bodied, heteronormative masculinity
BUT: these challenges are part of a cycle of crisis +
redemption — cultural center reaffirms its privileged
position by graciously redrawing boundaries of inclusion

Introduction

STAR BODIES AND THE POLITICS OF INCLUSION

In JANUARY 2014, THE POPULAR FEMINIST WEBSITE JEZE- *bel* offered a $10,000 reward for unretouched images from Lena Dunham's photo shoot with Annie Leibovitz, the altered versions of which were then appearing in the current issue of *Vogue*. *Jezebel* had long crusaded against fashion magazines and their representation of unrealistic female bodies, especially the practice of "Photoshopping" models and celebrities into monstrously unreal proportions. But the website was gearing up to make the Dunham shoot and the bounty for those "real" images the main event in its campaign for realistic women's bodies in the media, primarily because Dunham is often held up as a challenger to unrealistic body norms. According to *Jezebel*'s editor, Jessica Coen, "Lena Dunham is a woman who trumpets body positivity, who's unabashedly feminist, who has said that her naked body is 'a realistic expression of what it's like to be alive' and 'if you are not into me, that's your problem.'"[1] When someone claimed the bounty and *Jezebel* published the images, however, they revealed fairly limited retouching, although that did not keep the site from touting the "real" images as a victory for body type diversity.[2] And then Dunham herself criticized the site's antagonistic exposé—perhaps *Jezebel* should have applauded *Vogue* for putting Dunham in the magazine in the first place, she suggested.[3]

The back-and-forth debate surrounding *Jezebel*'s antics helped cement Lena Dunham's place in the culture as a prominent example of progressive, feminist body politics in mainstream media, but one whose meanings are still up for debate. With the success of her HBO series *Girls* (2012–), which focuses on the personal and professional struggles of a group of twenty-something women in New York (with a frank and unromanticized emphasis on their sexual exploits), Dunham has become a celebrity as much for the show itself (which she writes, directs, and stars in) as for being an out-

Remember this?

spoken, hip feminist icon. Affirming this status, Dunham told crowds at the SXSW festival that Hollywood has to change the way it casts and represents women with only a few character types and that she plans to work tirelessly to help enact that change.[4] She is also known for her willingness to display her naked body even though it deviates from Hollywood beauty norms, offering a prominent example for feminist body-acceptance discourses. Meanwhile, *Jezebel* (despite the recent tension) celebrated Dunham's 2014 gig hosting *Saturday Night Live* as a "feminist extravaganza."[5]

Dunham's stardom puts her squarely in the middle of cultural debates about women, feminism, and media representations, but as the *Vogue* incident suggests, it is her body that serves as the focal point for these debates. Is Dunham's body an "authentic" representation of average women, free from the manipulation of patriarchal mass media? Does her body pose a radical challenge to the kinds of bodies that US entertainment has allowed in the past, or does she glorify an unhealthy disregard for appearance and health, as the late Joan Rivers suggested by saying that Dunham's message to women is "Stay fat. Get diabetes"?[6] Does her insistent nudity break barriers for body-type diversity in the media, or is she just a narcissistic, postfeminist hipster who, like the character she plays, makes irresponsible sexual decisions?[7] Right-wing commentators have long despised Dunham's openly feminist politics—she has campaigned publicly for Planned Parenthood, after all— but their critiques mostly take the form of body shaming, as was the case in May 2015 when Dunham posted a revealing picture of herself on Instagram. In response to the photo, which shows her in lingerie, the hyperconservative pundits at Breitbart had a hysterical conniption, warning that the sight of the scantily clad Dunham would cause "emotional, spiritual, or psychological damage."[8] More than anything else, the meanings of Lena Dunham and her status as a cultural crusader hinge on how we interpret the shapes and contours of her body.

She is not alone in this regard. Dunham is part of a wave of celebrities since the year 2000 whose bodies challenge Hollywood beauty standards and cultural body norms in one way or another. Held up as examples of a new and seemingly more diverse entertainment industry, these stars provide assurances that the US media really are adapting to a changing culture, even if the images of these stars' bodies are still subject to intense shaming. A spate of performers seems to illustrate a shifting reality in stardom and celebrity culture in which one can become a star in spite of (or even because of) a body that deviates from social norms of beauty and health. From larger women such as Rebel Wilson, Amy Schumer, or Aidy Bryant who have found success in Hollywood despite an obsession with thinness, to women of color such as Mindy Kaling or Viola Davis whose weight or skin tone challenges

Hollywood's fetish for thin, ambiguously ethnic women, to performers with disabilities such as *Breaking Bad*'s R. J. Mitte or *Glee*'s Lauren Potter who are earning more nuanced roles than have ever been offered in US pop culture, the entertainment media are riddled with feel-good stories about the new opportunities for folks who would never have been stars in the past.

This book singles out six such examples that particularly exemplify the new body politics: Melissa McCarthy, the overweight comedian who starred in *Bridesmaids* and the CBS sitcom *Mike and Molly*; Gabourey Sidibe, the overweight African American actress who won rave reviews in *Precious* and starred in the third season of *American Horror Story*; Peter Dinklage, the dwarf actor who is currently a fan favorite in the HBO series *Game of Thrones*; Danny Trejo, who spent years playing muscled and grim-looking bad guys in action movies but has become a leading man with the immigration-themed *Machete* films; Betty White, a longtime TV star who has rejuvenated her career late in life with films such as *The Proposal* and her role on the TVLand sitcom *Hot in Cleveland*; and Laverne Cox, the transgender actress who is part of the ensemble cast of *Orange Is the New Black*. After decades of debate and discussion about diversity and inclusion in the media, the success of stars such as these hints at a new kind of body politics that makes space for a greater variety of bodies.

As the lingering tensions over the meanings of Lena Dunham's body suggest, however, the new body politics tell a complex story about what diversity means in the contemporary United States. The entertainment industry would like to promote stars like these as examples of its inherent meritocracy and inclusivity, to advance its narrative that talented performers will rise to prominence through hard work and individual merit despite their deviation from cultural norms. But stars with non-normative bodies actually provide far more complex narratives about individualism and diversity. Far from simply affirming the importance of inclusion in the entertainment media, each of these celebrity bodies acts as a site of contestation for the most pressing social issues of our day, including obesity, race, poverty, disability, immigration, aging, and gender identity. These celebrities resonate in contemporary culture because their bodies bear the burdens of our cultural anxieties, creating often-contradictory cultural spaces where ideas about inclusion, inequality, and cultural change clash with one another. Lena Dunham's celebrity, for example, has helped make room for progressive, feminist discourses about women and media representations, but the debates about how we interpret her body (is it a feminist challenge or a health risk; that of an "authentic" woman or an out-of-control, privileged brat?) make her body a place where the culture's anxieties about feminism, sex, and class can be processed.

This book argues that stars with non-normative bodies create powerful

This is main argument

challenges to the cultural centrality of white, able-bodied, heteronormative masculinity. These challenges, however, are part of a constant cycle of crisis and redemption in which the cultural center reaffirms its privileged position by magnanimously redrawing the boundaries of inclusion. The increasing presence of non-normative bodies in media content and public discourse, after all, draws both non-normative *and* normative bodies into debates about privilege and inclusion. At stake are not just the stigmas facing those who deviate from cultural body norms but also a crisis about the rigidity of those norms, about people with privilege refusing to change with the times. In other words, crises about inclusion often tell us much more about those with power and the accommodations they are willing to make than about those who would be included.

The crises posed by stars with non-normative bodies, then, draw *everyone* into a model of identity based on relentless self-transformation. In a postmodern, neoliberal era in which identity has become yoked to constant self-improvement, the inclusion of different bodies into the cultural fabric requires a public reassurance that those with such bodies are constantly working to be better citizens and consumers, if not through physical change then through disciplining attitudes, behaviors, fashions, etc. At the same time, the inclusion of non-normative bodies by mainstream media provides evidence that the cultural center can be flexible and self-transformative, rejuvenating normative identities through assurances that challenges to the center can be accommodated.

As some of the most public and visible challengers to shifting body norms, stars with non-normative bodies function as both the source of cultural crises and the solution to them, as their inclusion in the entertainment media proves how flexible and adaptable cultural privilege can be in changing times. Such gestures of inclusion signify an adapting but still dominant cultural norm: the presence of non-normative bodies is necessary to create a cultural crisis that can be resolved by the center's own tolerance of the margin.[9]

As this suggests, at stake for both those who are included and those who do the including is the idea of citizenship in a changing, more diverse world. As the mantra of diversity expands the number of populations that would seek not just inclusion but full, cultural citizenship,[10] what are the values that bind together those who have held privilege and power and those whose bodies have marked them as outsiders, as deviants, and as problems for the civic order? What are the dominant narratives, images, and discourses that can turn non-normative bodies into sites of appropriate citizenship? And how does this accommodation of difference help rejuvenate the citizenship of those with cultural power?

These questions of full cultural citizenship have only become more com-

[handwritten margin notes at top: neoliberalism: system of gov. that shrunk the welfare state + instead there is an emphasis on the free market - obsession w/ individualism / focus on individual responsibility + marketing yourself as a product]

plicated in the world of neoliberal economic policy. In contrast to the liberal nation-state that supports its citizens through social welfare programs, neoliberalism has encouraged the shifting of responsibility away from government programs and toward individuals acting on the free market. Promoting privatization over state control, neoliberalism has impacted a variety of programs and institutions central to economic mobility, from the slashing of welfare programs to the rolling back of consumer protection regulations.[11] These changes all align with a neoliberal worldview that places the costs and responsibility for community services such as education on citizen-consumers, helping spur economic stratification.

[handwritten margin note: Citizenship & consumerism]

The very concept of citizenship, then, has become fraught and controversial in a world of neoliberal policy. The transition to individual responsibility on the free market in theory should make the concept of citizenship outmoded, a relic of liberal nation-states as they systematize who is eligible for state support and benefits (rather than simply allowing individuals to participate in the free market). As the liberal nation-state slowly erodes in a world of neoliberal privatization, however, questions of citizenship and cultural belonging have intensified in the United States and abroad. If neoliberal citizenship can be practiced through consumption (or exploitation) on the free market rather than being defined by the state, then what are the new boundaries of national identity and cultural belonging? What "others" are acceptable to the fabric of a multicultural neoliberalism and what "other-others" (to use Sarah Ahmed's terminology)[12] must be excluded from cultural citizenship? Or, as Elizabeth Povinelli puts it, what "new justifications for belonging and abandonment" emerged in an era of neoliberalism?[13] What bodies are marked as dangerous threats to the economy and society, and what bodies are acceptable as participants in "free" exchange?[14]

According to Jennifer Wingard, these boundaries are policed not simply through economics and politics but through emotional rhetoric that "brands" certain kinds of bodies as "cautionary tales of what to avoid, whom to fear, and who is outside the norm of citizenship."[15] The images and narratives surrounding such bodies (for example, those of immigrants or gays and lesbians) function much like the branded objects of consumer capitalism as they are circulated around the culture, crystallizing the meanings of these bodies into a discrete set of emotions and affective associations that help obscure the real threats of neoliberal policy. "Part of the reason branding works," Wingard explains, "is because it creates an object upon which the American public can focus their emotions. Branding redirects the anxieties that the material conditions of neoliberal capital produce through unemployment, economic disenfranchisement, and changing demographics."[16] Rather than fostering a concern for widespread inequality and economic powerlessness,

Rebellious bodies provide stories about individualism + diversity
- celeb. body acts as site of social debate about social issues
  - obesity - disability - age
  - race - gender identity

these branded bodies provide an emotional outlet for any apprehension about the loss of political and economic power in a neoliberal economy.

For Wingard, immigrant and LGBT bodies are the most salient examples of branded bodies in the contemporary United States, since they are the two groups around which explicit discussions of citizenship and individual rights have taken place in recent years. Depictions of immigrant bodies crossing the border or LGBT bodies participating in marriage rites clearly function as charged, emotional images deployed to affirm traditional notions of citizenship. But a range of bodies function in similar ways, eliciting emotional responses that construct them as social and economic burdens. In the news media, obese bodies are stigmatized and dehumanized as "out of control," making them the focal point of a moral panic around obesity rates and their burden on the US health care system. Poor, urban black bodies have a long history of signifying both out-of-control violence and a drain on the US welfare system, a perspective that continues today despite erroneous claims that Barack Obama's presidency has ushered in a "postracial" America. Disabled bodies—especially the increasingly visible bodies of disabled veterans in the wake of the wars in Iraq and Afghanistan—continue to produce anxiety about how they can be accommodated within "normal" visions of labor and family life. As the nation's demographics change, elderly bodies are increasingly a source of cultural anxiety, from worries about aging masculinity (seen in erectile dysfunction ads as well as through aging action stars in films such as *R.E.D.*) to concerns that elderly Americans and their Social Security benefits will bankrupt the government and leave younger Americans high and dry. And transgender bodies are increasingly sites of moral panic as various groups resist new policies designed to make the gendered world more accessible to transgender individuals.[17]

In all these cases, the dominant images of these groups focus emotional attention on "out-of-control" bodies in order to intensify anxiety about which bodies are accepted and what distributions of government resources are appropriate for them. In the process, the real culprit behind losses of political and economic power—the highly unequal distribution of wealth and power in the United States, which is exacerbated by neoliberal policy—is ignored as the culture is drawn into heated but fruitless arguments about who belongs and who is bankrupting the system.

At the same time, the increasing cultural imperative to embrace a particular vision of diversity and tolerance as part of good cultural citizenship promotes the inclusion of such branded bodies into the cultural fabric. The projects of multiculturalism and political correctness of the 1980s and 1990s have helped normalize the values of inclusivity and tolerance to the point that bigoted actions or speech—whether racist, sexist, homophobic, or otherwise—are signs of irresponsible citizenship in media discourse and can carry steep repercussions. As Wendy Brown notes in her study of contemporary tolerance discourse, cultural tolerance has emerged as a foundational "telos of multicultural citizenship," a venerated individual trait in Western political discourse.[18]

Of course, this model of tolerant citizenship largely sees inclusivity as yet another project of individual self-improvement rather than an interrogation of social values and policies. As Brown points out, tolerance depoliticizes issues of social justice, reducing the pursuit of social equality to matters of individual prejudice or enlightenment.[19] Exemplified by the corporate world's embrace of diversity training and cultural competency as marketable skill sets, this perspective sees tolerance as something that individuals do in their day-to-day lives to demonstrate their ability to adapt to changing historical conditions, rather than as a means of seeking a foundational transformation in the community's values and priorities. As a result, the public's understanding of tolerance tends to revolve around narratives of individual success or failure. Those who have failed to master the new dictates of inclusivity are pilloried in order to make ourselves feel better, while those who champion tolerance are treated as icons in the hope that sharing their stories will demonstrate our own personal commitments. This is not to suggest that all efforts at education or self-improvement are narcissistic, or to deny the power of thoughtful media to challenge cultural privilege. Rather, as Brown argues, these meaningful projects tend to be drafted into much narrower and individualistic conceptions of the value of tolerance and social justice in neoliberal culture.[20]

So while stars with non-normative bodies raise tense cultural questions about the boundaries of citizenship and inclusion in the United States, their presence is also a valuable cultural resource for individuals and the entertainment industry to prove a commitment to diversity and tolerance. Their stardom demonstrates how to form anxiety-producing bodies into resonant narratives of individual success, all while providing feel-good narratives of inclusion and progressive change in the entertainment media. In the process, both those on the cultural margins and those in the center are drafted into a model of citizenship as individual self-improvement, not social change. Thus lost in the recent expansion of cultural citizenship, as Toby Miller explains, are the troubling facts of *real* social power—how entrenched structures and institutions shore up the interests of economic and cultural elites.[21]

This exploration of stardom and citizenship, then, aligns with existing theories of stardom that see stars not necessarily as "real" people but as mediated constructions that help manage the ideological contradictions of the modern world. Stemming from the foundational work of Richard Dyer,

Dyer!

this discursive approach to stardom analyzes the multitude of "texts" (films, TV shows, interviews, stories in entertainment journalism, gossip, advertisements) that constitute a particular "star text." Taken together, this ever-changing (and sometimes contradictory) conglomeration of media texts coheres into the image of a complete individual—the star. For Dyer, the "star text" resonates in a particular historical moment because it encapsulates particular ideological contradictions about gender, race, sexuality, or personhood in general. But rather than dwelling on the contradiction, we see those complexities smoothed out behind the charm, talent, and allure of the star as an individual. We do not see a bundle of contradictions about women's purity and sexual availability—we simply see Marilyn Monroe.[22] For Dyer, then, stardom becomes a key mechanism through which media culture articulates ideas about individualism and personhood within modernity, affirming the idea of a coherent individual in spite of the fragmented ideologies of modern, patriarchal capitalism.[23] A rich body of scholarship on stardom and celebrity has emerged since Dyer's work to explore the variety of meanings and social functions of stardom in the modern world, but his discursive and semiotic approach remains influential in scholarly discourse.[24]

Dyer's work on Paul Robeson, for example, provides a particularly relevant precursor to the case studies I pursue here. From the 1920s through the 1940s, Robeson was arguably the most important black star in US pop culture as a singer of popular black folk songs and an actor known for not just his singing but also his athletic physicality. Like other black performers, Robeson's popular appeal was profoundly corporeal, offering one of the most popular representations of what a black body ought to be, according to white culture: athletic, primitive, and extraordinary at musical performance. He was the epitome of black masculinity, according to his popular appeal. As Dyer argues, the white media constructed Robeson's stardom to both exploit the spectacle of the black body and contain it within "safe" discourses of his raw talent and meritocratic success. While making room for black stardom, these discourses affirmed white stereotypes about black bodies and white narratives about how blacks ought to succeed in white culture. And yet Robeson's body also sparked a set of black discourses about identity and success—some of which denigrated his status as a "sellout" to the white culture industries—that could never be fully contained by the dominant white discourses, despite the work of white media industries to frame the contours of his stardom. Robeson's complex and often contradictory star text opened a myriad of possibilities to "make sense" of his body that led to competing racial discourses. Or, to put it another way, the predominant culture could imagine a form of cultural citizenship for some black men organized around an athletic, musical, and muscular black masculinity, but the limitations and contradictions of this citizenship are always seeping out around the edges, yielding a range of competing pleasures and meanings in consuming star bodies.

Star bodies, then, negotiate the shifting norms of identity and citizenship, managing historical changes concerning race, class, gender and gender identity, and sexuality by both displaying and assuaging the tensions such changes create. In the process, the popular images of stars and celebrities manage the boundaries of sexual desirability and appropriate gendered behavior, classify raced and ethnic bodies as either acceptable or dangerous according to white bourgeois norms, or navigate queer bodies into spheres acceptable to heteronormative values. Hollywood's increasing attention to African Americans, for example, has yielded many more images of black bodies on screen, but black celebrities often occupy a contradictory space that hides continuing structural racial inequalities in the United States.[25] Or US pop culture fixates on mixed-raced celebrities like Halle Berry or Tiger Woods whose blackness can be both exploited for exotic cachet and simultaneously denied.[26] Likewise, gay and lesbian celebrities such as Ellen DeGeneres are more visible than ever, but their queerness must be contained within certain depoliticized spheres that are the least threatening to the heteronormative social order.[27] Star bodies, in short, help manage cultural body norms and the kinds of bodies privileged in US society. Thus Chris Holmlund shows that the "impossible" bodies of Hollywood celebrities help hide "impossible" contradictions about gender, race, and sexuality.[28]

The case studies I examine here, however, provide a radical challenge for the cultural functions of stardom. Stars with bodies that deviate from cultural definitions of the "normal" body on the basis of disability, obesity, race and ethnicity, transgressive gender identity, or some other characteristic bring into question cultural definitions of acceptable bodies and identities, at least within the limitations provided by capitalist, patriarchal culture. Stars with non-normative bodies visibly challenge the carefully constructed norms of US entertainment media, disrupting the steady stream of impossibly "perfect" bodies in popular culture. The plethora of such stars in today's media culture signals an important willingness on the part of media producers and consumers to transgress and potentially transform traditional body politics.

The crises evoked by such bodies, however, continue to provide the grounds upon which neoliberal culture can affirm its vision of diversity as self-improvement, creating the means through which privileged identities can use a commitment to diversity to reaffirm their place at the center of cultural norms. For the stars examined here, this process is reflected both on screen and off. In many of their most popular roles, McCarthy, Sidibe, Dinklage, Trejo, White, and Cox all find themselves in narratives where their rebellious bodies help those with normative bodies to become better, more self-actualized citizens. They often play roles as quirky sidekicks whose self-confidence or sense of individuality helps spur a process of self-improvement for those with more normative identities. Similarly, the off-screen personas of these stars demonstrate how their personal commitment to self-improvement or embrace of their individuality can provide educational lessons about self-acceptance for those at the cultural center. In this way, the rebellious possibilities of stars with non-normative bodies are most often contained by safer and less challenging narratives of self-confidence and self-acceptance that deflect substantive critiques of US body politics.

Exploring the functions of non-normative bodies within contemporary stardom, then, yields three insights, each of which will be discussed in further detail, about how stardom and diversity function in the contemporary United States:

1. Within the popular discourse of diversity, stars with non-normative bodies function as heroic icons whose images and stories can be used as social-justice currency for media industries and entertainment journalists. Not surprisingly, the images and stories making up this currency tend to individualize issues of social justice, creating a melodramatic narrative of bigoted villains and body image heroes.

2. The images and stories of stars with non-normative bodies can also function as currency for individual projects of self-construction thanks to social media. As such, the media circulation of body image heroes also serves a pedagogic role, illustrating how people who deviate from the cultural norm but aspire to cultural citizenship can actively manage their identity according to the dictates of neoliberal consumer citizenship. In other words, stars with non-normative bodies provide templates for self-transformation and self-actualization.

3. Gender identity plays an especially important role in managing the contradictions of non-normative stardom. Transgressions in race or ethnicity, body shape, age, or ability are all primarily managed by the projection of traditional gender roles, suggesting that gender functions as a kind of master category in definitions of neoliberal citizenship.

As I explore these complexities, it is worth noting that I myself embody the privileged norm against which these stars are all measured: I am a (relatively) young, white, able-bodied, generally fit, heterosexual, cis-gendered man. As such, it is not my intention to speak on behalf of any of the populations that may find themselves represented by stars such as Melissa McCarthy, Gabourey Sidibe, Peter Dinklage, Danny Trejo, Betty White, or Laverne Cox. There is important scholarship already in circulation and more waiting to be done that brings the voices of such populations into the scholarly discussion on media and diversity, both as authors and as subjects. I hope that this project can join in that discussion without taking up too much room at the table. What I hope to contribute, then, is an interrogation of the pleasures stars with non-normative bodies offer to individuals who—like me—have historically been at the center of cultural citizenship in the United States. What kinds of negotiations or accommodations do the culture industries demand of these stars in order for people like me to feel a connection with them, to feel that they are part of a shared sense of community values about individualism, the value of diversity, and personal responsibility? And what do these accommodations tell us about the blind spots of diversity rhetoric in the United States, the conversations that many folks like me are not willing to have?

BODY IMAGE HEROES AND DIVERSE STARDOM

Stars whose rebellious bodies manage popular ideas about identity and social norms of course have a long history in US pop culture. One of the most prominent examples is silent film comedian Roscoe "Fatty" Arbuckle, whose robust frame became part of his successful comedic persona but would later embody the excesses of Hollywood debauchery. When actress Virginia Rappe died after becoming ill at a raucous party at Arbuckle's house in 1921, Arbuckle was accused of rape and murder, with popular accounts offering the sensational story that he crushed the young actress with his weight while raping her with a bottle. Arbuckle was eventually acquitted of all charges, but he was ostracized within the film industry and only worked sporadically using pseudonyms following the scandal. As Sam Stoloff argues, Arbuckle's rotund body before the scandal offered a popular vision of transgression and buffoonery, with an enormous man whose persona was effeminate and much like that of a giant baby. But while these gendered and body transgressions resonated in pop culture, the scandal quickly transformed Arbuckle into a perverted monster whose weight came to represent the excesses of Hollywood wealth and the moral decay of the film industry.[29]

Similarly, Mae West's curvy body came to signify her persona's open sexuality and transgression of appropriate femininity in the late 1920s and early 1930s. West was hugely popular in the early years of the Great Depression for her sexual innuendo and performances of strong-willed, sexually liberated women that challenged traditional middle-class values. But like Arbuckle, West's gendered transgressions would make her an icon of Hollywood's excesses. As Ramona Curry points out, West's unruly popular persona portrayed women's sexual desirability as an empowering commodity and in the process "exposed contradictions in the well-established American capitalist practice of simultaneously exploiting and repressing female sexuality as a commodity under men's control."[30] In the early years of the Great Depression, then, West's popular image would become "a locus in a long-standing US controversy over 'movie morality,'" especially as the economic crisis threatened the cultural and economic stability of the middle class.[31] As Anne Helen Petersen describes it, West's films "appeared at a crest of the wave of objectionable films and provided a rallying cry for those clamoring for renewed censorship efforts."[32]

For decades, stars with non-normative bodies like Arbuckle and West remained few and far between, but with the ascension of multiculturalism as a political and cultural project in the 1980s and 1990s, a greater variety of stars and celebrities have gained popularity, reflecting the entertainment industry's attempts to woo more diverse audiences and appease cultural pressures to embrace the mantra of inclusivity. Like their predecessors, these new generations of stars with non-normative bodies produce images and narratives that smooth out the ideological contradictions of identity. As Dyer and other theorists of stardom attest, such stars embody the tensions of a culture that values individualism but distrusts those who stray too far from social norms.

But what *has* changed since the days of Arbuckle and West is the cultural context of individualism and diversity in the United States. Stars with non-normative bodies today exist in a cultural context in which the value and meanings of diversity itself are both ubiquitous and highly contested in public discourse.

After all, not that long ago, only academics (and the occasional progressive-minded film critic) really cared about how Hollywood represented women and minorities. Starting in the 1970s and building exponentially as higher education expanded throughout the 1980s and 1990s, a growing number of writers created a massive body of innovative work carefully analyzing the sexism, racism, elitism, Eurocentrism, and heteronormativity of the US entertainment media. Some scholars made polemical accusations that powerful, elite corporations use the entertainment media to maintain power and hide inequality. Others showed that everyday audiences use the media to negotiate with the cultural and social challenges of the modern world. But almost all of this research agreed that Hollywood provides images and narratives that generally affirm white, patriarchal, heterosexual, middle-class, and able-bodied values.[33]

Not surprisingly, these perspectives on media and cultural power largely remained tucked away in university libraries, college classrooms, and academic conferences. Entertainment journalism and the news media rarely engaged with issues like casting politics or stereotypes in any serious way, especially since such media increasingly operated within the same corporate entities that produced entertainment in the first place. Topical films or television shows that referenced race relations or women's rights might occasionally elicit discussions within the media of representational politics, but for the most part these were intellectual discussions that were assumed to be uninteresting to the general public.

But over the past few decades, our public discussions of entertainment media have increasingly become centered on issues of diversity and social inequality. Despite the fact that race/ethnicity, feminism, and political correctness became battlegrounds in the so-called culture wars of the 1990s—and remain controversial touchstones of cultural change today—the basic assumptions of these movements have entered the mainstream to a certain degree. US media culture has come to accept enough of the basic tenets of the multiculturalism movement that public accusations of racism, sexism, or homophobia have gained cultural power and can come with steep repercussions. For example, the career of actor Mel Gibson went into a tailspin after he was recorded making anti-Semitic comments in 2006 while being arrested for drunk driving.[34] While scandal has always played an important role in the shaping and reframing of celebrity personas,[35] more and more issues of diversity and inclusion serve as the backdrop of celebrity scandal, tearing down established stars caught uttering bigoted speech or turning regular folks into well-known public pariahs for their insensitive transgressions.[36] This is not to say that issues of diversity have displaced the long-dominant themes of celebrity culture and entertainment reporting, which still focus heavily on romantic gossip, lifestyle, and intimate behind-the-scenes portraits of celebrities. But a brief overview of contemporary entertainment reporting reveals a much larger space for debates about the media, representation, and social power.

For example, across entertainment journalism, issues of stereotypes and the complexity of roles for women, including feminist critiques of media content, are becoming central talking points, as Lena Dunham's popularity suggests. Female television protagonists are interrogated by critics (are they "strong" women with complex rationales?),[37] and as the stars of the baby boomer generation age, entertainment news sources from *Vulture* to *The Hollywood Reporter* are commenting on the ageism of Hollywood that forces older women out of leading roles but keeps pairing older men with younger women.[38] Even the Bechdel test, a basic measure of a film's gender equity that asks whether at least two women are shown talking to one another about something other than a man (a surprising number of films fail the test), became so commonly discussed in entertainment reporting that both Holly-wood.com and *Salon* ran stories wondering if it is already passé.[39]

The changing racial demographics of the United States have also increased the media's discourse on race and representation in entertainment industry productions, with the media not only reporting on the general lack of diversity on screen but also detailing the complex efforts to court diverse audiences by challenging assumptions about storytelling.[40] *Time* even reported on a detailed social science study tracking diversity on screen through diversity among Hollywood agents, showcasing academic work on race and representation that typically does not find its way into mainstream news media reporting.[41]

Moreover, activist organizations advocating for underrepresented groups have been able to capitalize on the entertainment industry's interest in diversity by using Hollywood films and TV shows to draw attention to discrimination. For example, disability rights organizations effectively forced a public debate about language, media, and power by staging a protest and boycott of the 2008 comedy *Tropic Thunder* over the use of the term "retard." Spearheaded by organizations such as the American Association of People with Disabilities and the Special Olympics, the protest suggested that the casual use of the "r-word" in the film and across other media contributed to the stigma and discrimination faced by people with cognitive disabilities.[42] Several critics and industry insiders stood up for the film, including the film's director and star, Ben Stiller, who argued that it does not affirm the use of the term but rather satirizes the shallow characters that do so.[43] While the protest had no significant impact on the film's box office revenues, it still succeeded in generating a discussion in entertainment journalism over Hollywood's representation of people with disabilities. A variety of groups use similar tactics to advocate for diversity and equity in the media, including the NAACP, the National Latino Media Council, the Asian-Pacific American Media Coalition, American Indians in Film and TV, GLAAD, and others.

This increasing attention to diversity is clearly due in part to the rising importance of market segmentation. Rather than aiming for mass audiences as in the golden age of broadcast media, entertainment companies are now more likely to target particular market segments such as Latinos/Latinas, African Americans, young women, etc. Appearing to denigrate the interests of these groups can have a much more detrimental impact on ratings today than in the past, when the intended audiences were much larger and more general. In a certain sense, the commodification of minority groups into "target demographics" has somewhat democratically meant that issues of diversity have become more economically and therefore culturally powerful (even though smaller, less affluent demographics—say, Native Americans—remain woefully underrepresented and stereotyped).

Attention to diversity also increased after the year 2000 because the Internet destabilized media industries, especially traditional news media and their role as gatekeepers of public discourse. With the ensuing proliferation of news websites and blogs, a much broader array of voices reflecting a range of perspectives entered the public conversation about the media and social power. And since traditional news outlets like CNN or the major broadcast networks have scaled back on news production costs, their websites or broadcasts often rely on these new voices for content or inspiration. The popularity of feminist websites such as *Jezebel*, for example, allows these smaller sites to help frame media discourse for more mainstream journalism by foregrounding stories that organizations like CNN or shows like *Entertainment Tonight* might otherwise overlook. Sites such as *Jezebel*, *Buzzfeed*, *Vulture*, *Upworthy*, and *Bustle*, along with more traditional journalism sites such as the *Daily Beast*, the *Huffington Post*, and *Salon*, also help circulate the stories coming out of more mainstream entertainment journalism by linking to and remediating them in online form. The result is a much more diverse set of voices influencing the major topics and trends in entertainment reporting.

This is not to suggest that contemporary media are necessarily more progressive. There are simply more voices, many of which actively condemn the "oversensitivity" of multicultural media critiques. In fact, media discourse since the year 2000 has been countered by backlash against various forms of political correctness, which is often seen by conservatives as anti-American and a moral failure. For example, when Phil Robertson, the star of the A&E reality show *Duck Dynasty*, made homophobic comments in an interview with *GQ* that became public in late 2013, he was quickly suspended from the hugely popular show and widely condemned in the entertainment media.[44] But almost as swiftly came a chorus of voices defending Robertson and condemning the supposed tyranny of political correctness. His supporters included Louisiana's governor Bobby Jindal and the conservative icon Sarah Palin, who tweeted, "Free speech is an endangered species. Those 'intolerants' hatin' and taking on the *Duck Dynasty* patriarch for voicing his personal opinion are taking on all of us."[45] Robertson was quickly reinstated on the show, indicating the power of the anti-PC discourse in pop culture. But for a media industry that thrives on conflict and controversy, claims of racism, sexism, elitism, and homophobia make for juicy headlines and continue to be a staple of entertainment reporting.

In this way, while more diverse voices have helped create new waves of entertainment reporting that are bringing nuanced questioning of media representation to the public, the appetite for social justice controversy also creates stories and story cycles that reduce complex issues to black-and-white moral dichotomies. Examine, for example, the brief 2015 controversy regarding comedian Amy Schumer, who had become a darling of media critics for her openly feminist comedy sketches. When *The Guardian* published a thoughtful essay online about Schumer's success with feminist comedy and her failures to address issues of race in the same way,[46] a flurry of stories followed that either defended or castigated Schumer, with most of them organized around the question of whether she is a racist. Instead of more nuanced discussions of white feminism, comedy, and race, the media coverage became an inquisition of Schumer's status as an acceptable celebrity role model.[47] Drafting a discussion of race into a melodramatic inquisition of Schumer's personal character, these media discourses obscured a bevy of larger issues about television and racial diversity, such as a lack of diversity among TV executives or the historical failure to support black women comedians.

Conservative critics tried to chalk up the Amy Schumer controversy to the evils of politically correct liberals stifling the free speech of one of their own, but the real dynamics here cross party lines: popular media discourses tend to reduce social justice debates to simplistic questions about individuals: who is "bad" and who is "good"? These debates often rely on the melodrama of celebrity scandal to articulate the values of diversity, creating a world of heroic progressives and villainous bigots that makes for good clickbait but ultimately occludes the long and complex history of oppression in the United States, as well as the deeply entrenched social and institutional structures supporting that oppression. Public discourses about diversity excel at creating celebratory narratives for some, while heaping shame and scorn on others. But the nuanced middle ground where the culture might grapple with the complexities of equality and opportunity is often too messy for a catchy headline on *Upworthy*.

Writers like Jonathan Chait see the kinds of public shaming that are common in this melodramatic world as examples of overzealous political correctness chilling difficult but necessary debates[48]—a position for which he was, ironically, personally condemned. The phenomenon he describes is not the stifling of public debate, however, but rather the insistence that public debate about diversity be filtered through the lens of neoliberal individualism. From this perspective, diversity is not a commitment to rectifying large-scale social and cultural injustice, but instead an individual project of self-improvement, a chance to demonstrate one's personal triumphs and magnanimity. Failures at this project—when people are publicly shamed for their language, action, and beliefs—become examples of the imperatives for self-discipline and self-transformation, not for social transformation. This is not to say that changing personal beliefs and practices is not an important aspect of social change, but rather that the gleeful cycles of shame and celebration tend to individualize discussions of diversity instead of asking harder questions. The increasingly prominent practice of online shaming campaigns focuses the culture's energies on assigning individual blame by creating more and more media villains. Desperately seeking individual scapegoats, the contemporary entertainment media love to blame individuals in order to deflect issues of structural power and inequality.

For example, Indian American comedian Mindy Kaling has been widely celebrated as a powerful role model, not only for being a successful woman of color who rose from the ranks of the sitcom *The Office* to write and produce her own sitcom, *The Mindy Project*, but also because she is slightly overweight (by Hollywood standards). And yet Kaling herself was criticized because her show does not have a large, multiethnic cast and her character only dates white men. When asked about such critiques at the SXSW festival in 2014, Kaling fired back, asking why no one critiques predominantly white shows about their casting practices.[49] As Kaling's response suggests, entertainment journalists are often more comfortable assigning individual blame than examining structural inequalities. Since Kaling has become an icon of the new diverse Hollywood, it becomes easy to scrutinize her actions and place responsibility on her shoulders for creating diversity in the media. It is far more difficult to consider the larger systems and structures in Hollywood that keep producing white-centric sitcoms, so instead individuals are both celebrated and targeted for their roles within this system.

A similar tendency was at work in the 2014 "Cancel Colbert" campaign on Twitter after an uncontextualized joke by the team at *The Colbert Report* went viral. On the show, host Stephen Colbert, who played a satirical caricature of a conservative political pundit, was discussing the critiques leveled at the Washington Redskins for using Native Americans as mascots. Redskins owner Daniel Snyder had tried to deflect the controversy by creating a charitable organization to benefit Native Americans that, incredibly, included the racial epithet "redskins" in the name of the organization, showing how little he understood the issues at stake. After poking fun at Snyder on the air, the team at *The Colbert Report* tweeted a follow-up joke: "I'm willing to show the #Asian community I care by introducing the Ching-Chong Ding-Dong Foundation for Sensitivity to Orientals or Whatever." The Internet was soon buzzing after Asian American activist Suey Park critiqued Colbert's use of Asian stereotypes and called for the cancellation of the show. A chorus of voices joined in on Twitter with the hash tag "#CancelColbert," and the controversy splashed across a range of mainstream news outlets, including an op-ed on CNN.com calling for Colbert's ousting (even after it was revealed that Colbert himself did not write the tweet).[50] As with the Kaling incident, what could have been a nuanced discussion of media stereotypes, their persistence in contemporary culture, and the efficacy of combating stereotypes with more stereotypes instead quickly turned into an interrogation of Colbert himself and his personal racial politics as the story became distorted through the lens of social media outrage.

As this suggests, the quick and easy outrage that social media facilitates often makes for heated but simplistic discussions of the issues at hand, leading Andrew O'Hehir to wonder if this emerging "Twitter politics" is an outlet for political disenfranchisement. In a highly unequal world in which the political power of the rich leaves so many feeling powerless and frustrated, the democratization of the media at least means that people can exercise their opinions with regard to popular culture. In lieu of exercising actual political power through a broken system of democracy, at least people can weigh in on whether Colbert crossed the line.[51]

The rising tide of social media shaming, however, makes the heroes of a seemingly more diverse Hollywood important and complex figures in contemporary culture. Stars with non-normative bodies are the inverse of the online public shaming phenomenon, providing resonant body image heroes that counter its rampant negativity. They provide uplifting and inspirational narratives affirming individual triumph and the progressive change of the culture, but they only exist in relation to the social pariahs of public shaming campaigns. This dialectic of shame and celebration makes social justice something individuals *do* in their behavior and language, not an idea that must be reflected in community laws, policies, and institutions. By exploring one half of this cultural economy through an analysis of body image heroes, this book examines the values and attitudes concerning diversity that are privileged by neoliberal culture. In a world in which we are so quick to blame individuals for the problems of inequality, why do certain narratives of individual success resonate?

STARDOM AND SELF-ACTUALIZATION

Given this tendency to focus on individuals as either heroes or villains in the public debates surrounding diversity, it is not surprising that celebrities have become central to the campaign to celebrate the newfound inclusiveness of the entertainment media. Celebrities, after all, have a long history of affirming the power of individual success in narratives that downplay structural inequalities. Celebrities have always helped perpetuate narratives of meritocracy, class mobility, and opportunity in US culture. As Karen Sternheimer notes in her exhaustive historical study of celebrity fan magazines, "Celebrity culture seems to provide a continual reaffirmation that upward mobility is possible in America and reinforces the belief that inequality is the result of personal failure rather than systemic social conditions."[52] And P. David Marshall tells us that the star system has always been an important cultural institution in the promotion of meritocratic ideologies; treating each star's rise from obscurity as "unique" only affirms the narrative that anyone could one day become a star.[53]

Historically, these narratives have revolved around issues of class, creating celebratory narratives about stars who became a new kind of nobility by rising from humble beginnings (but typically obscuring the fact that they were mostly white, young, and beautiful). In today's slightly more diverse Hollywood, however, we are treated to narratives of upward mobility for a variety of individuals outside of cultural norms. In addition to narratives about women's struggles against patriarchy in their rise to prominence (such as the ones about Lena Dunham, Kathryn Bigelow, and Amy Schumer) or celebrities of color overcoming racial discrimination (for example, Chris Rock, Mindy Kaling, Kerry Washington, Terrence Howard, or America Ferrera), entertainment journalism also offers its audiences a host of uplifting tales about stars with disabilities or different body types who have made it in Hollywood (including Marlee Matlin, Chris Burke, Warwick Davis, R. J. Mitte, Lauren Potter, and others). These narratives remind us of the power of individuals to craft their own destinies, even if discrimination and the statistical realities of inequality show that for many, such narratives are only fantasies.

And the statistical realities of inequality in the United States do remain grim. In addition to well-documented inequalities in income and wealth (with the richest 1 percent of Americans bringing home 20 percent of the income),[54] the likelihood of overcoming these inequalities and moving up the socioeconomic ladder continues to be slim, especially for those who come from underprivileged backgrounds. Rather than demonstrating that the United States realizes its ideal of being a "land of opportunity," the rate at which Americans rise into the middle or upper classes is lower than in other industrialized countries, including even Great Britain with its long history of class stratification. Thanks to economic changes ranging from the decline in manufacturing jobs that helped expand the middle class after World War II to the exponentially rising costs of higher education to the systematic gutting of its welfare system, the United States has come to lead industrialized countries in socioeconomic immobility.[55] While economists debate whether mobility is still decreasing or simply holding steady at low levels,[56] the widening gap between the rich and the poor has increased public scrutiny of economic inequality in the United States, with politicians on both the left and the right highlighting the low mobility rate in the wake of the 2008 financial crisis.[57] The feminization of poverty, the high correlations between economic class and race, and the high rates of poverty among the disabled mean that women, people of color, and the disabled bear the burden of this immobility more than other groups.

The stagnation of upward mobility in the United States (and elsewhere) is a direct result of neoliberal economics and its emphasis on individual consumers assuming responsibility for a variety of community services. Not surprisingly, then, the solutions to inequality within a neoliberal worldview are tied to individual consumption and self-transformation. The rise of neoliberalism affects not just economic policy but also the culture of individualism and consumerism in an increasingly privatized world. Neoliberalism promotes not only a model of citizenship as consumerism (privileging the "choices" of individuals on the private market over the ability of the state to provide support) but also a model of individualism based on adaptability and self-transformation. It is now the individual's responsibility to adapt to changing market conditions by constantly remaking one's skills, habits, and even identity to meet the shifting demands of the economy.[58]

Beyond the economy, in fact, individual identity in the age of neoliberalism increasingly revolves around projects of self-improvement, self-promotion, and the constant disciplining of one's identity. Thus, as Jayne Raisborough explains, "lifestyle media," or media organized around individual transformation and "self-improvement" such as self-help books or makeover TV shows, have ballooned in the era of neoliberalism. Referencing Michel Foucault's later work on governance as central to this phenomenon, Raisborough argues that "an ethos of transformation and re-creation . . . permeates most, if not all, aspects of our daily life and organization."[59] But far from a neutral vision of "betterment," these transformations tend to police the boundaries of race, class, gender, sexuality, and ability, often providing explicit lessons on how to "design out" exterior markers of inequality, whether through fashion, behavior, or the appearance of one's home.[60]

Brenda Weber also offers a detailed and compelling outline of this ethos of transformation in her examination of makeover TV shows, the glut of reality TV programs organized around the makeover of individual appearance, living spaces, cars, and other extensions of one's identity. These shows promote a model of identity based on the constant disciplining and transforming of one's external appearance, and the need for some to submit themselves to regimes of experts that can guide them to their "true" and "better" selves. These notions of identity, though, are deeply linked to the social norms of white upper-middle-class culture. As Weber explains, "On these shows, selfhood links to social locations and practices marked as normative, frequently designated through images that connote upward mobility, heteronormativity, consumer-orientation, conventional attractiveness, ethnic anonymity, and confidence."[61] Moreover, the logic of self-actualization that is pervasive across the genre suggests that individuals incapable of self-improvement might lack any real sense of identity in modern culture: "Those who are sloppy, cluttery, overwrought, overdrawn, and overweight can lay no legitimate claim to selfhood within the makeover's constitution of identity."[62] Such programs suggest that it is only through the mantras of self-transformation and self-improvement that a stable identity can be achieved in a chaotic world.

so confused by citizenship

At stake in this pursuit of selfhood, Weber insists, are the boundaries of citizenship in a world of neoliberal governance. The imperatives to maintain, transform, and claim a viable sense of self in makeover TV reflect the cultural borders of belonging (as articulated by mainstream media) and the necessity for that self to navigate the competitive world of neoliberal economics. As Weber explains:

> In its emphasis on progress, its desire to provide access to restricted privileges, and its insistence on free-market meritocracy, the project of citizenship imagined across the makeover genre comes deeply saturated with Americanness and this, in turn, imports neoliberal ideologies, which position the subject as an entrepreneur of the self, who does and, indeed, must engage in care of the body and its symbolic referents in order to be competitive within a larger global marketplace.[63]

The pathways to cultural citizenship imagined in makeover TV privilege self-maintenance and self-promotion as the requirements for cultural participation, reflecting a deeply American vision of competition and meritocracy.

Stars and celebrities play an increasingly important and pedagogical function in the cultural necessities of self-transformation and self-promotion. Of course, as P. David Marshall illustrates, stars have always been an important pedagogical tool for selfhood in the modern world, teaching individuals how to "engage and use consumer culture to 'make' oneself," typically through fashion and hairstyle but also through stylized models of social class, manhood, and femininity.[64]

Stars with non-normative bodies continue this long history by teaching appropriate pathways to self-transformation for those with rebellious bodies not so easily brought into line with white, patriarchal, ablest culture. As Raisborough's and Weber's writings suggest, one of the main focuses of neoliberal individualism is the active reworking of the body to fit cultural norms through exercise, surgery, and other means, but stars with bodies that dramatically deviate from cultural norms suggest other forms of self-making and self-promotion when physically reshaping one's body is just not an option. For example, as I discuss in chapter 2, Gabourey Sidibe has far fewer options than, say, Halle Berry when it comes to crafting a marketable image and narrative of African American femininity. Berry's stardom clearly relies on the traditional tropes of race and female sexuality to resonate as an exotic (but not too exotic) representation of black desirability, supported by her mixed-race background and typically sensual body. Sidibe, on the other hand, must craft a far different narrative of black femininity as an overweight and darker-skinned woman. Instead, her narrative taps into the rise of a "postracial" discourse after 2008 and media discourses of self-confidence, suggesting that her embrace of personal confidence and "girly" femininity can teach other women how to locate and claim their selfhood. In fact, Sidibe makes for a much more compelling model of neoliberal self-making than Berry, offering an uplifting narrative of merit and self-actualization that validates the possibilities of upward mobility for those who will never look like movie stars.

The stars analyzed in this book all demonstrate the pedagogical nature of stardom, illustrating a variety of pathways to self-actualization as the key to cultural citizenship. An explicitly normative star like Brad Pitt, whose physical beauty, whiteness, and masculinity cohere into a picture of cultural privilege, might offer aspirational lessons in manhood and glamour. But for the vast majority of the population who will never achieve those normative standards, stars with non-normative bodies reveal other avenues of self-making and other narratives of individual success. In fact, across the case studies, a web of discourses and narratives connect the various lessons of self-construction that stars with non-normative bodies rely on. For Melissa McCarthy, Gabourey Sidibe, and Peter Dinklage, the popular discourses of self-confidence are central to their public personas, while for Sidibe, Betty White, and Laverne Cox, postfeminist affirmations of girly femininity characterize their pursuit of cultural relevance. For White and Danny Trejo, nostalgia for a time when gender roles were supposedly simpler marks their popular appeal, while for Trejo and Peter Dinklage, the foisting of hard, hypersexual manhood on their public images has helped make them fan favorites. For all the stars, moreover, their construction as pioneers or challengers to Hollywood's "old" exclusivity marks them as popular icons of social justice. All these narratives serve as pedagogical tools, celebrity guides on the most relevant avenues to acceptable cultural citizenship—outside of actual body transformation—for those with the kinds of bodies that usually serve as sources of cultural anxiety.

The necessity to bring a broader range of people and bodies into the discourses of celebrity and self-promotion also aligns with the transformations of celebrity culture in the twenty-first century. For example, reality TV competitions and the "celetoids," or "those who command media attention one day and are forgotten the next,"[65] that such shows spawn provide a model for individual success in a world in which economic mobility is increasingly stunted. Conflating individual merit with successful self-promotion, celebrity culture in the world of reality TV affirms a superficial sense of meritocracy lost through neoliberal economics, according to Jo Littler.[66] In the face of vast inequality, Littler argues, the media have dramatically increased the production of reality TV competitions promoting the idea that fame and success can be achieved by "ordinary" folks if they work hard, are clever at reality show competitions, and show their skills at the "game" of self-promotion. Recognizing that the transition to celebrity offers a form of "symbolic validation" in a media-saturated culture, Littler suggests that celebrity itself—not just the financial rewards of economic mobility—has become a central goal of neoliberal individualism. Instead of questioning the structural distribution of wealth and power, people strive for celebrity status to save themselves from being designated as "ordinary."

Similarly, the expansion of what Marshall calls "presentational media," or the burgeoning social media platforms (Facebook, Twitter, Instagram, etc.) organized around the construction and circulation of an online self, has elevated the pedagogical importance of stardom and celebrity.[67] The rise of social media in the last fifteen years has created a new sphere within which individuals can carefully craft their own visions of selfhood. Posting images on Facebook, tweeting, "pinning" on Pinterest, and the myriad other ways that people manage their online individuality have provided a new frontier in self-making and self-promotion. The increasingly visible cultural work of stars and celebrities to maintain and reshape their public images via social media provides a model for everyone to navigate the world of mediated self-construction. As Marshall explains, the self-production modeled by celebrities "now serves as a rubric and template for the organization and production of the on-line self, which has become at the very least an important component of our presentation of ourselves to the world."[68] In short, users of social media get to practice on a smaller scale the kinds of image management essential to contemporary stardom and celebrity. Like celebrities, people can build networks of friends and followers within which they can promote images of themselves and their lifestyle to construct their own media-based personas.

Because stars with non-normative bodies provide such powerful narratives of individual achievement, they also function as a key currency in the everyday self-making projects of ordinary people, especially in an era of social media. Along with other narratives of the new diversity in entertainment media, stars with non-normative bodies can be deployed within these practices of self-promotion to help manage online identity. Linking to stories or videos about those stars (or other stories about media diversity) is a way to shape one's online persona, to use one's taste in popular culture to manage a sense of identity. Narratives of media diversity, then, can function as a kind of currency within social media networks, shared and exchanged in order to purchase certain values and tastes in the game of online self-construction. A link to a story about the most feminist new TV shows becomes part of a complex representation of beliefs and ideals for a Facebook user, contributing to their sense of online self and actual vision of individuality. This is not to suggest that people cynically deploy certain images or share different stories on social media solely as a kind of disingenuous self-promotion, but rather that the very act of social networking interpolates us all into a system of mediated self-construction.

Stars with non-normative bodies, then, are put to use by entertainment industries and the audiences who consume their stories as icons of tolerance and diversity. While managing the place of non-normative bodies within the cultural fabric, they also provide highly visible examples of the flexibility and capacity for self-reflection of those with privilege, helping to rejuvenate the cultural center as they are brought into the fold of contemporary citizenship.

GENDER AND DIVERSITY WITHIN NEOLIBERAL CITIZENSHIP

I focus on these particular case studies—Melissa McCarthy, Peter Dinklage, Gabourey Sidibe, Danny Trejo, Betty White, and Laverne Cox—because they represent the most popular examples of celebrities who reflect the most pressing social issues regarding bodies and inclusion: obesity, urban blackness, disability, Latino/a immigration, aging, and transgender identity. These celebrities have also (more or less) followed similar career trajectories, indicating a kind of standard pattern for celebrities with non-normative bodies. With the exception of Laverne Cox, they all emerged as icons of inclusivity with popular film roles in which they were heralded for challenging stereotypes: Melissa McCarthy in *Bridesmaids*, Peter Dinklage in *The Station Agent*, Gabourey Sidibe in *Precious*, Danny Trejo in *Machete*, and Betty White in *The Proposal* (although she was clearly well known for the 1980s TV show *The Golden Girls*, I will be focusing on White's late-career resurgence). While continuing their work in film, most then found their way into critically acclaimed TV shows that helped cement their celebrity personas beyond these initial roles: McCarthy on *Mike and Molly*, Dinklage on *Game of Thrones*, Sidibe on *American Horror Story*, Trejo on *Sons of Anarchy*, and White on her prank show *Off Their Rockers* as well as the comedy *Hot in Cleveland*. Although Cox's celebrity is still emerging, she found her star-making role in the Netflix-produced TV show *Orange Is the New Black* and is quickly becoming the most prominent celebrity face for transgender issues.

Across these career trajectories, these stars emerge as a coherent set because they all demonstrate the intersectional nature of managing identity and inequality. An intersectional approach to identity and social power recognizes that the categories typically used to organize power and privilege—for example, race, class, gender, sexuality, ability, etc.—are not singular, mutually exclusive categories. Rather, they overlap, reinforce, and intersect with each other in complex and multivalent ways. Moreover, these categories might work in tandem to help contain social and cultural transgressions. Certain forms of LGBTQ identity, for example, are more culturally acceptable when reinforced by gender and class identity; thus one of the most dominant images of homosexuality in the mainstream media is affluent and effeminate men who assist straights in fashion or décor. So while all the stars analyzed here deviate in one way or another from cultural norms of beauty and a "normal" body, in each instance the fears produced by such a deviation are displaced into other categories of identity in order to manage their persona.

As this suggests, the negotiations at the heart of cultural citizenship are not organized around assimilation into the dominant culture, but rather the fetishizing and consumption of (some) kinds of cultural difference. Deviations from cultural body norms produce cultural anxieties about excess and social decay, but those deviations can also become a source of popular appeal when managed by their intersections with other discourses or categories of oppression. These dynamics are by no means new. As Dyer's work argues, the intersections of race and masculinity helped manage Paul Robeson into an image of blackness that could be popular among white audiences. In the same way, the intersection of black masculinity with high social class was imperative to the popularity of Sidney Poitier, offering a seemingly safe vision of respectable black masculinity in the midst of the civil rights movement's challenge to white privileges.

For stars with non-normative bodies, however, the intersectional dynamics of their star personas are informed by the ascension of the "post-" discourses of contemporary culture: postfeminist, postracial, and the burgeoning hint of a postdisability worldview that I examine in chapter 3. Each discourse posits an end to the social justice activism of the 1960s through the 1980s, 1990s, and 2000s, culminating in a supposedly egalitarian world where cultural difference can be playful, fun, and an object of consumption.

As I explore in detail in chapter 5 (and reference in chapter 2 and the conclusion), postfeminism is a worldview that tries to move beyond the victories of second-wave feminism, the feminist movement that ascended in the 1960s and 1970s and was organized around workplace discrimination, reproductive rights, legal/policy inequalities, and other issues. Postfeminism sees the politicized perspective of second-wave feminists as joyless, antisex, and dismissive of the pleasures of femininity. Seeing the work of second-wave feminism as anachronistic for young women who have grown up in a more egalitarian world, the postfeminist worldview celebrates the consumerist pleasures of femininity (makeup and fashion), affirms the importance of traditional notions of heterosexual romance, and sees female sexuality as always empowering. The highly popular TV program *Sex and the City* exemplifies this worldview, defining women's identities and empowerment around shopping, sex, and the pursuit of marriage. Of course, as critics of postfeminism point out, this perspective fails to address the continuing inequalities faced by women, such as the persistent gender wage gap.[69]

Similarly, as I discuss in more detail in chapter 2 (and reference in chapter 4), postracial discourse in the United States refers to the belief that racial and ethnic equality has been achieved to such a degree that US culture and society has moved beyond the debates and discussions of stereotypes, bigotry, and media representations, especially after the election of Barack Obama as the first African American president. Often tied to a color-blind worldview suggesting that the discussion of racial inequality itself contributes to racial tensions, postracial discourse valorizes only a superficial diversity—having friends of different races, or consuming media with diverse casts and crew—that ignores the kinds of cultural or structural inequalities that continue to limit economic opportunity for many nonwhites. The television melodramas of Shonda Rhimes (*Grey's Anatomy, Scandal*) showcase this postracial worldview, offering exceptionally diverse casts, but casting them as affluent professionals tending to their love lives divorced from the stark racial inequalities of the contemporary United States.[70]

Finally, in chapter 3, I explore the emerging possibilities of a postdisability worldview in US media culture, especially around the increasing presence of little people in the media. Like postfeminism or postracial discourse, a postdisability perspective deploys the disabled body as a marker of progressive inclusivity, but either removes that body from the stigmas and discrimination faced by people with disabilities or else creates all-too-common "overcoming narratives" in which responsibility is placed on individuals with disabilities to overcome their impairments and prove their place in the community. In *Glee* the character of Artie, a wheelchair user who is part of the school's show choir, illustrates this trend. Artie in the wheelchair is simply one of many diverse bodies used to show how quirky the choir kids are—to affirm their status as underdogs—all while reaping the benefits for the show's "progressive" casting (although the casting of an able-bodied actor for the role did raise some protests from disability rights groups). While Artie's impairment and the challenges he faces are sometimes addressed by the show, the narrative as a whole conflates disability with a general view of cultural outcasts in high school who can overcome the odds.

Stars with non-normative bodies often affirm the power of the "post-" narrative as part of their inclusion in cultural citizenship. Indeed, their very existence adds weight to the argument that the "old" forms of cultural exclusion are giving way to new models of inclusion, even if their fame clearly exists alongside the same stereotypes of race, gender, disability, age, and transgender identity that have persisted for decades. The fact that people like McCarthy, Sidibe, Dinklage, Trejo, White, and Cox can be stars today bolsters the perception of the "post-" narrative. In turn, the stars' personas draw from a "post-" discourse to help frame their cultural differences as simply something fun and unique about their identities, interesting bodily differences that make them a marketable spectacle, but not something that should produce anxiety or force discussions of social justice.

In order to secure the status of their bodily difference as safe and appealing, the star personas I analyze all gravitate toward the power of traditional, middle-class gender roles as an intersectional category capable of assuaging the fears of race, ethnicity, obesity, disability, and transgender identity. For all the case studies, the anxieties raised by the non-normative bodies of the stars are countered with the insistence that they conform to bourgeois gender identity. McCarthy's transgressive flouting of "good taste" and patriarchal norms in her over-the-top comedy is situated within a discourse insisting that she is, in real life, a nice, polite, middle-class mom. As a dark-skinned, overweight black woman, Sidibe's stardom draws out the culture's prejudices surrounding black poverty, but her fame declares the power of fashion-loving, girly, self-confident femininity as the cure for economic disenfranchisement. Dinklage's rise to fame as a Hollywood leading man raises important questions about stereotyping and bigotry against little people (and people with disabilities more generally), but the discourses around his fame rationalize his success through an appeal to his rugged sexiness and appealing manhood. Likewise, Trejo's tattooed and muscled frame has long made him the go-to actor for roles about hyperviolent Latino villains, but his recent turn as an action hero suggests that Latino, macho paternalism and family life can rejuvenate multiethnic urban enclaves and reform the excesses of white culture. White's signature bawdy comedy, meanwhile, assures aging baby boomer women that continued youth and vitality come with a commitment to postfeminist attitudes about sex and romance. And while Laverne Cox is helping to publicize and humanize the stigmas facing transgender people in the United States, her stardom must balance the complex realities of transgender identity with a dominant media discourse that uses gender essentialism and the postfeminist pleasures of femininity to make sense of transgender women.

While the many categories of oppression policing the boundaries of belonging and citizenship in the modern world are significant, these case studies suggest that traditional, middle-class gender norms are a kind of master category within a neoliberal model of diversity, the category most sacred to the possibilities of cultural citizenship in a consumer culture. The assurances of traditional gender behavior and attitudes can help reframe bodily difference as a safe commodity, a bodily attribute that can signify a superficial commitment to diversity, but with the knowledge that it still affirms the centrality of gender and family roles to capitalist, consumer culture.

THE CASE STUDIES

For each case study, I examine a variety of media that compose the "star text" of each performer, a central feature of which are the films and television programs at the core of their public identity. Looking at the kinds of narratives that tend to be crafted around each star—along with the images and iconography used to represent them—this book explores the common set of meanings and ideas about each star's identity and body. How, in other words, has the entertainment industry deployed stars with non-normative bodies in certain kinds of roles, and why might those roles resonate within the cultural negotiations of diversity and identity?

I also analyze the discourses of entertainment journalism in magazine articles, film reviews, interviews, and other sources that refine and reframe the contours of each star's public persona. This kind of critical discourse analysis reveals the ways social power relations are inflected in the discursive practices of the media, seeing "texts not as truths but as discourses that act in the world in ways that both define and distribute power."[71] My analysis examines how discursive practices explain, rationalize, or construct the social world in accordance with dominant power relationships.

The discourses about these stars found in entertainment journalism most often express the dominant narratives concerning stardom as managed by a variety of institutional forces, from the star's publicist to Hollywood studio marketing departments, which actively work to maintain a certain public image for celebrities.[72] Entertainment journalism, then, functions as a space within which the core narratives and discourses that define a star's partly managed and partly spontaneous public persona are constructed and reconstructed as that persona changes over time. The range of discourses describing and framing a celebrity in entertainment journalism manage the central narratives that define their cultural meanings, providing a site upon which dominant narratives can be affirmed (or deconstructed, in the case of celebrity scandals).

Chapter 1, on Melissa McCarthy, explores the complex intersections of obesity, femininity, and social class in the age of the so-called obesity epidemic. This chapter asks how Melissa McCarthy, the comedian who has become the most prominent figure of overweight femininity in US culture, has become one of America's sweethearts in an age in which a medical rationale has been constructed for shaming and degrading obesity. Focusing on her negotiation of gender and social class to provide a middle-class model of feminist fat acceptance while performing excessively "trashy" characters on screen, this chapter demonstrates how assurances of middle-class femininity can obscure the contradictions of inclusion and shaming in the new body politics. In short, I explore how shoring up middle-class identity and disavowing "white trash" stereotypes can alleviate anxieties about obesity.

Chapter 2 then uses Gabourey Sidibe to explore the intersections of race, poverty, and obesity within a media context in which the election of Barack Obama serves as an example of a "postracial" society. Rising to fame after her 2009 film *Precious*, Sidibe is frequently used in the new body politics to demonstrate progressive inroads: she is an overweight black woman with dark skin in a culture that still privileges light-skinned African Americans. Her rise to fame also coincided with the debates concerning African Americans, racism, and the election of the first black president. Using the debates surrounding a "postracial" America as the backdrop for Sidibe's popularity, this chapter explores how her stardom articulates a model of postracial success based on the neoliberal mantra of self-confidence, which posits feminine self-assurance and the pleasures of girly femininity as the most appropriate models of self-making for those struggling with urban poverty.

Chapter 3 examines how masculinity and disability intersect in the rise of

Peter Dinklage to construct a narrative of meritocratic success. Dinklage has accomplished an unlikely rise to fame in an industry in which little people are most often used as surrealistic props or fantasy creatures. This chapter analyzes Dinklage's ability to move beyond this history of representation, considering how the construction of his persona as a pioneer and a sex symbol crafts a narrative of meritocracy within neoliberal individualism. Of course, the spectacle of Dinklage's sexualized body also borrows from the cultural tradition of the "freak show." Thus media discourses conflate Dinklage's talent with his good looks to insist on the meritocratic nature of his fame while still indulging in the exploitation of little people's bodies as a source of voyeuristic pleasure.

In chapter 4, the rise of Danny Trejo is firmly situated in representations of Latino immigrants. For much of his acting career as a bit player in action movies, Trejo's large, muscled body and pock-marked face functioned as a source of cultural anxiety: he embodied cultural fears about Latino labor and violence spilling into the United States. So how are these fears managed when Trejo became a leading action hero in Robert Rodriguez's action-parody films *Machete* (2010) and *Machete Kills* (2013), which explicitly lampoon US immigration policies? Analyzing the tendency for Trejo's heroic characters to violently take down caricatures of white elitism as a kind of "hyperwhiteness," this chapter shows how Trejo's machismo helps reform and rejuvenate whiteness in a new multicultural era, making way for new racial definitions and hierarchies. In the process, Trejo's stardom also posits the centrality of multiethnic families with tough patriarchs like Trejo to the norms of middle-class life in this new racial order.

The other bodies providing anxiety about the future of the United States, of course, are the aging bodies of the baby boomers as they pressure the US health care system and start to draw their Social Security benefits. This backdrop helps explain the late-career popularity of comedian Betty White. The recent resurgence of White, who starred in two TV series and several hit films in the 1980s and 1990s, revolves around her over-the-top antics and sexual humor as she debunks media stereotypes of the elderly as polite, passive, and insignificant. While White herself is no baby boomer, her fame coincides with an increasing cultural anxiety about the aging demographics of the boomers, especially baby boomer women, whose cultural worth has long been tied to beauty norms threatened by their aging. White's brand of bawdy humor, then, outlines how aging boomer women (and even nostalgic millennials) can claim cultural relevance by embracing postfeminist mantras of sexual pleasure and the power of romance. Acting as what I call a "prefeminist" icon, White provides a historical narrative suggesting that women did not really need second-wave feminism in order to reap the benefits of postfeminist culture.

As a means of conclusion, the last chapter examines transgender actress Laverne Cox as a test study in the limits of the new, neoliberal body politics. *Time* recently featured Cox on its cover, using her rising fame to indicate a "transgender tipping point" in US culture. But while the other case studies in the book are generally accepted as uplifting icons of the new inclusiveness, Cox's fame and the acceptance of transgender celebrity are still hotly contested and debated. Comparing Cox's fame to the public coming out of former Olympic champion and reality TV star Caitlyn Jenner as transgender, my discussion explores how and why neoliberal culture might embrace transgender identity within its vision of cultural citizenship, as well as the limits of that embrace.

CHAPTER ONE

Melissa McCarthy

CLASS AND CORPULENCE IN
THE OBESITY EPIDEMIC ERA

*M*OST CELEBRITIES SEEK COHERENCE IN THEIR PUB-
lic images, presenting a relatively narrow and simple persona for popular consumption. But if you happened to see Melissa McCarthy
in popular magazines during and then after her breakout role in *Bridesmaids*
(2010), you might think you were gazing at two very different women.

On the one hand, she has graced the covers of *Good Housekeeping, Ladies'
Home Journal, More, Parade,* and *People* as the picture of middle-class, wholesome, mom-next-door femininity, wearing a bubbly smile and casual attire
while offering uplifting assertions of self-confidence. In *Good Housekeeping*
she tells us, "It's what's inside that counts!" Her *Ladies' Home Journal* cover
promises instructions for "loving who you are"; her image on *More* assures the
reader of the "power of being yourself." Reflecting the magazines' readership,
these images of McCarthy promote her as a likable, "ordinary" (i.e., middle-
class and white), plus-sized woman whose fame affirms every heartwarming
platitude about self-confidence and inner beauty. Likewise, her covers on *Elle*
and *The Hollywood Reporter* shift this image into high fashion or old Hollywood glamour: on *Elle* she dons a stylish, flowing overcoat, while her black-
and-white image on *The Hollywood Reporter* has her all in black and wearing a
sleek, wide-brimmed hat. As with the other covers, here she suggests respectability and self-confidence, especially compared to the hypersexual images of
women that have become the standard for entertainment magazines.

On the other hand, the images of McCarthy in magazines such as *Entertainment Weekly* or *GQ* highlight her tendency for over-the-top, raunchy on-
screen performances. One *EW* photo spread pulls out all the bizarrely sexual
and violent energy of the star: McCarthy is dressed like the drag queen Divine
in John Waters's *Pink Flamingos* and brandishes an oversized, double-barreled
pistol that she points at the camera. A snarl across her face, her hair is vibrant

FIGURE 1.1. *Melissa McCarthy on the cover of* Ladies' Home Journal, *May 2012.*

red in a tall bouffant that matches the form-fitting red latex dress showcasing her curves. In *GQ,* however, these curves are used as a joke: McCarthy dons an oversized T-shirt with a cartoon of a slim but busty bikini-clad torso on the front. With short red hair and overdone makeup, she munches on a bag of nuts with a sour look on her face, a vision of "trashy" femininity. Instead of affirming superficial mantras of self-confidence, these images envision McCarthy as a dangerous challenge to bourgeois norms, whether through the marriage of queer sexuality and violence or through "bad" taste and a grumpy refusal to promote unrealistic beauty norms.

She does not have a say in how the covers are edited though (up close allows to ignore body)

FIGURE 1.2. *Melissa McCarthy dressed like Divine in* Entertainment Weekly, *October 2011 (EW.com).*

what they think main point is

McCarthy, then, bears an inordinate variety of contradictory cultural meanings, promoting fat acceptance and the normalization of overweight femininity while also offering an image of out-of-control feminine excess that threatens the very fabric of bourgeois society. On her CBS sitcom *Mike & Molly,* her performances address the day-to-day challenges faced by a lovable obese couple, while her film roles frequently portray her as a sex-crazed, raunchy, and often violent weirdo, from shitting in a sink in *Bridesmaids* to repeatedly punching Jason Bateman in the neck in *Identity Thief.* She is a glamorous figure on the cover of *Elle,* but in one of her most popular *Saturday Night Live* sketches she blasts an entire container of Hidden Valley Ranch onto her face while wearing a Mr. Spock sweatshirt. How, then, are these contradictions and the excess of meanings embodied by McCarthy managed and shaped into a coherent celebrity persona?

McCarthy's contradictions mirror those of neoliberalism and obesity in the United States. Increased media attention to the "obesity epidemic" has given a new, medical rationale to the long-standing practice of fat shaming (calling attention to and degrading celebrities—mostly women—for being or becoming overweight). As obesity continues to be treated as a cause for public concern in the mainstream media, coverage of this "epidemic" stigmatizes obesity as a moral failing warranting public scorn. Both news and entertainment media link obesity with excess, loss of control, and cultural

It's a personal problem

decline. Despite the fact that increasing rates of obesity are a social problem with a complex set of economic and environmental causes, in the mainstream media obesity is usually treated as inherently personal and psychological, an individual failure that must be met with discipline, therapy, and self-transformation. Those who do not take responsibility for their bodies warrant *neoliberal* scorn as burdens to themselves and to society.

McCarthy herself has been subject to this continuing trend in media culture. In a review of her comedy *Identity Thief* (2013), the prominent film critic Rex Reed called McCarthy "tractor sized" and a "hippo," prompting a media furor for his demeaning of the actress.[1] Fellow critic Richard Roeper condemned Reed's "mean-spirited name-calling,"[2] and the incident became so well known that Oscar host Seth MacFarlane even made a joke about Reed at that year's ceremony.

Instead of a well-publicized apology (the routine response to public shaming in today's celebrity culture), Reed doubled down on his comments. He told *Us Weekly* that he stood by his review, deploying the logic of the obesity epidemic to rationalize his rant about the actress:

dick →
> I object to . . . the disgusting attempt to pretend obesity is funny. It is not remotely humorous, and every obese comedian who ever made jokes about the disease are now dead from strokes, heart disease, high blood pressure, and diabetes. . . . I stand by all of my original remarks about Melissa McCarthy's obesity, which I consider about as amusing as cancer, and apologize for nothing.[3]

After Reed's nonapology, the uproar effectively died down, but by using the health risks associated with obesity to rationalize his harsh critique of the actress, Reed's comments showcase how the medical discourses surrounding obesity legitimize stigmatization and cruelty.

Of course, Reed emerged as the villain in this incident, illustrating a different trend in media culture. As I discuss in the introduction to this book, entertainment journalism and popular culture have also become increasingly attuned to feminist critiques of how body image is portrayed in the media. Popular websites such as *Jezebel*, among other media sources, frequently critique the popular media's cult of thinness, exposing the Photoshopping practices of fashion magazines and promoting the need for a variety of body shapes and sizes in the media. Such critiques often make their way into mainstream news and entertainment, as did the outrage over Reed's comments about McCarthy, which was covered on *Entertainment Tonight*, CNN, and a host of other news outlets. Although celebrity media coverage has been (and in many cases continues to be) one of the major sources of fat shaming and obsession with celebrity thinness, the general cultural acceptance that the media promote negative body images has led to contradictory narratives about women's obese bodies: they are signs of individual failure that must be disciplined into conformity, but overtly stigmatizing and mocking them contradicts discourses of inclusivity, acceptance, and female empowerment.

This seeming contradiction between fat shaming and fat acceptance in contemporary media culture is not really a contradiction at all, but rather two sides of the same neoliberal coin. The complex give-and-take between the stigmas of the obesity epidemic and the mantras of women's self-acceptance reflects the process through which the boundaries of neoliberal citizenship are clarified with regard to femininity and the overweight body. Reflecting an emphasis on self-transformation and self-improvement, these media debates explore what kinds of bodies must be reshaped in the interests of responsible citizenship and appropriate projections of self-confidence as a source of inner beauty. These are not really opposing trajectories, but rather two intersecting modes of self-actualization, each promoting projects of transformation that initiate the individual into the realm of neoliberal identity based on a vision of consumer citizenship. In short, the fat-shaming discourses and inner-beauty discourses are only slightly different modes of retooling one's identity to qualify for cultural belonging within capitalist culture.

McCarthy's stardom places her squarely in the middle of these trajectories: she offers a respectable model of uplifting self-confidence, yet she also gives excessive performances of vulgar, hypersexual, and violent femininity that link obesity to a loss of individual control. Her persona affirms the seeming power of "inner beauty," and yet she has made her career by playing characters whose outrageous behavior locates obesity as the source of moral and personal transgression. Combining and managing these seemingly contradictory impulses, her stardom illustrates how to differentiate acceptable modes of overweight femininity from those that should be the subject of derision.

Her stardom also illustrates the crucial role of social class in demarcating these boundaries. After all, McCarthy's most resonant performances are defined by not only violence, swearing, and hypersexuality but also excessive markers of low social class and "bad" taste, from the bowling shirt–clad Megan in *Bridesmaids* to Diane's permed bouffant in *Identity Thief* to almost every character she has played as a host of *Saturday Night Live*. Particularly in her work in film, McCarthy's humor has become synonymous with not only raunchy transgression but also trashiness and the flouting of middle-class respectability. Or at least she has proved adept at *performing* obese trashiness. By contrast, McCarthy's "authentic" self—as seen in entertainment journalism—is humble, well spoken, lovable, and classy. Working hard to distance McCarthy's real-life personality from the outrageousness of her on-

I hate seeing familiar representations of how I grew up on screen for us to critique as lower class + trashy.

37 :: *Melissa McCarthy*

screen work, entertainment journalists assure us that she is a down-to-earth midwestern mom who upholds healthy bourgeois values.

Failing to recognize this distinction between McCarthy's off-screen lovability and on-screen trashiness seems to have been Rex Reed's biggest mistake. While it was easy for the media to castigate the critic for his nasty insults about McCarthy's size, Reed's real transgression was suggesting that McCarthy herself is as crass as the characters she plays. When he targeted McCarthy, claiming that she "is a gimmick comedian who has devoted her short career to being obese and obnoxious with equal success," he collapsed this important distinction in her star persona.[4] But the image of McCarthy as an icon of middle-class fat acceptance must function in tandem with her onscreen trashiness in order to manage the boundaries of overweight citizenship in our neoliberal world. McCarthy's elaborate creations of "trashy" fatness on screen, in fact, are crucial to her articulation of middle-class, self-confident femininity, providing grotesque foils that celebrate the freedom to overturn bourgeois values while still stigmatizing the perceived excesses of obesity.

BODY IMAGE HEROINES AND THE "OBESITY EPIDEMIC"

McCarthy's career started with stand-up comedy in New York City in the 1990s before she moved to Los Angeles and eventually earned a spot with the comedy group The Groundlings. Her comedy work eventually landed her a seven-year run as the quirky sidekick and chef Sookie St. James on the comedic drama *Gilmore Girls* (2000–2007). After playing another quirky sidekick on the short-lived *Samantha Who?* (2007–2009), McCarthy finally landed the lead on a TV sitcom, *Mike & Molly* (2010–2016), as a schoolteacher who falls in love with an overweight police officer. But it was not until her Oscar-nominated role as the eccentric bridesmaid Megan in *Bridesmaids* that she became one of the most popular stars in contemporary Hollywood. The success of *Bridesmaids* helped her land starring roles in films that put female characters in traditionally male genres: *Identity Thief* (2013), a road movie, and *The Heat* (2013), a buddy-cop film costarring Sandra Bullock. After cameos in Judd Apatow's *This Is 40* (2012) and the blockbuster comedy *The Hangover III* (2013), McCarthy began writing and producing films with her husband, Ben Falcone, that included *Tammy* (2014) and *The Boss* (2016). She also starred in the 2014 comedy *St. Vincent*, alongside Bill Murray, and reunited with *Bridesmaids* director Paul Feig for the 2015 comedy *Spy* and the 2016 all-women *Ghostbusters* reboot.

Following the critical and box-office triumph of *Bridesmaids*, McCarthy's career became intertwined with discussions of female empowerment and positive body image in Hollywood. *Bridesmaids* itself was often discussed in the entertainment media as a triumph for women—the film was written by two women (Kristen Wiig and Annie Mumolo) and was celebrated as evidence that women comedians could outdo the highly popular raunchy comedy genre that has long been dominated by men. Critics singled out McCarthy's performance as particularly daring, and she was rewarded with a rare Oscar nomination for a comedy role. Her public persona, especially as viewed in popular magazines, saw her fame as proof of a new inclusiveness in Hollywood and a sign that women were gaining more prestige in the industry. As Karen Valby wrote in *Entertainment Weekly*, "What makes this sudden rush of recognition even more moving for McCarthy is the sense that hers are shared triumphs. The success of *Bridesmaids* put a shine on six gleefully funny actresses. And when her name was called at the Emmys, McCarthy was up on stage in a most righteous display of wit and solidarity alongside five other talented comedians."[5]

Out of the smart, funny women of *Bridesmaids*, however, McCarthy has emerged as a powerhouse, not only for the economic successes of her subsequent films but also because she quickly became a popular heroine for body image in Hollywood. In 2011 *Ladies' Home Journal* proclaimed that McCarthy is "proof you don't have to look a certain way to have wonderful things happen to you,"[6] and the magazine ran another feature on her in 2012 that stated, "Melissa McCarthy is giving women everywhere the confidence to embrace who they are."[7] *Good Housekeeping* described McCarthy as a challenger to a sexist film industry: "in an industry obsessed with youthful, toothpick-slim actresses, McCarthy has never let her age or her shape become an issue."[8] And *People* declared her a "new kind of movie star" and "Hollywood's reigning plus-size A-lister."[9] McCarthy even called out a film reviewer who had body shamed her in his previous writings, asking if he had a daughter and whether he thought he should be more careful about tying women's worth to their physical beauty.[10]

These discourses have made McCarthy the reigning queen of positive body image in the US media and a populist heroine. As a feature in *Redbook* put it, "She's sweetly silly, but also a ballsy barrier-breaker. She looks more like your neighbor than a Barbie. Instead of griping about Hollywood, she simply changed it. In short Melissa McCarthy is the movie star we've all been waiting for."[11] Thus the cover of a 2014 *Rolling Stone* declared McCarthy "Fearless, Fierce, and Funny" while picturing her as a tough, empowered crusader. On the cover, McCarthy, wearing a hip T-shirt, flexes her muscles while making an expression that is half smile, half grimace; she looks like a triumphant rebel taking her place as an industry powerhouse and cultural icon.

McCarthy has become a key figure in the new Hollywood inclusiveness, especially with regard to feminist media critiques of body image. Even mainstream media today readily acknowledge the popular narrative that Hollywood's obsession with thinness may be related to body image disorders such as anorexia and bulimia, despite the fact that the same media outlets still engage in fat-shaming coverage of female celebrities such as Oprah Winfrey, Jessica Simpson, Lady Gaga, and others. Celebrities such as McCarthy, Lena Dunham, Queen Latifah, Gabourey Sidibe, Mindy Kaling, America Ferrera, and others frequently provide entertainment journalists with feel-good narratives that demonstrate how progressive Hollywood casting (and entertainment journalism) can be these days.

Fashion magazines, with their Photoshopping practices and pole-thin models, often function as easy scapegoats for the evils of media beauty standards. In fact, after the Rex Reed incident, McCarthy again found herself at the center of a media and beauty standards scandal as critics at first lauded the fashion magazine *Elle* for including McCarthy on the cover of their "Women in Hollywood" edition, only to publicly shame the magazine for outfitting McCarthy with a loose-fitting jacket that hid the curves of her body.[12] The brief media debate about the *Elle* cover shows the penchant of entertainment journalists for manufacturing quick controversy around celebrity bodies with easy villains like the fashion industry. So when McCarthy revealed in 2014 that several prominent fashion designers refused to make a plus-sized Oscar dress for her when she was nominated for *Bridesmaids*, the fashion industry again bore the brunt of the criticism, with McCarthy again emerging as a populist heroine fighting elitist and sexist couture designers.[13]

The mainstream acceptance of such feminist media critiques can also be seen in the Dove True Beauty campaign, in which advertising for a massive line of beauty products is built around sentimental images that urge women to accept their bodies just the way they are instead of trying to look like fashion models. And when more and more news organizations included uplifting stories about plus-size models, the satirical news site *The Onion* was quick to mock the self-congratulatory trend, publishing its own slideshow of plus-size models with captions like: "Beauty comes in all shapes and sizes. We are goddamn saints for recognizing that and making a slideshow about it," and "Years from now, generations of Americans will remember and honor the day *The Onion* ran this slideshow. Historians will speak of a time when people had unrealistic standards of beauty and how this news institution changed all of that forever."[14]

Yet while entertainment journalism has embraced certain kinds of feminist body image critiques, US culture has increasingly become obsessed with preventing obesity, as a so-called obesity epidemic has occupied the attention of policy makers and the national media. News reports are constantly reminding the public that rates of obesity in the United States are on the rise while emphasizing the individual and social costs of being overweight. Michelle Obama even made childhood obesity and healthy eating the centerpiece of her time in the White House as the First Lady, signaling not only the widespread acceptance of a "crisis" narrative but also insisting that a solution can be found in individual, not structural, changes: personal eating habits, exercise, and lifestyle.

Putting aside the scientific and social veracity of such an "epidemic" and its basis in material reality, Natalie Boero argues that the media have helped construct obesity as a kind of moral panic, shaping its significance in the popular imagination. Examining coverage in the *New York Times* between 1990 and 2001, she demonstrates that the medical and policy debates in the United States have transformed obesity into a site of social panic that seems to threaten not just individual health but the social order itself. Suggesting that individuals' willingness to submit themselves to regimes of self-discipline and self-improvement is vital to the social order, the logic of the obesity epidemic stipulates that individual failures to conform to dominant ideals (of health, beauty, or normalcy) reflect a large-scale social malaise in addition to personal moral failures.[15]

Not surprisingly, contemporary media representing obesity (both in news and entertainment) often stigmatize the obese body and implicate obesity in moral and social failures, from imperatives to transform the obese body on a show such as *The Biggest Loser* to stereotypes linking obesity with laziness and gluttony.[16] Such stigmatization is routine in the world of the "obesity epidemic," where fatness—signifying loss of personal bodily control and the failure of Western patriarchy to control women's bodies—can be seen as a threat to "the dominance of western, imperial/militarized, white, middle-class, reproductive masculinity."[17]

Obesity, then, has become a central focus in the neoliberal discourses of self-transformation within contemporary media and culture. Boero's book *Killer Fat* details the creation and perpetuation of this "epidemic" in the news media, public health policy, medical discourse, and the diet industry, with each bolstering a massive weight-loss and self-help culture that has not only produced trillions in revenue but also helped shape the insistent belief that body shape and size is an external reflection of individual, psychological factors.[18] In particular, the diet industry and those in bariatric medicine have promoted the dangers of an "epidemic," in the process transforming public health policy to encourage individual weight loss (mostly though the purchase of diet products, exercise equipment, and medical interventions).[19] Within this neoliberal view of the body, consuming weight-loss goods and services is the only responsible way to discipline one's body and save US society from the "dangers" of being overweight.

The contemporary media, then, spend half of their time telling overweight individuals to discipline their bodies into conformity and the other half maintaining that self-confidence and inner beauty will triumph, as it did for Melissa McCarthy and other body image heroines. As I note above, these different trajectories in contemporary media culture are more complementary than contradictory, especially when examined from the perspective of social class.

After all, one of the key ways that images of obesity are linked to moral and cultural degradation is through appeals to low social class. Visual markers of "trashiness" or "bad" taste often function as shorthand for the shame of obesity. As Boero shows, the media's coverage of the obesity epidemic centers on issues of control, linking failure to manage one's body and its weight to the loss of social control.[20] But this narrative of "out-of-control" and overweight bodies envisions loss of control as a deviation from middle-class norms. In order to signify the horrors of obesity, overweight bodies in the media tend to be associated with working-class culture and its stereotypes: for example, tacky clothes, slovenly appearance, and fast food.[21] To signify that the epidemic is a kind of regression in the human species, many images and narratives of obesity depict it as a kind of backslide into "trashy" class values.[22]

The scandals that plagued the pop star Britney Spears in 2007 and her subsequent comeback provide a telling example of these dynamics. As Brenda Weber astutely teases out, the media discourses surrounding Spears's antics wove together issues of weight gain, sanity, and social class in describing the pop icon's fall from grace. Spears's weight gain of around twenty to forty pounds came to signify an unstable psyche and a supposed backslide into her "white-trash" southern roots. For Weber, this indicates that "the thin body is always one step closer to a Western ideal of empowered rational individualism and increasing class mobility."[23]

Thus one of the most popular phases of the weight loss show *The Biggest Loser* and other individual transformation shows is the makeover episode, where contestants can demonstrate their newfound control over their bodies by being brought into the fold of middle-class style and attire. The kinds of self-transformation dictated by neoliberal culture are not limited to the numbers on the scale—the physical transformation of the body must be constructed as a fundamental, psychological transformation of individual identity itself, with the weight loss and external appearance seen as a reflection of the contestant's internal discipline and self-acceptance. But far from an ideologically neutral vision of a "healthy" psychology, the contestant's initiation into middle-class taste and appearance aligns a "normal" outlook on one's body and lifestyle with bourgeois values and sensibilities. The audience cannot be assured that the contestant has really changed until they don the habiliments of bourgeois fashion.

Likewise, the media discourses of "inner beauty" and self-assurance are securely middle and upper middle class in their imagery and outlook, eliminating the anxious specter of "trashy" fatness. Examine, for example, the Dove True Beauty "Sketches" ad, in which women describe themselves to an FBI forensic artist only to have the sketch they help create compared to a sketch based on strangers' descriptions of them. Purporting to show how women's negative body image keeps them from realizing their true beauty, the ad also shows how steeped such discourses are in bourgeois cultural values. The women featured in the ad are in their twenties, thirties, and forties and represent a diversity of races and ethnicities, but they are all uniformly marked as middle and upper middle class in their clothing and appearances. By filming the ad in a massive urban loft with hardwood floors and impressive views, the video is located within the cultural milieu of privileged urbanites. In this cultural space, the discourses of inner beauty are acceptable and encouraged, but in the world of *People of Walmart* (a popular website showcasing the odd fashion and behavior of Walmart shoppers) obesity is a reflection of low-class values and a source of humor.

At stake in these class dynamics are the boundaries of ideal neoliberal citizenship. As Kathleen LeBesco notes, fatness has long excluded individuals from full cultural citizenship within US capitalism: "The fat person makes the ultimate bad citizen in that she or he reveals the American Dream for what it is: a fabrication. If we put stock in a philosophy of limitless individual achievement through hard work and intelligence, then what is a fat person but a sign that we can't always get what we want?"[24] Fatness has long been linked to overconsumption; it signifies an excessive appetite that showcases the ills of consumer culture, as exemplified in the animated film *Wall-E*, where fatness is linked to the laziness and complacency of a life in which all your needs are met by endless consumption. Thinness, by contrast, signifies disciplined consumption and thus a morally superior vision of citizenship (since overweight individuals are often blamed for social ills and for diverting food from the needy). This is especially true in an era of neoliberalism, where the ideal thin individual consumes food only along with exercise and weight-loss products in an endless cycle of sustenance and discipline.

But today the discourses of self-acceptance and self-confidence, when linked to the markers of social class, provide an alternative route to obese

airconditioning caused us to gain weight

cultural citizenship. The rising power of feminist media critique and aware-ness of body image issues have carved out a cultural space that is accepting of certain kinds of overweight femininity. Such femininities first and fore-most must demonstrate particular kinds of class markers and good taste in order to disavow the troubling combination of low-class status and fatness, which continues to signify moral failure, social decline, and bad consumer citizenship. However, these femininities must also ascribe to the mantras of self-acceptance and self-confidence, for these refrains facilitate participation in consumer citizenship by marketing the pathway to self-confidence. By cre-ating another level of self-help products aimed at inner transformation, these visions of overweight femininity can earn cultural belonging and citizenship.

McCarthy, then, helps demarcate these delicate boundaries. She can be a populist body image heroine who demonstrates what a classy vision of overweight femininity looks like for the consumers of women's magazines and celebrity culture in general. And yet she can also use her excessive and raunchy performances to shore up her vision of self-confidence by both mocking and appropriating the transgressions of "trashy" fatness.

PERFORMING TRASHY FATNESS

Central to McCarthy's demarcation of these boundaries are her zany, over-the-top performances of obese femininity, especially performances marked by stereotypes of bad taste and low social class. In *Bridesmaids* she plays Megan, the groom's oddball sister who wears oversized bowling shirts, carpal tunnel bandages, athletic sandals, and no makeup in her adventures with the other bridesmaids. Aside from her most memorable scene, in which she defecates into a sink in a swanky bridal shop, Megan curses like a sailor and claims that her "undercarriage" radiates heat when aroused. In *Identity Thief* she plays Diane, a con artist specializing in credit card fraud and iden-tity theft who is tracked down by one of her marks (Jason Bateman) and forced into a road trip while being chased by the mob and a devious bounty hunter. With her bright pink Florida home, blue-and-white gingham shirts, and overdone makeup, Diane screams bad taste, an impression only exacer-bated by her antics, from her seduction of a bolo tie–clad realtor to her ten-dency to punch everyone in the neck when threatened. In *The Heat* she plays a no-nonsense Boston cop who lives in the same rundown apartment build-ings as the trashy criminals she investigates. Wearing baggy, dirty clothes and sporting wild hair, McCarthy offers a fresh, gendered take on the working-class Irish cop so frequently seen on screen. And in *Tammy* she's a none-too-bright fast-food worker with no fashion sense and perpetually dirty hair.

FIGURE 1.3. *Melissa McCarthy as Megan with Kristen Wiig in* Bridesmaids *(Apatow Productions, 2011).*

Even when she plays a billionaire business mogul in *The Boss*, her character's style is crassly ostentatious, placing her foul-mouthed and hypersexual persona against a backdrop of tacky luxury.

These characters resonate not just because they authorize, for the most part, the mockery of obese, working-class femininity. One of the persistent compliments given to McCarthy's performances is that she takes these caricatures and endows them with a certain humanity and sympathy. But such characters are typically not meant for audience identification. Instead, they exist in a complex relationship with a middle-class foil in which their antics are stigmatized and ridiculed, yet are also seen as pleasurable and liberating. The freedom of their transgressions can then be appropriated as a means of enhancing the happiness and self-assurance of their bourgeois counterpart. So while McCarthy participates in a long line of female comedians who flout bourgeois patriarchy by creating grotesque inversions of "good taste," her performances often fail to challenge cultural norms, instead creating superficial icons of "bad taste" that middle-class women can celebrate as exemplars of self-confidence.

McCarthy, of course, is not the first corpulent woman to achieve success as a comedian in Hollywood by tackling the intersections of obesity and low social class. Her performance of outspoken and often crass femininity in fact reiterates the success in the 1990s of Roseanne Barr Arnold (known popularly as only "Roseanne"), whose star persona revolved around her representation of overweight, working-class femininity. Roseanne's persistent flouting of bourgeois cultural norms regarding femininity—her weight, her unkempt home on her sitcom, her mockery of men in power—led Kathleen Rowe Karlyn to describe her as an "unruly woman," a figure drawn from Mikhail Bakhtin's analysis of the carnivalesque. The "unruly woman" defies patriarchal authority by being everything that respectable women are not: loud, abrasive, large, and out of control. In her long-running sitcom (1988–1997), Roseanne's large figure, social class, and wisecracking persona made legible a series of cultural contradictions: "a fat woman who is sexually 'normal'; a sloppy housewife who is also a good mother; a loose woman who is tidy, who hates matrimony but loves her husband, and who can mock the ideology of true womanhood yet consider herself a Domestic Goddess."[25] These contradictions, of course, made Roseanne both popular and reviled, especially in the tabloids and other entertainment media, where she was often presented as overpowering, out of control, and a threat to "normal" definitions of womanhood.

McCarthy is the most salient example of the unruly woman in today's popular culture, giving her comedy the power to challenge entrenched cultural ideals surrounding appropriate femininity. Much like the women comedians (Kathy Griffin, Tina Fey, Sarah Silverman, Margaret Cho, Wanda Sykes, and Ellen DeGeneres) discussed by Linda Mizejewski in *Pretty/Funny*, McCarthy's comedy engages in "a transgressive comedy grounded in the female body—its looks, its race and sexuality, and its relationships to ideal versions of femininity."[26] Defined by the tension between being "pretty" and being "funny," this strand of comedy satirizes the culture's ideals of "pretty" (i.e., dominant definitions of womanhood). For McCarthy, this means making a mockery of bourgeois womanhood, gleefully embodying all that "pretty" women should not be in US culture: loud, vulgar, sexual, hungry, violent.

In this way, McCarthy's unruly comedy emphasizes the inherent paradoxes of overweight femininity in media culture. Because appropriate femininity in Western culture is grounded in ideals of thinness (to be a "good" woman is to control one's body, to not demand resources, to not take up too much space), fat femininity is inherently transgressive, a challenge to gender norms. But as Angela Stukator points out, the transgressions of unruly, overweight bodies are "neither intrinsically radical nor conservative; instead they are contradictory, conflicting, and paradoxical."[27] As much as the image of overweight femininity calls attention to the cultural norms of thinness and bodily control, the specter of the pushy, domineering fat woman is also "a product of the bourgeois imagination" that reinforces the very norms being transgressed.[28] In fact, in her analysis of the British comedian Dawn French, Anne Hole suggests, "The horror, fear, and anxiety which could be produced by the fat female body is diffused by making a jest about/against the fat woman" in most comic performances.[29] Despite the fact that comedians such as Roseanne or Dawn French expose and challenge the discrepancies between feminine ideals and the material realities of women's bodies,

FIGURE 1.4. *Melissa McCarthy as Megan defecating in a sink inside a posh bridal salon in* Bridesmaids *(Apatow Productions, 2011).*

the uncomfortable presence of overweight bodies in the media is diminished by making such bodies the butt of a joke.

These ambivalences are central to McCarthy's persona. Does her fame challenge normative constructions of femininity, or does it offer abject images that justify the derision of overweight women as out of control? Does McCarthy's corpulent body draw attention to the culture's unhealthy obsession with thinness and bodily control, or does it rationalize the stigma surrounding the overweight female body by making it an object of ridicule? While her roles all suggest a carnivalesque undermining of cultural norms, they all eventually end up compromised, affirming stereotypes of the overweight body as in need of discipline, control, and manipulation.

Part of McCarthy's cultural resonance and popularity stems from these contradictions. Her performances are simultaneously rebellious and reactionary, offering uncensored images of feminine transgressions that are often repressed in patriarchal culture, yet that justify the culture's stereotypes of obesity as violent, grotesque, and out of control. Her film roles demonstrate this cultural dilemma, joyfully wallowing in the pleasures of her transgressions while finding ways to bring those characters back in line with bourgeois values.

As a career-defining role, McCarthy's part in *Bridesmaids* perhaps best showcases these complications. On the one hand, her character Megan is a classic unruly woman: loud, assertive, sexual, and unafraid to flout the culture's definition of womanhood. She deflates the obsession with wedding culture and true womanhood by uncontrollably defecating in a pretentious bridal salon while wearing a pink gown. She is not afraid to mask her sexual desire by ridiculously pursuing a gentleman on a flight and is later rewarded with a prolonged, kinky sexual encounter with him during the movie's credits. On the other hand, however, the excesses of her performance seem to also make a punch line of her weight, affirming all of the culture's nasty stereotypes about overweight women. As Michelle Dean asks on *The Awl*, "why can't the buffoon be skinny?" Dean chafes against the celebratory praise of McCarthy's character as somehow radical or liberating, pointing out that "almost every joke was designed to rest on her presumed hideousness. . . . But if her failure to apologize for her size seems momentarily refreshing, one's satisfaction is instantly deflated by the fact that all the other characters in the movie find her so distasteful. The dominant feeling she seems to elicit from her fellow bridesmaids is one of horror."[30] For all its radical and unbridled bucking of feminine norms, McCarthy's body always seems to provoke anxieties about overweight femininity and tends to become the butt of jokes rather than a challenge to patriarchy.

In her other films, moreover, McCarthy's wild, sexually free, and ribald characters more often than not exist primarily to elicit laughs while helping a respectable, middle-class character loosen up. As is typical of Hollywood's vision of low social class, McCarthy's "trashy" persona is simply the vehicle through which the representatives of the middle class can achieve self-fulfillment by slumming it with McCarthy's charismatic bad taste. *Identity Thief*, for example, follows the generic conventions of the road movie and screwball comedy, using Jason Bateman's responsible, stick-in-the-mud family man as a foil to McCarthy's fast-talking, unruly woman. Diane's criminal antics — excessive drinking, shopping sprees, jet skiing — offer a critique of Bateman's Sandy Patterson, who acts as a bland representative of bourgeois patriarchy. Overly responsible and judicious, the real Sandy Patterson must learn to have a little fun — what good is cultivating an immaculate credit report if you do not have any fun with your family? Thus, much of the film wallows in McCarthy's zany humor as the pleasurable alternative to dull, middle-class masculinity, from her terrible but ardent road-trip singing to getting a free meal by telling the servers at a restaurant that Sandy's genitalia were blown off in Iraq. Indeed, the emasculation of Sandy is a running theme thanks to his feminine name, and the film suggests that Diane's transgressive behavior offers the means through which Sandy can "man up."

But if the real Sandy Patterson must learn how to be a better man from the low-class Diane, then Diane in turn must meet him in the middle (class) in order for a real friendship to be forged. Near the end of the film, Sandy and Diane go out on the town on the fraudulent credit card of Sandy's boss, but Diane arrives having shed all the visible markers of bad taste thanks to an expensive makeover. Newly classy, Diane now allows herself to be emotionally vulnerable, explaining to Sandy the traumatic childhood that led her down a criminal path. More reminiscent of the McCarthy seen on *Good Housekeep-*

FIGURE 1.5. *Melissa McCarthy as Detective Shannon Mullins, a violent and slovenly Boston police officer, in* The Heat *(Chernin Entertainment, 2013).*

ing or *People*, this Diane defines her weight and behavior as pathological, the result of psychological scars. So while her wild behavior props up the masculinity of Sandy, Diane must enter into middle-class norms of appearance and behavior—providing psychological explanations for her transgressions—in order to finally distance herself from low social class and earn Sandy's (and the audience's) respect.

A similar process informs McCarthy's buddy-cop film *The Heat*, only instead of bolstering middle-class masculinity, her working-class excesses help today's middle-class working women find themselves. In the film McCarthy plays Shannon Mullins, a tough Boston cop who curses at her supervisors, drags suspects out of their cars for beat-downs, and seems to enjoy a raucous sex life that she wants to keep casual. As in her other roles, the extremes of her character are emphasized through costuming: her hair is wild and unkempt, and she frequently wears baggy, patterned pants, vests over dirty T-shirts, and fingerless gloves. Playing a standard character type usually reserved for men—the tough, rebellious, but committed cop who loves the local community—Mullins is the perfect foil for Sandra Bullock's character, the FBI agent Sarah Ashburn, a by-the-book, careerist, and arrogant federal agent. Mullins lives in a disgusting (but heavily armed) hovel of an apartment in her crime-ridden neighborhood, while Ashburn lives in an immaculate but empty urban loft with all the amenities of middle-class professional life. Mullins's outfits are best suited for bar fights, while Ashburn prefers modest, professional pantsuits (and, in fact, in one scene Mullins can't tell the difference between one of Ashburn's business suits and her buttoned-up pajamas). Mullins curses in almost every line of dialogue, while Ashburn avoids swearing. Mullins has a complicated relationship with her large Boston Irish family, while Ashburn has no one in her life and even lies about having once had a cat.

As in *Identity Thief*, McCarthy's wild subversion of middle-class norms in *The Heat* helps to rejuvenate her bland, middle-class foil. Through her partnership with Mullins, Ashburn learns to loosen up, shed her uptight persona, and kick some ass. Ashburn starts swearing, dons an elaborate militarized get-up during an action scene, and starts bucking the stifling bureaucracies of law enforcement to exact justice, culminating in her shooting a murderous drug kingpin three times in the genitals. However, lest we think she has become too masculine, the film also suggests an impending romance with a fellow FBI agent (Marlon Wayans), whose romantic advances she had previously spurned. Ashburn starts the film as an overly professional working woman with good taste but no love life and bad relationships with her coworkers, a stereotypical vision of professional women who sacrifice relationships for career success. But the antics of McCarthy's Mullins rejuvenate Ashburn by repudiating careerism in favor of personal relationships—Ashburn does not get the raise she had been angling for, but she earns a close friendship and a boyfriend, which is what will really make her happy, the film suggests.

Rather than offering a truly carnivalesque or unruly figure (who overturns class values and subverts bourgeois norms), McCarthy's cinematic persona instead exists only in relation to middle-class self-actualization. Her performances of wild, violent, out-of-control corpulence conjure up a host of degrading stereotypes about obesity and low social class, but her characters become sympathetic instead of disruptive because they can help nice middle-class folks be happier in their day-to-day lives. Her "trashy" antics can be appropriated by the middle class to help them loosen up, but are contained or dismissed by film's end as the narrative focuses on bourgeois self-actualization.[31]

The carnivalesque possibilities and limitations of McCarthy's comedy are perhaps best seen in her popular turns as host of *Saturday Night Live*. McCarthy has hosted the show three times (in 2011 [season 37], 2013 [season 38], and 2014 [season 39]), each time earning huge ratings and rave reviews. In keeping with her other comedic performances, almost every character that McCarthy plays on *SNL* is rooted in the performance of one kind of excess or another, exemplifying the stereotypes of obese bodies in popular culture: the transgression of thinness in the media is often accentuated by excesses of violence, sexuality, and gluttony.

These excesses reflect the ability of the transgressive body to overturn and annihilate the hierarchies of bourgeois culture, to literally make a mockery of socially acceptable behavior and celebrate the destruction of class norms.

After all, many of these skits pair McCarthy with a well-intentioned middle-class white man trying to cope with and make sense of her bizarre behavior. Such foils only demonstrate that her characters undermine a stable sense of middle-class patriarchal authority. Her characters present a loud, sexual, violent, assertive challenge to the social norms that uphold Western cultural values. In this sense, her performances are similar to those of Chris Farley, whose stint on *SNL* (1990–1995) generated a series of larger-than-life, excessive characters who undermined acceptable social boundaries. Stephen Gencarella Olbrys traces Farley's vacillation between a rebellious "carnival-grotesque" that explodes social conventions and a hegemonic "burlesque" that structures his body as a site of humor and derision. In Farley's classic Chippendale dancer skit opposite Patrick Swayze, for example, Farley's sweaty, rotund and exuberant dancing body is judged next to Swayze's muscled, controlled, and idealized bare torso. Farley's performance hilariously undermines the male body norms that idealize muscle and self-discipline, but as the sketch progresses and Swayze's character wins their dance-off, Farley's body is described as "fat and flabby" as he is disciplined into class norms about weight and male beauty.[32] Similarly, McCarthy's performances offer vivacious, extreme, and at times domineering women who shatter expectations of appropriate feminine behavior, only to veer into images and narratives that make her body a source of discipline and shaming.

But while Farley's paradoxical persona became a cautionary tale about the dangers of transgression following the comedian's death in 1997, the rebellious transgressions of McCarthy's persona are contained by displacing them into class stereotypes. Her vivid depictions of sexual, violent, and gastronomical excess are matched on *SNL* by the elaborate and excessive markers of low-class "trashiness." As Barb Kellner, a woman with a business plan that involves eating leftover pizza around the city, she dons a pink tracksuit and huge, outdated glasses under her curly bouffant hairdo. As violent-tempered Shelia Kelly, a college basketball coach who throws toasters at her players, she sports an oversized pantsuit and unflattering short haircut. Season 39's Diane, a foul-mouthed, red-nosed, rib-eating woman who becomes the object of Bobby Moynihan's affection, drapes an unshapely cardigan over a frumpy brown dress while wearing more giant glasses. As Jennifer Evans, a stereotypical online comments section troll who once called the cartoon cat Garfield the "N-word," in season 37, McCarthy sports long stringy hair while wearing that same brown cardigan. And as Kathleen, a dim-witted game show contestant who proffers nonsensical answers like "Pass the mash!" in season 39, her stringy wig makes her look balding as she wears a frumpy brown turtleneck sweater. Clearly, the writers and costume department at *SNL* see McCarthy's characters as exemplars of bad taste and crassness.

The use of such class markers to contain transgressive expressions of female sexuality is apparent in the season 37 sketch "Arlene," in which Arlene (McCarthy) makes none-too-subtle sexual advances to her polite and un-interested coworker, Tim (Jason Sudeikis). As the sketch progresses, Arlene's overt sexuality overwhelms Tim's protestations as her antics become increasingly graphic and over-the-top. Rubbing his tie over her breasts, mock pole dancing on the string of a helium balloon, and licking and fellating the nose of a horse-shaped balloon, Arlene and her unbridled sexual desire (her "lady boner," as she calls it) cannot be contained by the rules of proper office decorum or middle-class romantic values. Tim protests that he is married and has children, but Arlene only pretends to toss his wedding ring aside while continuing to rub his chest.

These sexual excesses make a mockery of respectable, middle-class culture, using Tim as a nice, white, male, middle-class foil to Arlene's exuberant and uncontained sexuality. In a classic example of Bakhtin's carnival-grotesque, Arlene turns the rules of the dominant culture on their head: a bland site of corporate labor becomes a colorful place of dancing, rubbing, and sexual innuendo; appropriate feminine norms of passivity are tossed aside in favor of aggression; the nuclear family is dismissed as a hindrance to passionate sex; mock bestiality serves as a symbol for human sex acts; an overweight woman—normally a symbol of ugliness or asexuality—promotes herself as an object of sexual desire; and female sexual desire is made visible and masculine (her "lady boner") instead of being denied as impure. Her wild, open sexuality demonstrates the ability of corpulent femininity to overwhelm and elude the structures of male control.[33]

But obesity and low social class cohere in the figure of Arlene to transform this ludic rebellion against acceptable bourgeois values into a reactionary burlesque: Arlene's inversions of the social order can be contained by making her ridiculous as a trashy fat lady. As with McCarthy's other characters, Arlene exudes bad taste with her wacky, curled bouffant hair, brown sweater vest over a turtleneck, and (again) outdated, oversized glasses. Her appearance suggests another class inversion, setting her tacky appearance against the mundane but professional world of middle-class corporate life. But rather than enacting a transgressive critique of corporate labor, Arlene's appearance only marks her as an object of ridicule, establishing that the humor is rooted in the supposed discrepancy between professionalism and bad taste. The sketch also insists that transgression and desire are forced apart—her tacky costuming tries to insist that there could never possibly be any real desire for the corpulent body. Arlene is supposed to be funny precisely because her low-class appearance signifies undesirability, safely tucking away any impulses to find her rebelliousness—and the obese body—sexually desirable.

While these performances highlight the possibilities of transgression for McCarthy's humor in her unrestrained mockery of middle-class sexual norms, ultimately her work on *SNL*, much like Chris Farley's, disciplines her carnivalesque transgressions back into middle-class values, often by making her trashy fatness a source of humiliation. Neoliberal culture and the obesity epidemic have heightened the associations between corpulence, bad taste, and moral degradation, in many ways making obesity ripe for unruly humor exploring all that is "low" in contemporary culture. But in the end, such performances affirm the neoliberal dictate to discipline or reject the excesses of the obese body, calling attention to the desire to transform corpulence within the values of bourgeois culture.

THE "REAL" MCCARTHY: SELF-CONFIDENCE AND POSITIVE BODY IMAGE

In contrast to the excessive and confrontational characters McCarthy brought to life on *Saturday Night Live*, her monologues—the short stand-up comedy-style introduction each host offers near the beginning of the show—present McCarthy herself as a self-deprecating and lovable woman whose humbling failures to conform to Hollywood's strict gender and beauty norms reveal how ridiculous those norms are. Instead of the excessively low-class get-ups that her characters wear, McCarthy dresses in stylish clothes for her monologues, with her hair and makeup done according to current standards of beauty and class, even when those very standards are the source of her jokes.

Her season 38 monologue demonstrates this tendency best. Dressed in black tights and a black blouse with a stylish black cardigan over the top, her outfit is completed with dazzlingly bright red platform wedge high heels. But the style of her shoes trumps their practicality; McCarthy attempts to finish her monologue while completely unstable, desperately grabbing at the band members sharing the stage with her, flailing her arms wildly, using a stool for balance, and ultimately just crawling on all fours to keep her balance. McCarthy then attempts to complete the song-and-dance number while barely able to contain her frustration at the peppy cast member (Taran Killam) dancing around her. She then explains to the crowd that she primarily wears Crocs but wanted to get gussied up for the show.

Displaying a seemingly "authentic" persona, McCarthy gently pokes fun at herself in order to undercut the media's gendered beauty norms. She casts herself as a down-to-earth, "regular" woman who, like the vast majority of women in the world, cannot live up to the impossible expectations of women's beauty. The physically demanding feat of wearing ridiculous high heels—assumed to be a normal and natural way for women to demonstrate their sexual desirability—is made strange, unnatural, and hilarious when "real" women reveal what hard work it is to "act like a lady." Humbling herself before the audience, McCarthy suggests that the *performance* of desirable femininity in the media is a sham based on an unnatural and unrealistic set of expectations.

But if McCarthy's star persona shows that the culture's ideals of attractiveness are a carefully constructed performance, her *SNL* characters show that low-class values are also a performance, offering over-the-top exaggerations that the humble and genuine McCarthy can put on to garner laughs. Sandwiched between these two extremes, McCarthy's monologues normalize her performance of middle-class lovability as "real" and "authentic." She can make fun of the media's impossible beauty norms *and* offer caricatures of low-class obesity because the public accepts the authenticity of her middle-class, relatable persona. She can embody the contradictions between the obesity epidemic and the rise of fat acceptance only by appealing to the discourses of middle-class normalcy: obesity challenges the social order if it is crass and lower class, but at the same time the beauty standards of Hollywood such as extreme thinness are highbrow attempts to denigrate "authentic," middle-class women.

The popular magazine profiles written about her therefore frequently insist that the crass McCarthy seen in her films and on *Saturday Night Live* is not the "real" McCarthy. Her profile in *Rolling Stone*, while noting that McCarthy's character in *Bridesmaids* is a "take-no-prisoners alpha gal who bites Kristen Wiig on the ass," maintains that McCarthy in real life is "sweet and gracious, with a voice just a few decibels above a whisper."[34] And in *People* the writer assures readers that McCarthy is not the foul-mouthed, violent character she plays in *The Heat*: "The Melissa McCarthy who showed up to the Boston set of *The Heat* last summer with her two young daughters in tow could have passed for a friendly out-of-towner. Polite. Unassuming, even. 'A sweet, Midwestern mom,' as costar Michael McDonald puts it."[35] Resorting to the markers of appropriate femininity—a quiet voice, a gentle nurturer—such descriptions actively separate the transgressive performances of McCarthy from her sweet and polite "authentic" self. The excessive challenges to bourgeois cultural norms McCarthy offers on screen seem to warrant extra insistence that she is "really" a classy, appropriately feminine figure.

These discrete boundaries between on-screen excess and off-screen class explain why Roseanne in the early 1990s was a figure of cultural anxiety while McCarthy, despite the intensification of the obesity epidemic, is fast becoming one of America's sweethearts today. For Roseanne, there was very little differentiation between her on-screen working-class mom and her off-screen antics, which represented her as an out-of-control threat to patriarchal and bourgeois norms. Whether belting out a crude rendition of the national anthem at a baseball game (complete with crotch scratching and spitting) or delving into too much detail about her sex life with then-husband Tom Arnold, Roseanne's celebrity frequently mocked or made a mockery of the culture's definition of middle-class femininity. Such antics earned her much derision in the media as she came to be seen as a dangerous working-class figure (my polite, middle-class mother did not want me watching *Roseanne* for these reasons). McCarthy, on the other hand, taps into many of the same tensions surrounding overweight femininity and the cultural excesses of bad taste, but her celebrity assures us that her performances are the "safe" comedy of a quiet and sweet middle-class lady.

In many ways, then, McCarthy's celebrity is bookended between Roseanne and the rise of Lena Dunham, who has become a central figure in feminist media critiques of body image. If McCarthy's displays of crass, low-class femininity are *performances* compared to the *authentically* crass Roseanne, then McCarthy's seemingly authentic off-screen persona is simply more believable and more relatable than that of Dunham. While Lena Dunham has become a darling of critics and intellectuals for her outspoken feminist media critique and her willingness to bare all despite not looking like a model, McCarthy has achieved a broader, more populist success with raunchy, gross-out comedy. While both Dunham and McCarthy have become body image heroines in today's media culture, McCarthy's celebrity positions her squarely within middle-class, maternal femininity while Dunham appeals to hipster intellectuals.

Thus most of McCarthy's coverage in popular magazines insists that she is a friendly, lovable, midwestern mom rather than someone like the raucous characters she portrays on screen. In *Redbook*, her daughter, Viv, interviews her about princesses and macaroni and cheese.[36] In *Ladies' Home Journal* she talks about losing sleep thanks to kids, and her guilty pleasure of watching interior design shows.[37] In *People* McCarthy says that she skipped the Emmys to take care of her new baby.[38] And the release of *Tammy*—written and directed by her husband—led to a host of profiles of the film as a family affair, emphasizing McCarthy as a wife and mother.[39] It is no wonder *Good Housekeeping* proclaimed that millions of "everyday women" love McCarthy: "They view the immensely likeable working wife and mom as a regular-gal role model."[40]

These conceptions of McCarthy largely define her performance on the CBS sitcom *Mike & Molly*, in which McCarthy plays a lovable, overweight schoolteacher who meets an overweight police officer at an Overeaters Anonymous meeting. Following the courtship and eventual marriage of the two eponymous characters, the show offers a fairly stark contrast to McCarthy's film performances, dealing with the everyday antics of a standard romantic sitcom, only with obesity as a key theme. Disavowing the excessive representations of "bad taste" for which McCarthy is known on the big screen, the show helps cement her associations with everyday middle-class audiences.

While the show is sometimes criticized for making its own variety of fat jokes or failing to make the characters likable,[41] it is largely celebrated for its very existence; as an obesity-themed sitcom in an era when overweight people are only typically represented on weight loss shows, *Mike & Molly* is defined by its concept rather than its comedy. In fact, the fat-shaming controversies that tend to pop up around McCarthy's celebrity often make the show seem like a feel-good response to the snide comments of Rex Reed and others. For example, after a blogger said she was "grossed out" by the thought of McCarthy and her costar Billy Gardell kissing, the show's producer, Mark Roberts, promoted the idea that *Mike & Molly* epitomizes Hollywood's new inclusivity, saying, "the theme of our show is that everyone deserves love and we should accept each other no matter what we look like or where we come from."[42]

Reflecting these platitudes, in popular magazines McCarthy has become synonymous with the idea of self-confidence as the key to personal success. Portrayed as a celebrity who overcame Hollywood's weight obsession, she is able to serve as inspiration to "regular" women. *Ladies' Home Journal* declared, "Melissa McCarthy is giving women everywhere the confidence to embrace who they are," while *Good Housekeeping* sees McCarthy as "living proof that self-acceptance and perseverance can make any dream come true."[43] What makes McCarthy so inspiring, according to profiles like these, is her ability to shrug off the mean-spirited fat shaming of contemporary Hollywood and to maintain her self-confidence in a world that stigmatizes obesity. For example, *People* reported that she has given up on dieting to change her figure and instead focuses on health, and with that change of attitude has come success:

> In a weight-fixated culture, she's been attacked for being fat and cheered as a role model. Warned she wouldn't work because of her size, "I thought, I'll show you!" she told *People* in 2011. In 2003 she dropped 70 lbs. on a liquid diet: "I'll never do that again—I felt starved and crazy." Now an Emmy winner and Oscar nominee, "I'm still working on [my weight]," she said, "I just want to live a healthy lifestyle."[44]

So when that blogger made headlines expressing disgust at McCarthy kissing, entertainment media widely covered McCarthy's ability to dismiss the insult without taking it personally, saying that she hoped the blogger does not have a daughter.[45] Helping cement her status as a middle-class role model, McCarthy tends to respond to fat shaming with a shrug and a smile, only more proof that her self-confidence is seemingly unshakable.

In this way, McCarthy's celebrity dovetails with popular debates concerning women and self-confidence, a discussion that intensified in 2014 prior to the release of *Tammy* with the publication of *The Confidence Code* by Katty Kay and Claire Shipman. Building off the success of the tech executive Sheryl Sandberg's 2013 book *Lean In*, which explores why women still lag behind men in high-level leadership positions, *The Confidence Code* is a self-help manual on the "science and art of self-assurance" for women. The authors suggest that one of the key reasons behind continued workplace gender inequality is confidence; women's own insecurities about their self-worth and reluctance to promote themselves and their ideas are holding them back compared to their more self-assured male counterparts.[46] The book was widely reported in the US media as the authors tapped into a powerful narrative of confidence as central to women's empowerment. The shampoo brand Pantene, in fact, made confidence and women's empowerment a central theme of their Shine Strong ad campaign, including an ad admonishing women for apologizing too much that drew widespread attention.[47]

But as Kay and Shipman were making the rounds on morning television and the Pantene ad "Not Sorry" was racking up views on YouTube, controversy began to surround these feel-good messages about respecting yourself. Feminist media critics condemned the individualistic messages of the confidence gap discussion, suggesting that such narratives blamed women for their own oppression while ignoring the political, economic, and cultural discrimination structured into Western culture. As Jessica Valenti wrote for *The Guardian*'s US edition, if women are not insecure, then they are not paying attention: "Women's lack of confidence could actually just be a keen understanding of just how little American society values them."[48] Likewise, it was easy for critics to condemn Pantene's stylish women's empowerment ads as superficial pandering: buy our shampoo and you will get that raise you have always wanted!

The backlash against the "confidence gap" pinpointed its roots in neoliberal capitalist culture—by focusing on women's confidence, these approaches to inequality simply offer self-help mantras that market consumer products rather than exploring the complex reasons why inequality persists. By shifting responsibility away from the economic structures of US capitalism that devalue women and women's labor, such discourses place the responsibility for gender inequality on the shoulders of individual women who must transform themselves—from their behavior to their appearance—to be taken seriously within patriarchal culture. And as the Pantene ads suggest, the means through which this transformation should take place is consumption—buying the right kinds of products that will build self-confidence. Of course, confidence seems to be linked to the culture's beauty standards, according to Pantene: being confident and being beautiful are one and the same in the ads.

In the midst of these cultural debates, McCarthy became the poster child for self-confidence rhetoric, but not by being traditionally beautiful and classy like the women in the Pantene ads. Instead, her ability to perform wild and wacky caricatures of bad taste is cast as a challenge to Hollywood's high-brow perfectionism for women. McCarthy herself frequently promotes this philosophy as central to her comedy. As she told *Ladies' Home Journal* in 2012:

> One of my favorite things is playing someone who's utterly confident—even if they are, just, like *wrong*. They're off the beaten track. They're not polished or perfect, but they're so solid in their shoes. And I always think, *Now that's someone who's interesting.* They don't give a s---- what they're supposed to be, or how they're supposed to look. I find them mesmerizing. I think there's greatness in not caring what other people think.[49]

For McCarthy, this greatness is also clearly tied to social class, to individuals who deviate from bourgeois norms. Later in the same interview, her example of these mesmerizing individuals is "the woman at Walmart who's happy in her cat sweater," using the popular meanings of Walmart stores as a locus of low social class to suggest this carefree attitude. And when espousing this theory to *Entertainment Weekly*, she makes it clear that grotesque performances are her way of transgressing Hollywood's gender norms, saying, "I don't find anything interesting about someone perfect. . . . I'd rather talk about a rash than [hair] extensions. I'm always saying 'what if we black out my teeth?'"[50] For McCarthy, self-confidence and bad taste cohere in figures like the Walmart cat lady or Arlene on *Saturday Night Live*, making them philosophical challenges to Hollywood's glamorous but unhealthy promotion of "perfect" (high-brow) women.

In US pop culture, with scant roles for women who actively challenge notions of appropriate femininity, this vision of self-confidence can be radical. Only a handful of stars such as Mae West or Roseanne have achieved success equal to McCarthy's based on comedy that so blatantly demolishes the culture's notions of wholesome womanhood. As one critic explains it:

> McCarthy never let the need to seem "feminine," or "likable," or even remotely appropriate, get in the way of a good joke. Which, I would argue, is exactly why she's been so popular with female moviegoers: For women, who are trained to spend every moment of their lives worrying about how other people see them, McCarthy's on-screen persona is an untamed, foul-mouthed, ketchup-hurling Id, a woman who acts on every impulse that pops into her head, without a second's guilt or self-doubt.[51]

But the use of low social class to achieve this barrier-breaking id suggests that social stigma is merely shifted around, not necessarily challenged. The self-confidence that McCarthy models off-screen is *not* that of Arlene on *SNL*, who casually tosses aside good taste and bourgeois sexual norms. Instead, McCarthy is lauded in popular magazines for being a nice, polite, middle-class woman who excels at *pretending* she can be Arlene (or any of the other zany, "trashy" characters she portrays). Figures like the Walmart cat lady are appropriated as idols of self-confidence, but only when they can be used by "regular," middle-class women to affirm life lessons about self-assurance (much as McCarthy's characters most often function to rejuvenate the bland lives of her middle-class foils). McCarthy's celebrity persona suggests that the wild, ribald characters she portrays are not objects of identification but more like mascots—exaggerated representations of the working class that middle-class women can rally behind in the quest for neoliberal self-assurance.

McCarthy's 2015 comedy *Spy*, in fact, made these dynamics central to her character, finally allowing her to be the "regular" middle-class lady for whom the performance of zany trashiness facilitates her own self-actualization. In the film, McCarthy plays Susan Cooper, a CIA analyst who assists field agent Bradley Fine (Jude Law) by providing critical information through his earpiece from the safety of her desk back in Virginia. She is also in love with Fine, a James Bond-esque figure. But when Fine is killed and the identities of all the field agents are discovered by a criminal mastermind, Cooper volunteers to become a field agent since her identity is still unknown. She is sent to Europe and given a series of secret identities, all of which disguise her as trashy, zany American tourists: women with horrible sweaters, tacky hair, a penchant for cat fashion, and who travel with anti-fungal spray and hemorrhoid wipes. After working through these identities, however, she finally

FIGURE 1.6. *Melissa McCarthy as the CIA agent Susan Cooper (disguised as a crass American tourist) in* Spy *(Chernin Entertainment, 2015).*

cracks the case when she creates her own more confident alter ego—Amber Valentine, a foul-mouthed but glamorous mercenary—and gains the confidence of the film's villain, played by Rose Byrne.

Continuing the "girl power" trend of McCarthy's collaborations with director Paul Feig, *Spy* systematically undermines the masculinist pretensions of the spy genre, poking fun at the narcissistic male agents whose success relies on the intelligence and labor of the (mostly female) technicians back in Virginia. Jason Statham, in fact, plays a caricature of his action-film persona who constantly lists the heroic (and impossible) feats of strength and violence he has committed, even as he constantly bungles his mission and needs to be saved by Cooper's fast thinking. Cooper, moreover, relies on the help of her office buddy, Nancy, played by comedian Miranda Hart (between Law, Statham, and Hart, it is unclear why the CIA employs so many English agents). The film ends, then, with Cooper saving the world (she recaptures a stolen nuclear bomb), getting over her crush on Fine (who, as it turns out, only faked his death to go undercover), and spending some quality time with her buddy Nancy as the office oddballs finally get to be the heroes.

The key to Cooper's self-actualization as an empowered and skilled female field agent is the same characteristic that allows the nice, middle-class McCarthy to become a comedy icon: taking on caricatures of often trashy femininity. While disguised as a series of tacky American tourists, Cooper finally unleashes her natural capacity for violence (which she kept hidden as Fine's assistant), and as the prolific curser Amber Valentine, she finally comes into her own as a field agent. Mirroring the dynamics of McCarthy's star persona, *Spy* demonstrates the importance of McCarthy's trashy masquerades to the articulation of middle-class, professional femininity.

CONCLUSION: *TAMMY* AND THE FUTURE
OF THE MCCARTHY PERSONA

McCarthy's 2014 comedy *Tammy* seemed to mark a different direction for her on-screen persona and her off-screen control of her brand. Written by McCarthy and Ben Falcone, and produced by McCarthy (along with Will Ferrell and Adam McKay), *Tammy* offered McCarthy the opportunity to play a larger role in shaping her character and the contexts of her comedy. Would she continue to play excessive and out-of-control icons of trashiness, or could she craft a more nuanced version of her persona?

McCarthy plays the eponymous hero of the film, a foul-mouthed and dim-witted young woman facing a life crisis. After losing her job at a fast-food chain and coming home to discover that her husband has been dating their neighbor, she embarks on a road trip to Niagara Falls with her alcoholic grandmother, played by Susan Sarandon. Hilarious antics ensue, including a parking lot brawl with bratty teenagers over a case of beer, a bumbling robbery of a fast-food joint, and a raucous Fourth of July party with some wealthy lesbians (Kathy Bates and Sandra Oh). The film follows Tammy's maturation and tumultuous relationship with her grandmother, who helps Tammy find her way and start a new connection with a gentlemanly farmer (Mark Duplass) that they meet along the way, despite the fact that Tammy does a short stint in jail for her "robbery" (she gives the money back the next day).

Crass and classless antics still define McCarthy's humor in the film. When Tammy is fired for being late, she scrapes her dandruff into a bin of lettuce and licks a tray of burgers about to be served. She gushes over a tacky wooden sculpture of a red, white, and blue eagle. She wears hideous T-shirts, including one with a cartoon bear saying "mahalo" that ends up incriminating her. But the antics of Sarandon as Pearl, including guzzling booze with her oxycontin and having drunken sex in the backseat of her Cadillac as well as affairs with the neighborhood ice cream man, quickly take over the film. As Pearl's behavior spirals from the comic to the tragic (publicly humiliating Tammy over her weight, or admitting to making a pass at Tammy's father), Tammy finds herself cleaning up the messes of an out-of-control wreck rather than making those messes herself.

In this way, *Tammy* carves out a much more human and vulnerable character than McCarthy has portrayed in the past. As Sady Doyle argues, *Tammy* never makes its heroine the butt of jokes about fatness or sexuality, instead showing the real struggles of a woman who wants to be fierce but is stung by rejection. And the film offers her a genuine romantic plot instead of jokes about fatness and food fetishes.[52] Rather than a caricature of self-confident raunchiness, McCarthy's role in *Tammy* actually lets her be a person.

If *Tammy* adds nuance to McCarthy's vision of crass self-confidence, it still does so only by insisting on bourgeois self-actualization. Not surprisingly, Tammy's maturation and self-awareness coincides in the film with a makeover that flattens her unkempt hair and dons her in middle-class attire (thanks to the wealthy lesbians). Just as in *Identity Thief*, the trappings of middle-class style act as a visual cue for personal growth and individualism, changing her from a caricature into a real person. This transformation, moreover, is accompanied by a rather simplistic affirmation of bootstrapping: while moping after her grandmother fat-shames her in public, Tammy is scolded by Kathy Bates, who tells her to buck up and just work hard for herself. Noting that lesbians have not always been in style, Bates's character says that she overcame all the discrimination she faced by simply working hard in order to claim her slice of the American dream.

This ham-fisted moment of meritocracy highlights the centrality of neoliberal individualism to the McCarthy persona, despite its more humanized form in *Tammy*. Sure, discrimination exists, but those who choose to work through it will be rewarded, and all Tammy needs to do to get her life together, the film suggests, is simply decide to work hard at making herself a success. The film's resolution, then, sees Tammy, now with better hair and slightly more fashion sense, finally getting her grandma to Niagara Falls, reconnecting with her love interest, and finally setting off on her own in a new city. Achieving her own bourgeois self-actualization, she will finally channel her confidence into a respectable existence for herself.

In this way, Tammy's transformation reveals the possibilities for cultural citizenship encoded across McCarthy's persona: for women who do not qualify for the culture's cult of thinness, respectable femininity in a neoliberal world can be achieved by ignoring stigma, discrimination, and harassment and instead focusing on yourself. Work harder. Be confident. And feel free to use the specter of "trashy" femininity to show how self-confident you are, as long as you are *really* a nice, polite, middle-class lady.

CHAPTER TWO

Gabourey Sidibe

OBESITY AND POSTRACIAL FEMININITY

GABOUREY SIDIBE'S OSCAR NOMINATION FOR BEST actress in 2010 challenged popular conceptions of who gets to be a movie star, especially for black women. Unlike Halle Berry (the last African American woman to be nominated for the best actress before her), Sidibe does not look the part of a typical Hollywood leading lady. While Berry is a mixed-race, light-skinned former beauty pageant contestant, Sidibe is a dark-skinned young woman who weighs around three hundred pounds. Her nomination for her performance in *Precious: Based on the Novel "Push" by Sapphire*, along with the slew of other awards she won for that role, seemed to suggest a new, more progressive direction in Hollywood and celebrity culture, especially since the film provides a gut-wrenching tale of urban despair focusing on domestic abuse, incest, and illiteracy in 1980s Harlem. In the wake of the 2008 election of Barack Obama as the first black president, Sidibe's successes added fuel to the growing media discourses that US culture was entering a "postracial" era that could celebrate the successes of African Americans and other people of color. As *USA Today* proclaimed, "roles for black, Asian, and Latin actors are scarce in Hollywood, but surely Sidibe [and others] are having their moment."[1]

In the years after her debut in *Precious*, Sidibe has only built on this progressive narrative, finding a steady stream of high-profile acting jobs that once would have seemed unimaginable for a woman of her appearance. After work as a supporting actress on the Showtime series *The Big C*, she joined the ensemble cast of the hit FX series *American Horror Story* for seasons 3 and 4 and also could be seen in independent films such as *White Bird in a Blizzard* (2014), *Life Partners* (2014), and the horror-comedy *Gravy* (2015). She also took on recurring roles on Fox's hip-hop-themed family melodrama *Empire*

FIGURE 2.1. *Gabourey Sidibe as Andrea Jackson in* The Big C *(Showtime, 2011–2013).*

(produced by the director of *Precious*, Lee Daniels) and the Hulu comedy *Difficult People*.

Sidibe emerged on the scene in US pop culture just at the right time to feed the media's newfound concern with race relations, or at least with the question of whether race still mattered in a post-Obama world. Her success in the entertainment industry paralleled the rise of media discourse on race, especially as she became a high-profile, feel-good story demonstrating the seeming irrelevance of race and gendered beauty standards.

Ironically, of course, as the media became obsessed with the idea of a post-racial America, massive inequalities kept pointing to the relevance of race. Popular success stories like those of Lupita Nyong'o—another dark-skinned black woman who won the best supporting actress in 2014 and was voted that year's "Most Beautiful Woman" by *People* magazine—spawned a host of self-congratulatory media discourses about diversity and changing beauty standards.[2] And yet while Nyong'o graced the cover of fashion magazines, the skin tones of poor black men continued to mark them as appropriate objects of violence in a series of high-profile police brutality cases during the 2010s that sparked nationwide debates about racial inequalities.[3]

Sidibe's rise to fame, then, coincided with, and contributed to, a set of contradictory racial discourses in US culture which are deeply invested in determining the kinds of bodies that can truly belong within the social fabric. What kinds of black bodies can be embraced as objects of beauty and popular consumption, and what kinds of bodies can be denied their rights and punished by government institutions? What kinds of black bodies can be seen and celebrated in popular media, and what kinds are best obscured, to be seen only in fleeting glances on surveillance video? And what kinds of black femininity can be deemed appropriate, especially for black women who challenge dominant beauty norms surrounding weight and skin tone? This chapter examines such questions by analyzing the process through which Sidibe's overweight black body has been accepted within US pop culture, especially as it participates in the discourses of a seemingly postracial America.

Sidibe, of course, is an odd entrant into a media culture invested in only certain kinds of black women's bodies (typically those that are thin, light-skinned, and sexualized). As with Melissa McCarthy, Sidibe's popular persona must navigate the cultural stigmas of weight in a culture obsessed with the so-called obesity epidemic, but the images of black obesity carry a more stigmatizing set of signifiers. Throughout the history of the US visual media, after all, corpulent, dark-skinned black women have been deployed in two stock roles that still find their way into pop culture: the lovable "mammie" figure and the gluttonous "welfare mother."[4] Moreover, the recent moral panic in the US media over obesity has only intensified the stigma against overweight black bodies, marking them as objects of revulsion and deploying their images to signify the horrors of low social class. Research on images of obesity in the news media show that African American women evoke higher levels of disdain and bias than images of obesity in any other category.[5] So while the color-blind rhetoric of the anti-obesity movement posits a seemingly universal notion of "health" as the marker of responsible citizenship, the pathologizing of racial/ethnic cultures suggests that the rhetoric of health masks the governance of white, middle-class cultural values, in which images of bodies of color are used to signify the degradation of obesity in pop culture. As Scott Stoneman argues, "The intersection of the war on obesity with a continuing class antagonism toward racialized ethnic others is a consequential part of understanding the construction of the normatively healthy body, harnessed as it is to a privileged notion of whiteness."[6]

Thus when overweight stars such as Melissa McCarthy perform "trashiness" but insist on wholesome, middle-class values, they are in part distancing themselves from the racial undertones of obesity. McCarthy's public persona as a nice midwestern mom who can appear on the cover of *Good Housekeeping* affirms a sense of bourgeois whiteness that is brought into question by her weight and its associations with low social class, especially since her humor relies on exaggerated visions of "white trash." White obese bodies in the media, in other words, must disavow the threatening associations of blackness, or at least the stigma of being not quite fully white.[7]

Gabourey Sidibe's fame, then, poses even more stringent cultural challenges to conceptions of health and beauty that are tied to assumptions of whiteness, with her weight and dark skin epitomizing the culture's stereotypes of poor black femininity. For Stoneman, in fact, images of lower-class obesity such as Sidibe's performance in *Precious* participate in what Hancock calls a "politics of disgust": such images inhibit any forms of political solidarity between groups of citizens by linking marginalized groups to seemingly revolting and disgusting imagery.[8] Stoneman in fact argues that no matter how moving the narrative of individual empowerment might be in *Precious*, the visual imagery of lower-class, overweight black femininity cannot actually invite identification and empathy, providing instead powerful visual stereotypes affirming the degradation of blackness.

As with Melissa McCarthy, Sidibe's persona has sought to transcend such stigmas by celebrating individual self-confidence. Sidibe is most often represented as a strong, outspoken young black woman who locates her self-assurance beyond the quest to conform to cultural beauty standards, providing a challenge to the dominant models of young stardom. Her seemingly unshakable self-confidence allows her to transcend the stigmas she faces and has paved the way for her unlikely success—or at least that is how the story goes.

The previous chapter explored some of the pitfalls of such self-confidence rhetoric when it comes to obesity, arguing that appeals to self-confidence are just another mechanism of a neoliberal culture that wants individuals to transform themselves instead of instituting real social change. This chapter will extend that critique to the context of a supposedly postracial America in which people of color must transform or "improve" themselves in lieu of cultural or structural changes that would alleviate conditions of inequality. Despite the fact that Sidibe emerged as a star in a film depicting the harsh realities of black urban poverty, her star persona has come to embody the dictates of a neoliberal, postracial worldview that prioritizes consumption and the trappings of celebrity over community and education as the earmarks of black aspiration.

At the same time, Sidibe's inclusion alongside McCarthy and other exemplars of white body positivity (Lena Dunham, Amy Schumer, Rebel Wilson, and others) demonstrates the subordination of race to a generic celebration of femininity and womanhood in popular media. Sidibe's career shows how popular narratives of a postracial culture rely on feel-good appeals to women's empowerment that occlude the structural realities of racial injustice in America. In the process, Sidibe's fame illustrates the tendency for the media to use black women's bodies as symbols of a postracial sisterhood while positing highly individual and highly gendered solutions to inequality.

Post Obama

NAVIGATING RACE IN A POSTRACIAL WORLD

The term "postracial," while used sparingly in US media discourse in the 1990s, emerged in the mid-2000s as a popular adjective and talking point for journalists and cultural/political pundits, especially during and after the 2008 presidential campaign.[9] As Catherine Squires explains it, the definition of the term has been somewhat fluid during this period, but it generally refers to a belief that the United States has moved beyond the explicit racism of the country's past and the contentious debates surrounding racial identity in the post–civil rights era. Instead, a supposedly postracial world is one in which race no longer matters: racial identity is fluid and the country has created enough opportunities for people of color that even a black man can be elected president. Of course, the idea of a postracial United States was always contested: almost immediately after the term surged in use, a host of media discourses emerged critiquing and ridiculing the idea of a postracial United States, pointing to the many existing realities of racial inequality as evidence that race still matters in the everyday lives of people of color.[10]

The campaign and election of Barack Obama illustrates these contradictory trends. His election spurred a host of optimistic prognostications about a new, postracial America. Obama's campaign slogans of "hope" and "change" resonated with those who sought to put the challenges of the civil rights movement behind them and tapped into the aspirations of young black people who desire a world in which they do not face the same obstacles encountered by previous generations.[11] And yet the media discourse surrounding Obama's campaign was also marked by intense discussions of racial inequality, race-based fears about his presidency from his detractors, and none-too-subtle racist vitriol against him and his family.[12] Indeed, one of the biggest ironies of the so-called postracial era is that the media still seem to be constantly discussing race relations, albeit in contradictory ways—the achievements of people of color are celebrated as examples of a changing culture, but persistent inequalities continue to erupt into national news stories, such as the 2014–2015 furor over policing, violence, and racial profiling.

At the heart of these postracial discourses are two overlapping assumptions: (1) a valorization of color-blindness as a virtue, and (2) an assumption of individual choice central to a neoliberal worldview.

Building off the work of Eduardo Bonilla-Silva, particularly his book *Racism without Racists*, Sarah Nilsen and Sarah E. Turner describe a vision of "colorblind diversity" prominent in US culture and media that, while posed in the language of antiracism and diversity, undercuts an understanding of racial inequality. Color-blindness, while sometimes referring to an attitude in which race is never acknowledged, more often refers to an attitude in which diversity is acknowledged superficially but is divorced from issues of cultural stigma or structural barriers to parity. Seeing the world through a color-blind lens might mean touting one's nonwhite friends, or seeking diverse entertainment media to affirm a sense that race has no impact on one's personal beliefs or the opportunities afforded to people of color.[13] White teenagers, for example, might use a color-blind lens to consume hip-hop as a sign of their commitment to diversity while ignoring issues of poverty, lack of economic opportunities, police brutality, and other factors experienced by many black communities that have helped create the cultural context for hip-hop.[14] To be postracial is to deploy this color-blind logic and ignore the continuing expressions of racial inequality.

As this suggests, if racism exists, then from this perspective it is only manifest in individual racism—bad or uneducated people who harbor racist ideas—but never in structural or institutional discrimination (seen, for example, in residential segregation or law enforcement strategies that result in massively high incarceration rates for some people of color). In this way, postracial beliefs reflect a neoliberal worldview emphasizing individual choices on the free market as holding all responsibility for social problems. As Squires notes, "Post-racial discourses obfuscate institutional racism and blame continuing racial inequalities on individuals who make poor choices for themselves or their families."[15] For example, the "school choice" narrative suggests that parents are responsible for choosing the right schools if their child falls behind, rather than recognizing the role of systemic underfunding of education, especially in districts serving minority populations. Or when the recent mortgage crisis meant waves of foreclosures in black and Hispanic neighborhoods, the media blamed borrowers for not making sound financial decisions rather than investigating predatory lending practices.[16] Inversely, this neoliberal, postracial perspective also transforms certain kinds of racial identity into a marketable commodity that individuals should deploy in their own self-presentations, since it is assumed that in a culture which superficially celebrates images of diversity, one can flexibly deploy a preferred racial/ethnic identification for purposes of self-promotion.[17]

This tendency toward superficial, color-blind diversity is perhaps most visible in the entertainment media, which have sought to lure increasingly important nonwhite audiences with more diverse casting. But often these attempts at diversity obscure the structural and cultural discrimination faced by people of color. As Bonilla-Silva and Austin Ashe point out, programs such as *Grey's Anatomy* or *The Office* are celebrated for their racial inclusivity. In fact, the creator of *Grey's Anatomy*, Shonda Rhimes (an African American woman who also produces *Scandal* and *How to Get Away with Murder*, both of which have female African American leads), is lauded for her color-blind casting, ignoring race in the casting process and creating remarkably diverse shows compared to the rest of the network lineup. But the image *Grey's Anatomy* presents of a multiracial group of affluent doctors tending to their melodramatic careers and love lives fails to reflect the realities of inequality and race in America. Instead, the show offers a utopic vision of a world in which nonwhites achieve at the same levels as whites and in which structural inequality does not seem to exist. Meanwhile, a show such as HBO's *The Wire* attempts to represent the effects of urban decay and globalization on black communities, earning critical acclaim but never an audience.[18]

As this suggests, celebrity culture occupies an important place in postracial media discourse, offering examples of individual success that affirm the irrelevance of race to attaining personal success. Figures such as Oprah Winfrey, Barack Obama, Shonda Rhimes, and others have engendered lengthy discussions of race and opportunity in US media. After all, these public figures seem to demonstrate the inherent meritocracy of US culture and the possibilities for transcending race. How, then, does Sidibe take her place alongside these other postracial icons?

SELF-CONFIDENCE AS RACIAL TRANSCENDENCE

The central tenet of Sidibe's overcoming-racism narrative is the power of self-confidence. As I discuss in more detail below, for Sidibe's character in *Precious*, escape from poverty, illiteracy, and abuse comes through structural support systems: caring social workers, teachers, and other government representatives who make a difference in their communities. But for Sidibe's postracial persona, the power to overcome must not come from government support or strong communities, but rather from within the individual. In her coverage in popular magazines, Sidibe becomes synonymous with an unbridled confidence that holds the key to racial transcendence.

Within this narrative, the primary obstacles Sidibe has overcome are her weight and dark skin tone, especially when confronted by film reviewers who could not seem to move beyond her appearance. As Stoneman describes in his analysis of *Precious*, blackness, and obesity, several high-profile film critics made disparaging remarks about Sidibe's character and the actress's physical appearance in the film.[19] In Armond White's diatribe against the film, he said that Sidibe was "so obese her face seems bloated into a permanent pout."[20] In *The New Yorker*, Anthony Lane wrote that Sidibe is "grimly overweight, her face so filled out that the play of normal expression seems restricted."[21] And in *New York* magazine, David Edelstein said that Sidibe's head is like a "balloon on the body of a zeppelin, her cheeks so inflated they squish her eyes into slits."[22] For such critics, Sidibe's physical appearance acted as a source of fascination and disgust, prompting rhetorical flourish in order to try to capture what they saw as the spectacle of her fatness.

Across Sidibe's career, however, these kinds of overly stigmatizing comments were the exceptions in the media's coverage of her. In fact, most explicit discussions of Sidibe's weight function in tandem with discussion of race to show how physical appearance often leads to stereotyping and lost career opportunities. Sidibe is an unlikely star, and the story of her rise to fame is set against the stifling beauty norms of Hollywood stardom. As reported in her first profile in 2007 in the *New York Times*, her appearance not only singles her out for teasing but also typecasts her into the realm of comic sidekicks: "Ms. Sidibe is larger than the typical starlet at the casting agency, and her skin is darker. When she was younger, she was teased about her appearance. More recently, when she hung out with her theater friends, some other girl, taller or skinnier, always got all the attention. 'I was comic relief,' she said. 'The best friend.'"[23] Other articles, including some in black-centric publications, continue this comparison between Sidibe and the idea of a standard movie star in terms of race and weight: "In an entertainment industry of size zeros, colored contacts and an emphasis on 'exotic' or racially ambiguous beauty, Gabby is definitely a stand out. She has dark, ebony skin that radiates the warmth of her African ancestors, and her plump, round figure is not the type often found in magazine covers."[24] Sidibe's deviance from dominant beauty norms not only marks her as different but also acts as a source of stigma. As one reporter notes, "Sidibe says she endured years of teasing for her weight and dark skin. 'People told me my whole life that I'll never really be anything,' she says."[25] She also told *New York* that her friends and family still pressure her to lose weight and shame her about her food choices,[26] and in an interview in *Jet* Sidibe describes the pain of being called "skillet" and "midnight" because of her dark skin.[27]

As with the progressive casting of Peter Dinklage in *The Station Agent* discussed in the next chapter, Hollywood's casting gatekeepers—studio executives and casting agents—take on the role of villains in Sidibe's celebrity narrative, functioning as bigots whose assumptions about beauty and stardom inhibit diversity in the entertainment media. *Precious*'s director Lee Daniels told multiple interviewers, "You cannot call a Hollywood agent and say, 'Hey, got any 300-pound black girls?'"[28] Acknowledging the near impossibility of getting "a movie about a fat black girl financed,"[29] Daniels was quick to cast the structures of Hollywood as racist and sexist, situating his casting of Sidibe as a progressive challenge to the industry.

If Sidibe's non-normative appearance is constructed as a source of discrimination that has limited her career possibilities, the solution to this discrimination, as prescribed in Sidibe's narrative, is not systemic change prompted by directors such as Daniels. Instead, that narrative details her seemingly unshakable self-confidence as the source of her success. For some reporters, she always offers a "unique brand of confidence,"[30] while for others she is "bubbly, confident and outspoken."[31] Her stylist says, "She loves herself and is incredibly confident,"[32] while the editor of *Ebony* says, "She is more confident in herself than anybody I've ever met!"[33] *New York* magazine depicts her as "armed with . . . an unshakable confidence,"[34] and even Oprah has lauded Sidibe's self-assurance: "It's like she's from another planet, because she's so evolved, so confident, so secure about who she is."[35] *USA Today* quipped that "if Sidibe could bottle up her buoyant self-assurance and sell it, she'd be richer than Bill Gates,[36] and *Seventeen* relied on Sidibe to help readers "get killer confidence!"[37]

These exuberant proclamations about her confidence levels are supported by Sidibe's own discussions of her self-worth. She often discusses her own confidence and its source in interviews:

> People always ask me, "You have so much confidence. Where did that come from?" It came from me. One day I decided I was beautiful, and so I carried out my life as if I was a beautiful girl. I wear colors that I really like, I wear make-up that makes me feel pretty, and it really helps. It doesn't have anything to do with how the world perceives you. What matters is what you see.[38]

According to Sidibe, she had to cultivate this sense of confidence as a young woman exposed to the beauty standards of the culture. She told *People* that when she was around fifteen, "I decided for myself that whatever people said, and no matter what I look like, I was going to be happy with myself."[39] At some point in her life, she said in another interview, "I learned to love myself, because I sleep with myself every night and I wake up with myself every morning, and if I don't like myself, there's no reason to even live the life."[40]

As Sidibe indicates, the source of her confidence is purely internal, something that people must find within themselves. "My confidence (cannot) come from an outside source. I have to believe that I'm valuable," she told *Jet* in 2010.[41] Similarly, she told *People*, "It's like a force I gained inside, and ever since it's worked for me."[42] This force of self-assurance, she told *Essence*, is the root of her fame and accomplishments:

> It took me years to accomplish something many women—plus-size or not—spend their entire lives striving for: self-acceptance. I finally figured out that I was worth something despite not looking the part

based on mainstream standards of beauty. Ultimately, inner beauty and self worth is what it's all about. I truly believe that if you are open and welcoming, the blessings will come. My life is a testament to that.[43]

Much like Melissa McCarthy, Sidibe has become "a symbol of self-love and empowerment,"[44] particularly in a culture that constructs and valorizes a postracial ideal. These discourses insist on a color-blind, neoliberal worldview where individual choices and behaviors can seem to provide solutions to deeply entrenched structural inequalities in US society. Sidibe's persona acknowledges the existing discrimination and prejudices of the social world by referencing the challenges she has faced as an overweight, dark-skinned black woman, but these racial discourses are displaced in the articles celebrating her self-confidence, proffering up changes in individual outlook as a solution to racism and prejudice. In a postracial world, apparently it is only the bad attitudes of the marginalized and dispossessed that keep them from attaining fame and success.

In this way, Sidibe's fame dovetails with the popular discourses linking self-confidence and women's empowerment that were discussed in more detail in chapter 1. Focusing on women's levels of confidence as explanations for the gendered pay gap or underrepresentation in science and technology careers, these popular discourses proffered a neoliberal solution to issues of social equity: women must change their own appearance and attitudes toward success rather than demanding social change. Individuals must take responsibility for self-transformation in response to structural barriers to success. Sidibe's status as an icon of self-confidence adds racial discrimination to the list of social ills that self-assuredness and self-transformation can cure.

Sidibe's brand of flirty self-confidence, however, also indicates how issues of gender intersect with postracial discourse. After all, her confidence is not simply that of a talented young woman looking for more artistic challenges. Instead, it is highly feminized and youthful rather than aggressive or professional. Sidibe is frequently described as "bubbly,"[45] "giggly,"[46] "girly,"[47] and "sassy."[48] Her love of fashion and photo shoots frequently illustrates her self-assurance in the stories,[49] and her confidence is often explained by insistent references to her love life. For example, one reporter noted, "Director Lee Daniels was blown away by Gabby's confidence and presence, and has been quoted in several interviews speculating about whether Gabby has a few boyfriends at her beck and call."[50] Another asks, "Is she still juggling four or five boyfriends?" to which Sidibe replies, "Yes, but I don't want to get serious enough to call them boyfriends."[51]

Such references to her femininity and heteronormativity help frame her confidence as feminine and unthreatening, suggesting that for women—and perhaps especially black women—the mantras of self-confidence must fit within the boundaries of acceptable femininity. Her transgressions in body type can be accommodated by framing her self-confidence within the typical definitions of femininity: she is "girly" and "bubbly" and likes fashion. In other words, Sidibe's challenge to the long-standing stigma against overweight black femininity can only be accommodated through assurances of traditional, heteronormative girlhood, perhaps explaining why most of her major roles have her playing teenagers (even though she was twenty-six when *Precious* came out and is currently thirty-three). By containing the image of Sidibe within the bounds of girlhood—boyfriends, fashion shoots, and makeup—the popular discourses of her fame restrict her challenge to Western body norms to areas in which her assertiveness and confidence are culturally diminished.

Drafting her self-confidence into the realm of fun, Sidibe's playful femininity has also allowed her body to become an object of consumption for a largely white (and color-blind) body image movement. The popular discourses of body positivity, and in particular the fat-acceptance movement, have been historically dominated by assumptions of whiteness and in particular white femininity. While overweight people of color are overrepresented in degrading and stigmatizing representations of obesity in US culture, the images of body positivity in the media are overwhelmingly white and most often those of white women.[52] Moreover, popular discussions of body politics having to do with weight are almost exclusively related to white femininity and color-blind gender politics. So when women of color like Sidibe (or Oprah, Queen Latifah, America Ferrera, and others) are celebrated within the discourses of women's body positivity, they are often being deployed as color-blind examples of inclusivity that address a vision of universal womanhood, thus failing to engage with the body politics of race.

Ralina Joseph explores these dynamics using the 2007 weight gain scandal of former supermodel Tyra Banks, who was chastised in the tabloids over a slight weight gain that resulted in unbecoming photos of her in a bikini. Banks went on the offensive on her daytime talk show and in interviews, calling out the sexism behind the attacks and the racial undertones of their interest in her slightly larger derriere. But as Joseph demonstrates, Banks—who rose to fame as a black supermodel by cultivating a postracial "everywoman" persona that allowed her to effectively deploy her racial allure as a commodity—capitalized on the controversy by airing a program on her show titled "Racial Injustice: Who's Got It Worse." The episode explicitly addressed racial and gendered injustices, but culminated in cross-racial handholding and a universal celebration of womanhood. "This episode," Joseph explains, "is emblematic of the way the *Tyra Banks Show* solves problems of racism, patriarchy, and discrimination: magically equalizing all through multicultural celebrations of 'women.'"[53] In this way, Banks demonstrates the power of celebrity to embody the merger of postracial and postfeminist ideologies.

Likewise, Sidibe's status as body image heroine relies on the same erasure of race under the generic umbrella of womanhood. For example, in 2014 Sidibe was asked to deliver a speech at the Gloria Awards and Gala, hosted by the Ms. Magazine Foundation. The other keynote speaker was Amy Schumer, the white comedian who is also celebrated as a body image heroine because she doesn't look like a supermodel. Both Schumer and Sidibe delivered speeches on the topic of confidence, with both celebrating their own capacity to move beyond other people's opinions about their bodies. Other than a couple of references to her skin tone and the fact that most kids in her neighborhood did not have parents who went to college (although Sidibe's did), race did not play a large part in her speech—it stayed consistent with the coverage of popular magazines by focusing on her inner strength as a solution to social barriers. In fact, her speech was remarkably similar to Schumer's, and reports of the event offered an image of cross-racial unity under the banner of feminism: a white woman and a black woman standing together to celebrate the power of confidence to overcome persistent discrimination and social injustice. Operating within a color-blind framework, the discourses of confidence and self-actualization ostensibly address the concerns of women everywhere, but actually address only the concerns of white, middle-class, professional women.

PRECIOUS OR NOT PRECIOUS? RACE AND NARRATIVES OF PERSONAL TRIUMPH

That the context of racial inequalities could be occluded in Sidibe's public persona is rather ironic. Her star-making role in *Precious* so viscerally depicts the devastating conditions of black urban poverty that her fame at first seemed destined to be synonymous with poor blackness. But as her self-confident persona came to dominate media coverage of her rise to fame, Sidibe seemed to break free from her character Precious, becoming a living embodiment of the kinds of individual success that Precious could only fantasize about. So while *Precious* the movie ostensibly offered a heartbreaking account of the challenges faced by young, poor black women, Sidibe's popular image of a self-confident, "girly" young woman overshadowed the message of the film. In essence, Sidibe offered a resonant narrative of individual achievement based around consumption, celebrity, and playful femininity that displaced *Precious*'s lessons about community, education, and social services.

Precious tells the tale of sixteen-year-old Claireece Precious Jones, an abused, illiterate young woman in 1987 Harlem who has already had one child and is pregnant with another (both the result of being raped by her own father). At home, Precious suffers horrible emotional and physical abuse at the hands of her mother (played by Mo'nique), and in the course of the film she learns that she is HIV positive. After she is kicked out of school for becoming pregnant, her principal directs her to an alternative school that works with disadvantaged students, where she meets a dedicated teacher (Paula Patton) who helps her learn to read and develop a sense of self-worth. With the help of her social worker (Mariah Carey), Precious eventually confronts her mother and sets off on her own with a commitment to educating herself and her children.

Although the film became a critical darling after successful screenings at Sundance and Cannes (and with some promotional help from Oprah Winfrey), *Precious* also produced its fair share of controversy regarding race and representation. Mirroring the 1985 controversy surrounding Steven Spielberg's *The Color Purple*, which some critics argued portrayed African American men in a negative light,[54] *Precious* became a target for some high-profile commentators who thought the film perpetuated stereotypes and negative images of African American communities. The controversy was spurred on by the contrarian film critic Armond White, who provocatively argued, "Not since 'The Birth of a Nation' has a mainstream movie demeaned the idea of black American life as much as 'Precious.' Full of brazenly racist clichés (Precious steals and eats an entire bucket of fried chicken), it is a sociological horror show."[55] Other critics joined in, questioning why representations of black poverty and violence become popular with white audiences and Oscar voters while other more "positive" representations of blacks and the black community are ignored. But others pushed back, including Sapphire (the author of the novel upon which the film was based), who argued that images of Sasha and Malia Obama in the White House, while powerful, cannot be the only images of black children in popular culture: "Black people are able to say 'Precious' represents some of our children, but some of our children go to Yale."[56]

While these are important questions about race and representation, it is not surprising that the discussion around *Precious*'s vision of race in America became highly individualized. These kinds of questions place responsibility on filmmakers and producers, especially black filmmakers and producers, to

FIGURE 2.2. *Gabourey Sidibe as Claireece Precious Jones in* Precious *(Lee Daniels Entertainment, 2009).*

determine what an "authentic" or ethical representation of blackness should be. In a media culture that either valorizes diversity heroes or vilifies racist scoundrels, the core of the *Precious* debate focused on Lee Daniels and the responsibilities of black artists, especially since Daniels admitted he was at first embarrassed to screen *Precious* at Cannes because it showed realities of black life that he was not sure he wanted to share with the world.[57]

So while the media debated whether to celebrate or condemn Daniels and his work, it helped occlude other pressing questions regarding *Precious* and its vision of race in America, primarily how and why such a stark vision of urban poverty attained mainstream popularity. How, in other words, can a film that clearly illustrates the structural realities of racial inequality become a hit in a culture high on the possibilities of a postracial future?

For some reviewers of the film, this tension is navigated by constructing the film's setting—1980s Harlem—as a kind of fantasy space, denying its relevance to contemporary America. The hyperbolic construction of the "squalid"[58] and "brutal"[59] world in which Precious lives helps to reframe the historical realities of urban poverty into sensational fantasies that are safely contained in the past. Several reviewers linked the film's vision of 1980s Harlem to the "gothic" excesses of Victorian potboilers or a Dickensian melodrama.[60] Others saw the setting as more demonic, calling it a "1980s Harlem version of hell"[61] or a "hellish corner of 1980s Harlem."[62] These rhetorical flourishes indicate how the historical realities of urban poverty can become lurid fantasies—indeed, one critic held up *Precious* as an example of how "movies can take us places we never imagined."[63] The safe, middle-class "we" being addressed indicates how the imagery of racial poverty can become a sensational space for cinematic armchair anthropologists.

As a hyperbolic fantasy, 1980s Harlem can then serve as the backdrop to a story of individual triumph, making the film a celebration of individual grit against sensational odds instead of an exposé on race and urban despair. Critics swooned over the film's "inspiring message,"[64] "ultimately uplifting" narrative,[65] and "message of hope."[66] Even A. O. Scott, who briefly situated the film against the politics of Reagan's and Clinton's welfare reform, still emphasized a narrative of triumph and self-actualization, calling the film "less the examination of a social problem than the illumination of an individual's painful and partial self-realization."[67]

This framing of the *Precious* narrative around inspiring messages of hope and self-actualization helps to deny the relevance of race to the film, suggesting that at its core *Precious* is a universal tale about overcoming adversity. Joyce King in fact made this argument explicitly in *USA Today*, claiming that the film transcends race and poverty and speaks to a universal, human experience: "Its wrenching story of despair, then hope, is the tie that binds. Not race. . . . [T]he moral of the story goes beyond the color of one's skin and delves deeply into the humanity that resides within us all."[68] Or as Lynn Hirschberg claimed in the *New York Times*, "Precious is a stand-in for anyone—black, white, male, female—who has ever been devalued or underestimated."[69] These universalist claims reorient a narrative about poverty, race, and urban despair into a postracial tale about the "human spirit," tossing aside any acknowledgment that some populations are asked to overcome more odds than others.

The cinematic narrative of triumph, then, becomes blurred with the narrative of Sidibe's own success as a star, especially as critics grappled with the question of how much Sidibe is like her character Precious. Because of her powerful performance and the physical similarities between Sidibe and her character, reviewers at times drew parallels between the actress's rise to fame and Precious's emotional growth. Sidibe herself made these connections when interviewed by her costar Mo'nique, saying that she and Precious "have the same body, I guess, so we both had to grow up with people staring at us and people judging us based on what we looked like." These similarities, she continued, are "what I brought to Precious and what kind of brought her out of me."[70] Because she and Precious have experienced the same stigmas about weight and race, their stories became intertwined as similar examples of personal triumph. Of course, in other interviews, Sidibe fought back against the parallels between herself and her character: "They [the press] try to paint the picture that I was this downtrodden, ugly girl who was unpopular in school and in life, and then I got this role and now I'm awesome," Sidibe told *New York* magazine. "But the truth is that I've been awesome, and then I got this role."[71]

As Sidibe became a better-known figure, especially "in her bubbly appearances on the talk-show circuit,"[72] popular magazines followed her lead, distancing Sidibe from Precious and constructing the actress as the anti-Precious—a self-assured and vivacious young woman who stands in contrast to the emotionally closed character. *People* declared that "Sidibe couldn't be more different from the role that landed her a Best Actress nomination,"[73] while *Entertainment Weekly* called her "a happy-go lucky young woman who is nothing at all like her downtrodden character."[74] Lee Daniels also chimed in, saying, "Physically, she resembles Precious, but she doesn't talk like her or walk like her. She's not that girl."[75] Bill Condon, director of *The Big C*, said, "The thing to know about Gabby is that she is not Precious."[76] Even Oprah commented on the connection, saying, "She's a superb actress, because Precious's story is nothing like her story."[77] Ironically, considering that the "uplifting message" of *Precious* centers on the emergence of the title character as a self-fulfilled young woman, Precious becomes a symbol of introversion and despair when compared to the actress that brought her to life: "While Precious is shy, Gabourey is full of confidence. While Precious is ashamed of her large size, Gabourey is proud of her pounds."[78] Or as another reporter put it, "In person, Sidibe is as sunny as Precious is withdrawn."[79] Such descriptions distance Sidibe from her career-making character while still linking the two, with Precious viewed as an important foil for understanding the actress.

Perhaps the most telling descriptions of their relationship come from those who see Sidibe as the living embodiment of Precious's fantasy life. In the film, Precious retreats into vibrant, colorful fantasies of fame in which she becomes a confident and radiant young woman. She glides down red carpets swarmed by paparazzi or dances gleefully on a fashion show runway when the realities of her existence become too much to handle. Lee Daniels suggested that these are the sequences in which the audience gets to see the "real" Sidibe. He told *New York* that "Sidibe grew to be herself by the end of the movie. Not even herself, but a fraction of herself. To play Precious, she had to unwork all her confidence, and speak lower, slower, and gutterally. Only in fantasy sequences . . . do you see who Sidibe is, bubbly and giggly."[80]

This connection was also developed in a profile in *Harper's Bazaar*, in which the writer claims, "When you see her in *Precious*, you're convinced that she is the character, but really she's the character who has fantasies of walking down the red carpet."[81] In this way, Sidibe's outgoing persona becomes an idealized fantasy for poor, oppressed women like Precious, a set of attributes worth aspiring to.

FIGURE 2.3. *Gabourey Sidibe as Claireece Precious Jones imagining a life of glamour in* Precious *(L'ee Daniels Entertainment, 2009).*

By blurring the lines between Precious and Sidibe, then, these discourses obscure the film's more responsible vision of individual empowerment for poor black women. In *Precious*, the vivid and surreal fantasies of fame and fortune that help Precious disassociate from reality are escapist and possibly unhealthy. In the film, she learns to seek more grounded goals: understanding her own self-worth, finding her voice, and educating her son. Her fantasies of fame are slowly eclipsed by the promise of education. These promises are made visible in one scene in which images of US history and the civil rights movement swarm around her in class, projected on the classroom walls in a surreal style that suggests her colorful fantasies of fame are being replaced in her imagination by an awareness of her power as a citizen and student.

Precious's story of increasing self-awareness, however, is eclipsed in entertainment journalism by Sidibe's rise to fame. Sidibe becomes a stand-in for Precious (they share the same body and have faced some of the same stigmas), but she emerges as an even more evolved Precious who gets to live out Precious's most grandiose fantasies. In this process, the slippage between Sidibe and Precious glosses over the attributes celebrated in the film, such as finding avenues of self-expression, seeking education, and building a supporting community, in favor of trappings of celebrity like red carpets, fashion, talk shows, and individual charm. While Precious moves beyond these consumerist fantasies, Sidibe's fame insists that the pleasures of celebrity are the real reward of self-empowerment, obscuring the film's message about the power of education. By being Precious and yet not Precious, Sidibe's star persona provides a bridge linking the racial poverty and despair in the film with the excesses of celebrity culture, valorizing the escapist fantasies of meteoric individual success instead of the imperatives to empower and educate black women while repairing black communities.

Sidibe, then, becomes a perfect postracial icon, an emblem not just of individual triumph over racial inequality, but of a particular vision of achievement based on celebrity and consumption. Her associations with Precious help connect her persona to conditions of poverty and oppression (even though the Harlem that the middle-class and college-educated Sidibe grew up in is very different from that of Precious). This is especially true given that Sidibe's appearance is so strongly linked to popular cultural stereotypes of gluttonous, black femininity: even more so than Melissa McCarthy's white corpulence (discussed in chapter 1), overweight black women such as Sidibe are linked with low social class, represented as a drain on society, and denied their place as responsible citizens in the public imagination. But these associations with black urban poverty become simply a colorful backdrop to Sidibe's story of overnight fame, a nod to social oppression that only underscores the magnitude of her triumph.

This success, of course, is facilitated by Sidibe's charm and "sassy" fabulousness, offering the veneer of stylish womanhood behind which Precious and issues of black communities get left behind. Why settle for Precious's story—finding a modicum of self-awareness and community support—when Sidibe's narrative promises fame, fortune, and magazine covers? Reflecting a neoliberal worldview that valorizes celebrity status and normative femininity as the measure of success in modern life, Sidibe's fame becomes a much more resonant blueprint for transcending the oppressions of race in America than Precious's story will ever be.

A POSTRACIAL PERFORMER

Not surprisingly, then, Sidibe's career after *Precious* has seen her take on several roles as a feisty sidekick to a white bourgeois woman on a quest for self-assurance, indicating a tendency to deploy black self-confidence not as an end in and of itself but as a highly visible marker of white diversity and self-actualization.

Her first major role after Precious was in the Showtime series *The Big C*, starring Laura Linney. Like other popular cable TV series (such as *Weeds* or *Breaking Bad*), *The Big C* revolves around a seemingly normal middle-class character who begins to transform her or his life when confronted with tragedy. In the show, Linney plays Cathy, a suburban teacher who is diagnosed with terminal cancer and given around a year to live. Cathy promptly

FIGURE 2.4. *Gabourey Sidibe as Andrea Jackson with Laura Linney as Cathy Jamison in* The Big C *(Showtime, 2011–2013).*

reevaluates her life, kicking her well-intentioned but immature husband (played by Oliver Platt) out of the house, trying to develop a relationship with her selfish teenage son (Gabriel Basso), rediscovering her sexuality, and taking an interest in the life of her student, Andrea, played by Sidibe. Over the course of the show's four-season run, Cathy's cancer diagnosis has her constantly reevaluating her life and relationships as she battles the disease and finds some success with experimental treatments, but eventually dies at the series' conclusion.

Sidibe's role as Andrea builds off the narratives of postracial and gendered self-confidence that have surrounded her career. Andrea is a witty, bubbly teenage girl who does not hold back her at-times biting commentary about those around her. In season 1, when Cathy's son Adam disrespects his mother, Andrea calls him out and pelts him with a paintball gun in an attempt to make Adam mind his mother. As the show progresses, Andrea becomes a fixture in Cathy's family. Cathy promises Andrea's family that she will help Andrea raise her grades and go to college, and Andrea later moves in with Cathy's oddball family as Cathy tries to make good on that promise.

Andrea's role in the narrative exemplifies the logic of color-blindness in popular media today. While Andrea's blackness is acknowledged and occasionally commented upon in the series—in one narrative arc, in fact, she disappears to Africa in order to get in touch with her ancestral roots—her race is largely irrelevant as she takes her place as yet another kooky but lovable fixture on the show alongside Cathy's radical environmentalist brother, her gay best friend/fellow cancer patient, and her son's anal-sex-loving Christian girlfriend. The sharp-witted and assertive black woman is just another odd-ball node in Cathy's crumbling middle-class normalcy. The idea that Andrea might not be afforded the same privileges as the rest of the mostly white and affluent cast of characters is never really considered in the show because everyone has their own personal issues to deal with, whether cancer, bipolar disorder, or grief. These interior issues take priority, and as Cathy helps steer Andrea through school and toward college, the material realities of educational inequality in the United States (and in suburban Minneapolis, the setting for the show) are repressed beneath a narrative in which Andrea simply needs to focus under the strict guidance of a white teacher.

Mirroring Sidibe's star persona, issues of gender and weight take priority for her character in *The Big C*, helping to disavow the relevance of her race. After all, Andrea is first introduced in the series against the backdrop of weight and health issues. Cathy, having just learned about her own cancer prognosis, tosses aside the curriculum in her summer school history class, at times giving up on her mission as an educator and at others trying to teach her students important life lessons that have nothing to do with the class. In this last category, she takes a personal interest in Andrea's weight, offering her one hundred dollars for every pound that she can shed in an effort to inspire the teenager. This narrative establishes Andrea's weight and gendered conceptions of beauty as the personal obstacle that defines the character, even though Cathy gives up on this intervention as the two become friends.

Moreover, the culmination of the narrative for Andrea in the series only highlights the vision of highly feminized confidence that defines Sidibe's public persona. In the show's final season, Cathy has successfully guided Andrea to college, where she is seeking a degree in fashion design. Andrea has been struggling in her class workshops as she deals with Cathy's impending death, but before Cathy dies, Andrea regains her artistic flair and earns a prestigious internship with fashion designers in New York. Situating Andrea's success in the highly feminized field of fashion design, the show channels her intelligence, sharp wit, and no-nonsense attitude into a realm of professional success that affirms traditional feminine sensibilities (is it so hard to imagine that Andrea might make an excellent politician or journalist?). This narrative maneuver accomplishes the same policing of assertive femininity seen in popular magazines which insist that Sidibe represents a "bubbly" confidence: a popular image of feminine self-confidence, especially black, feminine self-confidence, must disavow the specter of the harping nag or the pushy bitch through assertions of traditional "girly" femininity.

Andrea's self-fulfillment, however, only exists in relation to Cathy's journey of self-discovery—this is, after all, Cathy's show. Andrea is simply one of many oddballs that Cathy picks up along the way and that help punctuate coming to terms with herself and her mortality. Just as Sidibe can function as a black icon of self-acceptance for the largely white discourses of confidence and changing beauty norms, Andrea is a quirky sidebar to Cathy's voyage, a figure that assists white womanhood in coming to terms with itself.

Sidibe's role in season 3 of *American Horror Story* also placed her in a narrative about white women and self-fulfillment, but this time issues of race and racism played a more visible role in the development of her character. As a series, *American Horror Story* often dramatizes prominent cultural and historical themes in its macabre tales of supernatural brutality: season 1, set in a haunted house in Los Angeles, takes up school shootings, the housing crisis, and masculinity crises (among other issues), while one of the major themes of season 2, set mostly in an insane asylum in 1960s New England, is the rise of feminism and women's career ambitions in US history. Continuing this trend, season 3 is focused on a school for witches in post-Katrina New Orleans, explicitly dramatizing tensions between the mostly white and privileged witches and poor black practitioners of voodoo. Within this narrative, Sidibe's character plays a key role in resolving these racial tensions, articulating a postracial vision of the future of the witches' coven (all while helping a white witch gain confidence and assume a position of leadership).

In the show, Miss Robichaux's Academy appears to be a normal, private boarding school but is actually a school that helps witches develop and control their various powers. Almost all of the students are descended from the witches of Salem, Massachusetts. Sidibe plays Queenie, the only black witch at the school; she is the descendant of Tituba, the slave who originally gave the Salem witches their magical powers, and can act as a human voodoo doll, inflicting whatever violence she unleashes on her own body upon the subject of her choosing.

While facing a crisis of leadership, the coven also confronts a threat from Marie Laveau (played by Angela Bassett), an immortal black voodoo priestess who has seen hundreds of years of American racism. The witches and Marie Laveau have had a truce since the 1970s that demarcates different territories in the city, a reference to race and urban segregation as Laveau clearly occupies the poor black areas of New Orleans while the witches inhabit areas of white, upper-class opulence (Laveau operates a run-down beauty shop, while the school is in a stately mansion with a sparse but elegant whitewashed interior). But the truce is falling apart as the coven's "supreme," Fiona (Jessica Lange), starts to antagonize Laveau. As part of the breakdown of the truce, Fiona digs up Delphine LaLaurie (Kathy Bates), a wealthy nineteenth-century slave owner known for the violent horrors she inflicted on her slaves and whom Laveau had made immortal and then buried alive.

Sidibe's character Queenie quickly becomes a token in the struggles be-

FIGURE 2.5. *Gabourey Sidibe as Queenie with Kathy Bates as Delphine LaLaurie in* American Horror Story: Coven *(FX, 2013–2014).*

tween Fiona and Laveau, who temporarily woos Queenie away from the coven to join forces with the voodoo priestess. But Queenie truly becomes a mediator of the racial tensions of the show as she takes on the task of educating and transforming Madam LaLaurie. Faced with the racial realities of contemporary America—including the prospect of a "darkie" like Obama as president—LaLaurie becomes distraught. Begrudgingly, she and Queenie develop an unlikely friendship as Queenie tries to teach the brutally racist nineteenth-century aristocrat to accept African Americans as equals. The women bond over fast food, and Queenie saves LaLaurie's life. In one scene, Queenie even forces LaLaurie's severed but still alive head to watch all of *Roots*. Despite the growing affection between the two, LaLaurie eventually gives up on her project of self-improvement, deciding that she is happiest torturing black men as she disembowels the school's black gardener.

Queenie's failure to reform LaLaurie, however, helps her chart a postracial future for the coven, especially as she recognizes that Laveau is as much of a threat to the coven as Fiona, whose intentions to kill any possible next "supreme" have come to light. Recognizing that the same magic keeps both Marie Laveau and Madam LaLaurie alive, Queenie conspires to have that magic revoked, ensuring that both women die. The last time we see the two enemies, they are both trapped in the underworld, with Laveau forced to torture LaLaurie over and over for eternity.

By linking the fate of the racist LaLaurie and the racial crusader Laveau, the narrative suggests that the only way to move forward is to let the past die: LaLaurie was buried alive for hundreds of years before Fiona unearthed her, an appropriate metaphor for a racist past that is repressed but still very much alive just below the surface of US culture. In order for the remnants of this racist past to actually die, however, the show suggests that militant antiracism has to go with it. Laveau, after all, is linked to antiracist crusading and the civil rights movement. She punishes LaLaurie for her racism in the nineteenth century, and in one flashback we see her exacting justice in the early 1960s against a white lynch mob that had murdered a young black child for trying to attend a segregated school. The tension between Laveau and the white witches is also based on race—Laveau accuses the witches of having stolen voodoo magic that was not theirs (a nod to the tendency for white culture to appropriate black cultural forms). From Laveau's perspective, her war with the witches is a form of racial justice, eradicating white enemies in the name of black empowerment. But the narrative clearly aligns the audience with the witches, making Marie Laveau an antagonist who must be dealt with for the coven to thrive. When Queenie decides that both Laveau and LaLaurie have to die, she acts on her belief that the remnants of racism *and* the fight against racism must be put to rest to clear a path for a post-racial coven.

With the specter of race and race relations banished to the underworld, Queenie can then take her place in a narrative about white womanhood and self-actualization. Believing Fiona to be dead, Cordelia (Fiona's daughter, played by Sarah Paulson) leads the remaining students in the house through a series of dangerous tests to determine which of them will take over as the coven's new "supreme." Several young witches die along the way. In the process, however, Cordelia, who had never shown much magical skill, realizes that it was her mother's constant insults and disappointment that kept her from developing as a witch. With newfound self-confidence, she sails through the tests and assumes her mother's position as the new "supreme." Queenie, who is disqualified for not being able to revive the dead in one test, literally takes her place at Cordelia's side as a key adviser as the coven enters into a new era of prosperity. The coven is able to move past its own infighting and create new bonds of sisterhood only after the racial tensions that marked the New Orleans turf war have been laid to rest.

CONCLUSION

The final scene of *American Horror Story: Coven* shows Sidibe's character Queenie standing alongside Cordelia (along with the other survivor of the coven, Zoe, played by Taissa Farmiga) as swarms of young women enter Miss Robichaux's Academy eager to discover their own inner power. Most of

FIGURE 2.6. *Queenie (Gabourey Sidibe) and Zoe (Taissa Farmiga) take their places beside the new coven leader, Cordelia (Sarah Paulson), in* American Horror Story: Coven *(FX, 2013–2014).*

these young women are white, with a few ambiguously ethnic faces mixed in, but the scene speaks to a larger category of empowered womanhood that ostensibly transcends race. With Queenie at her side, Cordelia will help these young women prosper and develop strengths inside themselves that they never knew they had, a vision of sisterhood and support the show's producers clearly see as resonant in contemporary American culture and gender politics. Of course, the show's own logic betrays this transcendent vision of postracial sisterhood. While they might be scattered around the country, any witches that will earn admittance to the school will presumably be descendants of the Salem witches of northern European ancestry. There do not appear to be any black faces in the crowd who, like Queenie, are descendants of Tituba. While the show attempts this gesture toward racially transcendent sisterhood, the specter of bloodlines and racial purity cannot be erased so easily.

The show's closing image illustrates the dominant narrative of Sidibe's place in contemporary US culture, showing how postracial discourse can rely on generic visions of women's empowerment to shore up the idea that race no longer matters. This vision of gender equity in turn must eschew any recourse to structural or cultural change, insisting that women's attitudes (or else their physical bodies) must change and adapt in order for them to achieve individual success. Lost in the mix of these negotiations are the women like Precious: poor black women for whom self-confidence can never really do the work of community support systems and for whom the allure of celebrity can never provide the same empowerment as education.

As a postracial icon, the image of Gabourey Sidibe promises a world where race is present but irrelevant. The feel-good success story of a vivacious and overweight young black woman who is taking on a bigoted system is powerfully appealing—it provides a clear challenge to the kinds of black bodies that popular media are normally willing to accommodate. In this light, Sidibe's fame effectively illustrates the allure of postracial discourse in the United States. Thanks to her continuing success, her charm, and the heartwarming affirmations that inner beauty still counts for something in media culture, Sidibe's story uses the power of stardom to sell a postracial vision of individual triumph. Who is not moved by her story of success or charmed by her personality? Like other stars, Sidibe provides a resonant image of personhood, of a likable and charismatic individual whose personal story outshines questions of social structures, politics, or policy.

But as likable as Sidibe is, her story is also organized around a series of assumptions about race, femininity, consumption, and confidence that hold *individuals* accountable for *social* problems while subordinating issues of race to the concerns of white middle-class womanhood. Her fame certainly offers more varied images of black femininity than US media culture has in the past, but her success suggests a limited set of pathways to acceptance for those whose bodies defy cultural norms.

CHAPTER THREE

Peter Dinklage

MERITOCRACY AND THE
WORLD'S SEXIEST DWARF

*P*OP CULTURE AFTER THE TURN OF THE MILLENNIUM
suddenly seemed obsessed with little people. The *Austin Powers* sequels (1999 and 2002) made a minor star of Verne Troyer for his role as "Mini-Me." Prominent little people actors Warwick Davis and Danny Woodburn kept active careers going on film and television, with Davis even starring in his own TV show called *Life's Too Short* in 2012–2013, although both actors primarily took on roles as elves and other mythical creatures in movies like *Harry Potter* and *Mirror Mirror*. Meredith Eaton earned not one but two regular roles on prime-time television with CBS's *Family Law* (1999–2002) and later on ABC's *Boston Legal* (2004–2008). And controversial television shows exploited the spectacle of little people engaged in wild antics, from Jason "Wee Man" Acuña on *Jackass* (2000–2002) to the Spike TV program *Half-Pint Brawlers* (2010–present), in which a troupe of little people put on outrageous and dangerous wrestling acts. Cable channel TLC of course took another approach, offering a pair of programs detailing the everyday lives and struggles of little people: *Little People, Big World* (2006–present) and *The Little Couple* (2009–present). The success of these shows led to a new reality TV concept: take the idea from an established reality program, but do it with little people. Animal Planet's *Pitt Boss* (2010–2013) showcases the work of Shorty Rossi and a crew of other little people who rescue pit bulls (building off the success of *The Dog Whisperer* and other animal-centric programming); and TLC's *Little Chocolatiers* (2010) follows Steve Hatch and Katie Masterson's chocolate-making business (building off the success of *Cake Boss* and other cooking-themed shows). Not to be outdone, in 2014 Lifetime launched a *Real Housewives* spin-off called *Little Women: L.A.* that follows the lives of six little women entertainers in Los Angeles.

This renewed interest clearly exploits little people in ways Hollywood has

FIGURE 3.1. *Peter Dinklage as Finbar McBride in* The Station Agent *(Miramax, 2003).*

long capitalized on. From *The Wizard of Oz* to *Harry Potter*, little people are frequently used as comic displays, mythical creatures, or icons of the surreal.[1] Or, continuing the tropes of the US sideshow, little people in Hollywood are used as voyeuristic spectacles, a chance to ogle bodies that deviate from cultural norms. The little people dotting the entertainment landscape since the year 2000 exemplify these tendencies in ways that range from the surreal to the mundane to the melodramatic.

And yet the increasing presence of little people in pop culture over the last decade and a half also reflects the rise of diversity and inclusivity rhetoric in the United States. Alongside the comic spectacle of "Mini-Me," US pop culture also gave us the Roloffs, the family featured in *Little People, Big World*, who showcased the humanity of little people and the real struggles they face. In addition to "Wee Man" staging bar fights on *Jackass*, pop culture also gave us the smart and sexy Bethany Horowitz, Eaton's character on *Boston Legal*. Reflecting the cultural power of the disability rights movement—which has celebrated a range of different bodies such as Lauren Potter, an actress with Down syndrome who appeared on *Glee*, and R. J. Mitte, the actor with cerebral palsy who starred in *Breaking Bad*—performers with disabilities are increasingly seen as evidence of inclusion and acceptance. Their roles, in turn, become politicized: each appearance is judged as either groundbreaking or a backslide into old stereotypes. In either case, bodily difference and the politics of representation continue to define the little people on US screens.

Then there is Peter Dinklage. Since his role in *The Station Agent* in 2003, Dinklage has become the most prominent and acclaimed little person in

Hollywood's history. But while other little people performers have become either ridiculous caricatures ("Mini-Me") or feel-good examples of inclusivity (*The Little Couple*), Dinklage has somehow transcended these two poles and become simply a star. Handsome, with a commanding baritone voice and a central role in one of the hippest cable TV shows on the air, *Game of Thrones*, Dinklage has achieved a remarkable feat: no longer just an industry pioneer always breaking new ground for little people, he is quickly becoming simply a talented actor and charismatic star who just happens to be a dwarf (the term he prefers). Warwick Davis attempted this feat in the late 1980s with his star-making turn in *Willow*, but Davis was still relegated to many science fiction roles as Ewoks, aliens, elves, and leprechauns. By contrast, Dinklage is finding his way into nuanced roles that do not call for little people and rarely make reference to his size at all, such as his performance in the 2014 blockbuster *X-Men: Days of Future Past* or the 2015 comedy *Pixels*.

This chapter explores how and why Dinklage has become the first bona fide dwarf celebrity in today's Hollywood. Although his success is clearly tied to his talent, good looks, charm, and careful choice of roles, Dinklage's rise to prominence also reveals a complex historical context that has made room for a dwarf celebrity. As with Melissa McCarthy and Gabourey Sidibe, Dinklage's fame touts the power of diversity and inclusion, making it possible for him to be celebrated as an industry pioneer and popular sex symbol, but his stardom is predicated on narratives of individual merit, especially the power of self-confident charisma to overcome cultural stigmas. While his rise to fame has helped draw attention to the persistent stereotyping of little people in the media, Dinklage's stardom also promotes a neoliberal vision of hip self-confidence that puts the onus on individuals—not society or the film industry—to adapt in the face of discrimination.

As this suggests, Dinklage's celebrity persona is organized around the foundational tensions between meritocratic capitalism and social inequality, balancing narratives of success based on talent and charm against the recognition of discrimination and denied opportunities. In this way, Dinklage's celebrity reflects US cultural anxieties about labor, citizenship, and non-normative bodies, especially issues of welfare, work, and disability. The disability rights movement, after all, has been highly successful at condemning media stereotypes and combating cultural stigma. Today, disability has taken its place alongside race, gender, and sexual orientation as a category worth celebrating (or at least not openly deriding). Images of people with disabilities are more frequently used in entertainment media and advertising to demonstrate inclusivity, and examples of disability stigma are openly contested in media culture (as seen in a petition circulating on the Internet that asks the Walt Disney Company to create a special-needs princess to offset their insistence that all princesses should be "beautiful, super thin, able-bodied, neuro-typical, straight women with perfect singing voices").[2]

The gains in cultural status of disability, however, are not necessarily reflected in policies concerning welfare and labor in the United States. Doctrines of neoliberal individualism prompted the dismantling of welfare systems starting in the 1980s under the logic that "dependency" kept the poor from taking responsibility for their own economic position. Such policies have been a target of the disability rights movement as neoliberal policies see accommodations for people with disabilities as a form of dependency or unnecessary government regulation.[3] The elimination or privatization of these support systems in an age of globalization has only increased an emphasis on self-sufficiency over social responsibility.[4] Ignoring the very clear structural inequalities and discriminations faced by people with non-normative bodies, neoliberal policies assume a model of individual responsibility that pressures people with disabilities to heroically overcome the obstacles they face.[5] At the same time, people with non-normative bodies are often excluded from the labor market not necessarily because their impairments impact their ability to perform tasks, but because of employer stigma concerning the concept of "disability." Seen as a drain on social resources for seeking welfare or accommodations, some people with non-normative bodies are then excluded from the very jobs that would provide more independence, especially as the scale and pace of labor in the United States increases, "disabling" bodies that would be "able" under different circumstances.[6]

As this suggests, labor and independence are central to the question of cultural citizenship for people with non-normative bodies. People with non-normative bodies have historically been denied many of the legal rights of citizenship, either through structural impediments to participation or because of patronizing efforts to "protect" them that strip them of individual rights (through institutionalization, sterilization, etc.).[7] But one of the central means by which they can demonstrate their ability to participate in the public commons is through labor contributions. Culturally, the power of the "overcoming narrative," common in media representations of disability in which individuals with impairments "overcome the odds" to achieve personal success,[8] is not just that it showcases the triumph of the human spirit, but that it insists that some non-normative bodies can become appropriate vehicles for labor and work. Overt cultural discrimination against people with disabilities is taboo in a diverse and inclusive world, but society is much more comfortable extending notions of citizenship and belonging to non-normative bodies that use talent and perseverance to claim a place in the labor force.

Peter Dinklage's fame mediates these tensions regarding individual labor and non-normative bodies. As with other celebrities, Dinklage's popularity both exploits and assuages cultural tensions,[9] in his case tensions about individuality, talent, and the structural barriers to inclusion that persist in contemporary US society. Dinklage has emerged as a star who challenges past stereotypes and yet offers a model of individual, meritocratic success. His celebrity offers the cachet of diversity, but couples it with an apolitical disposition that laughs off any supposed political meanings to his fame. The culture uses Dinklage to highlight the oppression of those with different bodies, but then uses him to insist that those stereotypes are all now in the past. His fame insists that we dwell in the inherent contradictions between meritocracy and the realities of structural inequality.

In Dinklage's case, these contradictions seem to disappear because he is just so hip, cool, self-confident, and sexy. He walks his dog in Brooklyn sporting casual but fashionable hoodies. He frequents hip bars and gets compared to classic Hollywood icons. He wears designer suits and pals around with other celebrities from the indie film scene. Dinklage's persona—as much as it highlights the stigma and oppression faced by little people—creates the fantasy of a charming and handsome dwarf in a world where hard work and merit really do pay off. In this way, Dinklage helps clarify the boundaries of cultural citizenship for those outside the definitions of a "normal" body: his fame suggests that bodies normally viewed as problems in contemporary capitalism can become acceptable models of individualism through appeals to talent, good looks, hip style, and the insistence that politics have no place in his fame. Not surprisingly, the discourse of self-confidence so prominent in the personas of Melissa McCarthy and Gabourey Sidibe equally informs Dinklage's hipness, illustrating the same problematic focus on self-transformation described in chapters 1 and 2. Of course, instead of the sassy assertiveness of those female stars, Dinklage typically exudes a more masculine, cool composure that offsets the emasculating stereotypes of men with disabilities.

To explore the dynamics of this persona, I discuss here the major narratives that surround Dinklage's fame and reflect the tensions of disability and its role within US culture. First, I explore the establishment of Dinklage's stardom in the 2003 independent film *The Station Agent*, showing that he emerged as a star challenging Hollywood discrimination while simultaneously denying the political message of the film. Next, I examine the contradictions of Dinklage as a role model, showing how his persona distances him from causes or political stands. Then I explore Dinklage's status as a charming, self-confident sex symbol, showing that the discourse of his handsomeness reinvests in traditional masculinities in order to make room for a dwarf celebrity. To conclude, I examine how the mantras of self-confidence prevalent in other celebrities with non-normative bodies inform Dinklage's persona, suggesting the possibilities of a "postdisability" worldview in contemporary US culture.

THE STATION AGENT: A HOLLYWOOD REBEL

From its outset, Dinklage's career has been tied to a critique of Hollywood and its portrayals of little people. After graduating from Bennington College in Vermont in 1991, Dinklage moved to Brooklyn and eked out an existence trying to run a theater out of an abandoned warehouse with a friend. The theater failed, and Dinklage was evicted.[10] He continued to find occasional acting jobs, although he turned down many good-paying jobs as elves or leprechauns because he found them demeaning.[11] His first film role was well suited to his idealism—it came in 1995 in Tom DiCillo's *Living in Oblivion*, a satirical independent film about the making of independent films. Dinklage plays Tito, a little person actor hired to act in a dream sequence in the film-within-the-film directed by Nick (played by Steve Buscemi). Fed up with Nick's stereotypical usage of little people to signify the bizarre and surreal, Tito screams at Nick before storming off the set:

> Have you ever had a dream with a dwarf in it? No!!! *I* don't have dreams with dwarfs in them. The only place I have ever seen dwarfs in dreams is in stupid little movies like this. Oooooh . . . make it weird. Put a dwarf in it. Everyone will go whoa, whoa, whoa! It must be a dream. There's a fuckin' dwarf in it. Well, I'm sick of it! You can take this dream sequence and shove it up your ass!

Calling out directors such as David Lynch who frequently use little people as a signifier of surrealism, Tito's diatribe draws attention to the limited roles available to little people in Hollywood as well as the cultural stereotypes of little people as bizarre "others."

That same year, Dinklage also worked on an off-Broadway play called *The Killing Act*, directed by Tom McCarthy, about P. T. Barnum. Dinklage played the famed sideshow performer Tom Thumb and struck up a casual friendship with McCarthy. So when McCarthy ran into Dinklage on the street years later, it inspired him to rethink a script he was writing about an introverted loner who inherits an abandoned train station in New Jersey. Determined to write the character for Dinklage after their encounter, McCarthy helped propel Dinklage to minor stardom.

The result was the 2003 film *The Station Agent*, which became a critical darling and commercial success after premiering at the Sundance Film

FIGURE 3.2. *Patricia Clarkson as Olivia Harris, Peter Dinklage as Finbar McBride, and Bobby Cannavale as Joe Oramas in* The Station Agent *(Miramax, 2003)*.

Festival. Dinklage plays Finbar McBride, a socially isolated train enthusiast whose only friend dies and leaves him a small, abandoned railway station. Fin moves to the station to seek isolation, but instead finds himself drawn into the complicated lives of those around him, including Joe (Bobby Cannavale), a loquacious young man running his father's snack truck, Olivia (Patricia Clarkson), a woman struggling to recover after the death of her son, and Emily (Michelle Williams), the local librarian dealing with an unplanned pregnancy. Dinklage was quickly identified as the breakout star of the film, and his performance was nominated for a host of awards, including an Independent Spirit Award and a Screen Actors Guild Award.

Dinklage's role in *The Station Agent* was quickly celebrated not only for his performance but also because it challenged a long history of Hollywood stereotyping. In contrast to other kinds of non-normative bodies, which tend to be ignored and occluded from cultural representations, little people have long participated in the US entertainment system, first as prime attractions of the sideshow, and then as spectacles in the Hollywood film industry. According to Betty Adelson, in fact, around 9 percent of the members of the Little People of America are connected to the entertainment industry in some way.[12] But the roles available to them have been severely limited and stereotypical, often "othering" little people as mythical creatures, as angry and violent, or as comedic spectacles.[13] Reflecting Rosemarie Garland-Thomson's claim that in cultural representations "the physically disabled body becomes a repository for social anxieties about such troubling concerns as vulnerability, control, and identity," images of little people in the United States often provide an opportunity for able-bodied audiences to safely gaze at and contemplate physical difference rather than seeking out audience identification or empathy.[14]

Compared to Hollywood's usual portrayal of little people on screen, *The Station Agent* offered nuance, compassion, and humanity for its lead character. As Adelson notes, this was one of the "first films to realistically portray the inner emotions of, and social reactions to, a dwarf."[15] Dinklage's character Fin is socially isolated but not angry: the film documents the stigma and name-calling he experiences because of his size, but his non-normative body does not define him. He develops deep and realistic friendships with other people struggling with their own personal issues, and Fin even becomes a romantic lead without the film indulging in jokes or making a spectacle of a sexualized, dwarf body. Compared to the stereotypical representations of little people that continue to pervade some Hollywood films, *The Station Agent* stands as a bold challenge to treat them with dignity, nuance, and respect.

Discussions of the film in entertainment journalism were quick to foreground these political themes, using them to call out Hollywood's shameful history of stereotyping. One film reviewer noted, "Dinklage (4ft 5in) finds there aren't that many parts for dwarves that don't involve Snow White or custard pies,"[16] while another compared Dinklage's performance to more contemporary spectacles of little people: "Outside of Mini-Me, Wee Man from Jackass and the Oompah Loompahs, it's been pretty thin pickings for actors of restricted growth."[17] Before *The Station Agent*, another reviewer noted, Dinklage seemed destined for "marginalized roles for freaks, magical figures and oddballs."[18] Dinklage, then, emerged as a hero of inclusivity: "A lot of the good will this movie has generated is due to Dinklage, who single-handedly overturns decades of screen stereotypes, in which dwarves have been used as freaks, jokes, arty symbols or surrealistic garnish."[19]

If Dinklage was a new role model, then bigoted Hollywood executives became a common target in discussions of the film's success. Noting that several executives characterized *The Station Agent* as too risky — "It's a little movie, in which almost nothing happens, starring a dwarf!"[20] — Tom McCarthy told interviewers that people tried to dissuade him from making the film, and he had a hard time selling it to studios: "So many people had passed on the script — openly and insultingly. People would say, 'Could you lose the dwarf?' Like that would make it work better."[21] One executive reportedly asked McCarthy, "Can't he [the main character] just be really short?"[22] And according to Dinklage, the studios were hesitant because they could not accept the idea of a dwarf in a romantic role: "Dinklage said the real problem for the studios was that a little person was playing the romantic lead. 'They loved everything else, it was just having someone like me there that kind of freaked them.'"[23] Casting Hollywood executives as the bigoted villains, entertainment journalists frequently touted the film's progressive casting as a key selling point.

Alongside the condemnation of Hollywood's stereotypes, film reviewers also highlighted the day-to-day struggles of little people as a stigmatized population. As one reviewer notes, "Outside, besieged by a lifetime of un-wanted attention—stares from the idly curious and shouts of 'Hey buddy, where's Snow White?' from the simply brutish—he [Fin] retreats into his cocoon of quiet."[24] Throughout much of the discussion surrounding *The Station Agent*, critics reminded their readers of "the alienation, the social anxiety and the loneliness that can characterize what it means to be a dwarf in these modern day times."[25]

But for all the insistence on the film as a political milestone for the rep-resentation of little people, those discussing Dinklage's triumph were also hesitant to see his career and prominent roles as overtly political statements about a minority group. In the reviews and discussions of *The Station Agent*, the importance of dwarfism to the main character is negotiated in a way that acknowledges social stigmas while attempting to see the character outside the discourses of dwarfism.

Several reviewers, for example, related Tom McCarthy's narrative of the script's development, in which the general story idea about social outsiders was crystalized when he ran into Dinklage on the street and witnessed the kinds of coping skills Dinklage used in his day-to-day life. McCarthy decided then and there to make the film about a dwarf.[26] The backstory indicates the centrality of the experiences of little people to the development of the char-acter, but both McCarthy and Dinklage have downplayed the significance of dwarfism to the film, denying that it is a "coming-of-height story."[27] In several interviews, McCarthy stressed that this is not a film about dwarfism per se: "We didn't want to deal with dwarfism. . . . The film is about discon-nection with friendship and community. Dwarfism was a cause of his situa-tion, but it takes a back seat to a bigger message."[28] Dinklage echoed these sentiments: "The lovely thing about Tom's movie is that, yeah, it is addressed, but it's not the overwhelming thing that the movie's about. It's about these three characters and the dwarf thing sort of gets lost in the shuffle."[29] Avoid-ing the typically sentimental clichés that tend to come along with "positive" images of disability in the media, such as the optimistic disabled person who perseveres in the face of adversity or the hardworking "supercrip" who over-comes all the obstacles, the film and its coverage in the entertainment media emphasizes a kind of depth of character that is not defined by disability.[30] But in doing so, these discussions also distance the film from a more overtly political message, creating a kind of culturally safe space to mention discrimination while insisting that the film's themes are universal, not political.

Ironically, such insistence transforms Dinklage's success story itself into a stereotypical "overcoming narrative," even as it is denied that *The Station Agent* relies on this stereotype. A public discussion of Hollywood's stereotyping and the lack of quality roles for little people might seem to suggest a broad structural critique of Hollywood discrimination: little people remain stereotyped because of persistent cultural stigmas and systematic discrimination against them. But by showcasing Dinklage's success, this critical insight instead becomes the background to a highly individualistic narrative: hardworking and talented individuals can overcome adversity to succeed through grit and determination. As in other "overcoming" narratives, very real and concrete structural inequalities that disable those with bodily impairments are recast as simple obstacles that effort and talent will overcome.

THE TALENTED AND ALOOF PIONEER

After *The Station Agent* (and a hilarious cameo in the comedy *Elf* [2003] as a grumpy children's author), Dinklage would chart a career in independent films and television that showcased him as both an industry pioneer and a hardworking and talented performer. Focused on finding work that would not pigeonhole him as only a dwarf actor, he took on smaller roles that did not necessarily revolve around his height, such as an eye-patched journalist in *Penelope* (2006) and a lawyer opposite Vin Diesel in *Find Me Guilty* (2006). Or he found roles that potentially exploited his height but at least represented little people in new, complex ways, such as his role as the secret gay lover of a family patriarch in both the British and American versions of *Death at a Funeral* (2007, 2010). He would also find his way into guest spots in critically acclaimed television shows such as *30 Rock* (as Liz Lemon's accidental love interest) and *Nip/Tuck* (as a male nanny who becomes Julia's lover). And even when he took on the kind of role he typically spurned—a mythical dwarf in *The Chronicles of Narnia: Prince Caspian*—Dinklage insisted to entertainment reporters that this role was more nuanced than other fantasy roles for dwarfs.[31]

It was *Game of Thrones*, however, that really propelled Dinklage into stardom, earning him an Emmy and a Golden Globe for his portrayal of Tyrion Lannister on HBO's violent and sex-filled fantasy series based on the novels by George R. R. Martin. Set in the fantastical kingdom of Westeros, the show explores the intricate political intrigue of the realm as various families vie for power, often showcasing the moral corruption of power and privilege.

FIGURE 3.3. *Peter Dinklage as Tyrion Lannister in* Game of Thrones *(HBO, 2011–present).*

Tyrion Lannister is the dwarf son of Tywin Lannister, a wealthy and ambitious lord who ruthlessly promotes his family's interests. The youngest of the Lannister children, born after twins (and incestuous lovers) Cersei and Jaime, Tyrion is reviled by both his father and sister because his mother died giving birth to him. A Machiavellian thinker but with a surprising moral compass, Tyrion starts the series as a lovable cad whose fondness for booze and prostitutes is matched by his love of reading and quick wit. He is a privileged son who both despises his father and seeks his love and recognition. As the series progresses, moreover, he evolves into a man of true leadership—much more so than the king (his nephew) that he serves—as he seeks his own power and to serve the family name.

Tyrion is a role tailor-made for Dinklage's star persona. The role showcases the stigma faced by little people, with Dinklage delivering lines like, "all dwarfs are bastards in his father's eyes." And yet Tyrion never seems to be defined by his stature, offering a complex and likable character with multifaceted motivations. He is a sexual character who frequents brothels, but he is capable of poignant intimacy. Politically ambitious and at times duplicitous, he is still pained by the injustices he has witnessed and the barbarism of characters like his father. He drinks, often to excess, but never becomes the stereotype of the embittered "freak" drowning his sorrows. And above all, Dinklage's Tyrion is smart and witty. Dinklage, in fact, gets to deliver many of the show's best lines. When Cersei tells Tyrion he isn't half as clever as he thinks he is, he quickly replies, "That still makes me twice as clever as you." Tyrion is at once a politicized role—he struggles with the stigmas that little people in the real world face—and yet also a highly complex character that requires the gravitas and nuance of a performer such as Dinklage.

Tyrion's outsider status catches up with the character in season 4, when he is put on trial for poisoning his nephew, the king. While his nephew Joffrey was a sadistic monster who took every opportunity to mock Tyrion's dwarfhood, Tyrion is innocent of the crime. His father knows of his innocence, but puts Tyrion on trial anyway, where Tyrion denounces the whole process and the larger community for wanting to see him as a monster because of his dwarfism. It is another of the rare moments when the character's dwarfism becomes overtly politicized, yet because of the detailed character development and Dinklage's tremendous importance, the scene avoids any schmaltzy identity politics.

Game of Thrones has elevated Dinklage's stardom because it also showcases his talent, or at least it is the type of critically celebrated cable TV show that gets marked as "quality television" and conveys respectability upon its stars. This marker of "quality," then, becomes central to a narrative of Dinklage's stardom that is both meritocratic and apolitical. He got where he is because of his natural talent, and his fame should not be politicized: he is just an actor looking for good roles.

The emphasis that entertainment journalism places on his talent, however, should be understood not simply as a reflection of his work, but as a discourse that has come to define the Peter Dinklage narrative in entertainment media. Many actors and actresses are quite talented and capable of complex performances, but they become defined as popular figures for other characteristics. Jennifer Lawrence, for example, is defined by her relaxed, unpretentious "cool girl" status more than by her acting chops, despite the fact that she won an Oscar for her performance in *Silver Linings Playbook*. Ryan Reynolds's work in independent films such as *Fireflies in the Garden* (2008) or in thrillers such as *Buried* (2010) reveals real talent, but his fame revolves around his puppy-dog handsomeness in romantic comedies or his attempts to become an action star. Some actors, likewise, cultivate a discourse of quality in midcareer, even though they might be just as good (or bad) as they have been all along, by selecting key roles to highlight certain kinds of performances. Matthew McConaughey achieved this feat in 2013, steering clear of romantic comedies and taking on more serious (if somewhat similar) roles. Sometimes, regardless of actual measures of talent, some stars become marked by the discourse of "quality" actors and actresses.

It should not detract from an assessment of Dinklage's talent, then, to consider why he is defined by his status as a "quality" actor. Part of this status relates to his choice of roles, which tend to be in independent films that fulfill the culture's expectations of "art cinema," and on cable television, a contemporary bastion for edgy shows and racy performances that are assumed to have a high degree of quality to them. Dinklage's continued connection to the New York theater world—in 2004 he starred as Richard III in an off-Broadway production, and he is married to theater director Erica Schmidt—also helps affirm the discourse of his talent, relying on the class assumption that theatrical work suggests talent in ways that commercial cinema cannot.

In this way, the emphasis on Dinklage's natural talent also helps enforce the "overcoming narrative" established by the coverage of *The Station Agent*. Because Dinklage's stardom is linked to discourses of political correctness and a critique of Hollywood stereotyping, his performances are almost always political, each representing a possible challenge to the status quo due to the very fact that Dinklage is the star. As such, his casting is always somewhat suspect, suggesting the specter of tokenism or affirmative action. But the discourse of quality keeps such suspicions at bay, assuring the culture that Dinklage has earned his place through merit rather than as an icon of inclusion.

Endearing Dinklage even further to this meritocratic narrative, he also insists that he should only be judged by his roles and actively dismisses any political meaning to his fame. In a 2004 profile in *GQ*, for example, Dinklage relates a narrative about his personal politics that illustrates his political detachment. While riding the subway, he was approached by another dwarf who also happened to be an actor. The man told Dinklage that he would not be playing Christmas elves again and thanked him for being an inspiration. As the writer suggests, however, this did not sit well with Dinklage:

> And yet now, a few minutes later, Dinklage is unsure of what to make of the encounter. "If an actor comes up and talks about liking my work, that's great," he says, leaning forward, both palms flat on the table. "But when it turns into . . . a *cause*? That's not why I do this."
> He slugs some beer from his plastic cup.
> "I do this to pick up chicks!"[32]

Deflecting any serious political discussion with his trademark wit and charm, Dinklage leaves open the possibility that he is a role model, but then humorously dismisses it.

Similarly, in lengthy profiles of the actor and his life, Dinklage acknowledges the difficulties of adolescence as a little person, but is quick to make jokes and insist that his suffering is no different than anyone else's. In *Rolling Stone*, he argues that "High School sucks for everyone," not just little people.[33] And in *GQ* he jokingly dismisses his teenage angst: "So you wear a lot of black clothes, start smoking and are just angry. . . . You go from listening to Asia to Depeche Mode. . . . It's not torture. Just high school."[34]

So when he made it big in *The Station Agent* and started fielding questions about his struggles finding work, he was quick to dismiss his role as a kind of activist. "I'm just an actor," Dinklage said. "I like good roles. It's hard to be, like, a spokesperson or be up on a soapbox."[35] And of being an industry pioneer, Dinklage has said, "As an actor, I just like to play juicy roles. . . . [The responsibility for social change] should be put on some people who are actually making decisions or policies like politicians, not for an actor who just wants to work and pay the bills."[36] He has even denied (somewhat incredibly) that he faced any more difficulties than other young actors looking for quality roles: "I have no complaints because I am getting scripts and I have the luxury of turning roles down. I have friends who are so tired because they only get the handsome best friend role; the same with beautiful women. I am not complaining about how limited my roles are because every actor's are."[37] When pressed about this statement, though, he followed it with a joking retraction: "No, I don't really believe what I'm saying at all. I'm in complete denial. Thanks for catching me. I just like to compare my pain with others."[38]

The very real dismissal of casting discrimination (even half-jokingly) that Dinklage offers here suggests a concerted effort to frame his fame as highly individualistic and distanced from identity politics. Apart from one brief blip in his career in which he drew attention to a recent "dwarf tossing" attack in his 2012 Emmy acceptance speech, Dinklage has remained distant from activism. As *Rolling Stone* puts it, "Dinklage doesn't necessarily feel a sense of responsibility to other people his size. 'I just want to work,' he says."[39] This is clearly a shrewd career move: he does not want to be defined by political causes in order to access better and more mainstream roles. He does not want to be locked into the "little-people-are-people-too schmaltz," as one writer described the inclusive tendency in Hollywood today.[40] He knows that being defined by political activism will limit the roles that come his way. The shrewdness of this strategy, however, reflects the culture's apprehensions about diversity and acceptance of individualism. While entertainment journalism often celebrates the inclusion of different bodies, Dinklage seems aware that this inclusion is tokenistic and can pigeonhole an actor's career.

By avoiding the political meanings of his fame, then, Dinklage's life story is drafted into highly individualistic narratives about transcending social stigma. In order for the culture to accept him as an actor who "just wants to work," all political arguments about discrimination are tossed aside as excuses or complaints. One writer makes this point bizarrely clear in describing Dinklage's upbringing in New Jersey: "There isn't much to complain about, not that he ever did much of that—his parents never moved anything from the high shelves in their house, just expected him to get on with it, to climb up for what he wanted, and that's what he's always done."[41] The image of a young Dinklage struggling to get himself a glass of milk (and learning an important lesson about self-reliance) helps cement a narrative of hard work and individual perseverance. He succeeded where other little people performers did not, this anecdote suggests, because he never "complains" about the structural inequalities he faces, choosing instead to just work a little harder. Any attempts to accommodate individuals who face steep barriers to success—even providing a stool for a dwarf child—are acts of mollycoddling that ruin their work ethic.

Dinklage's success in the industry, then, is also framed as being a result of his personal choices: by refusing stereotypical but well-paying roles, he has promoted himself as a "quality" actor who never compromises his ethics. In *Rolling Stone*, for example, Dinklage discusses the dilemma between poverty and principles:

> [Dinklage] remembers bleaker days when most acting gigs on the table required pointy, jingling hats, as apologetic agents check in each holiday season to see if he was desperate enough to play a Santa elf. "I said, 'No'" Dinklage says. "It was hard. I was wondering, 'How am I going to pay the rent?' You need the work, that's how you make your living. But I'm going to play roles that are appropriate to my size—it's all about how real it is."[42]

Taking this principled stand, of course, worked out for Dinklage, who eventually found more lucrative and appropriate roles (although one wonders how many little people performers try a similar strategy and are simply unable to maintain a professional career). And by acknowledging the limited roles available to little people in entertainment, this discourse allows Dinklage to reference identity politics without being defined by it—he gets to criticize the entertainment industry while still insisting that his persona is defined by his choices and his talent, not by political challenges to the status quo.

This logic implies that individuals struggling against forms of discrimination are ultimately responsible for overcoming those obstacles themselves, in this case by choosing to stereotype themselves in certain roles. Dinklage has made this logic fairly explicit, in fact, as one writer explains:

> He wishes other actors his height would reconsider certain roles—particularly ones that involve answering to the names Dopey or Sneezy or Sleepy. "I just feel like it's the responsibility of people my size to persevere a bit more about what they do. Because it will just

perpetuate itself if you agree to do these things. *Mirror Mirror—*
I have a friend who was in that movie, and he was like, 'Why did I
do this?'"[43]

By placing some responsibility for continued stereotypes on the little people
who perform in stereotypical roles, Dinklage not only obscures the cultural
assumptions and structural conditions that perpetuate stereotypes of little
people, but also positions himself as a talented, hardworking actor who has
succeeded precisely by avoiding politics. He refuses stereotypical roles *and*
roles that politicize his body too much, suggesting that he has succeeded
through "fair" competition on the casting market.

In this way, Dinklage is the ideal neoliberal role model in a world concerned with diversity. He demonstrates the increasing inclusiveness of Hollywood while insisting that he earned his inclusion through his raw merit. His
persona hints at the stereotypes little people have faced (and sometimes continue to face), but he suggests we can move beyond those stereotypes if everyone just tries a little harder and relies on their natural talents.

THE CHARMING SEX SYMBOL

Sex appeal has consistently been a central means through which this
narrative of Dinklage's "natural" talent is secured in his popular persona. His
fame, one critic claims, offers a "meritocratic twist" for an actor who does
not "meet a certain physical ideal,"[44] and yet much of the media coverage of
Dinklage also emphasizes how much he does, in fact, "meet a certain physical ideal." Calling Dinklage "the newest thinking person's sex symbol," one
writer gushes over his "soft kissable lips, a strong jaw, and knockout blue
eyes."[45] Another calls him "dark-haired and striking, with a deep, sexy voice
and eyes more than one reporter has called 'soulful.'"[46] Several critics refer to
him as the sexiest dwarf in the world,[47] while another refers to him as "classic
leading man material: dark, handsome and moodily charismatic."[48] Captur-
ing the assumed dissonance between dwarfism and sex appeal, one reviewer
says that Dinklage's character in *Game of Thrones* "may be no taller than a
mailbox but women everywhere have fallen for his sharp wit and steamy bedroom antics in this medieval fantasy drama."[49] *Buzzfeed* even created a slideshow of sexy Dinklage pictures demonstrating his cool charm and appeal.[50]
As *GQ* described his power back in 2004, "Peter Dinklage walks into a bar
. . . and women swoon, agents hustle, and gossip ignites over the young actor
of the moment."[51] He has achieved fame where other little people performers
have not because, quite simply, he is one hot dwarf.

The persistent attention to his sexual allure and "classic leading man" good looks is often seen as a pivotal moment in disability rights. Cara Egan, a former vice president for the Little People of America, has celebrated Dinklage's rise to fame, citing his inclusion in *People*'s list of "sexiest men alive" as a culture-changing moment for little people and their place in mainstream media.[52] The idea that a dwarf might be considered not just an acceptable object of sexual desire but even an enviable one is a radical transformation in cultural norms. In popular culture, little people and people with disabilities in general are most often desexualized and displaced from narratives of romance.[53] So the sexualization of Dinklage and the gushing descriptions of his "soulful" eyes represent a major challenge to this popular representational trope.

And yet the sexualization of Dinklage might also objectify his non-normative body as a site of alluring taboo. Reflecting the perceived novelty of combining dwarfism and sex appeal, these discourses also suggest a continued cultural fascination with sex and the "other" made manifest in the history of the US sideshow.[54] The sideshow and the continuing use of people with non-normative bodies in the media rely on the mechanism of staring to produce the idea of bodily difference and perpetuate the hierarchy between non-normative bodies and bodies deemed "normal." As Rosemarie Garland-Thomson argues:

> Staring at disability choreographs a visual relation between a spectator and a spectacle. A more intense form of looking than glancing, glimpsing, scanning, surveying, gazing and other forms of casual or uninterested looking, staring registers the perception of difference and gives meaning to impairment by making it aberrant. . . . Staring thus creates disability as a state of absolute difference rather than simply one more variation in human form.[55]

But since explicit staring at the non-normative body is socially taboo, spaces like the sideshow and now visual media allow able-bodied audiences to indulge in the spectacle of the non-normative body, providing a safe position that affirms the bodily difference of the on-screen spectacle rather than inviting identification with little people or others who deviate from the bodily norms of Western culture.

The history of voyeurism in the representation of non-normative bodies raises serious questions about the pleasures of little people in the media today, even concerning shows such as *Little People, Big World* that are celebrated for their "positive" portrayals of different bodies. Dan Kennedy, who writes about the culture of dwarfism, applauds the show's portrayal of the Roloffs as

FIGURE 3.4. *Tyrion Lannister (Peter Dinklage) gets intimate with a prostitute in* Game of Thrones *(HBO, 2011–present).*

just a normal family, but also suggests that its popularity is rooted in the pleasures of gazing: the show "wallows in what it purportedly deplores, allowing us to feel good about ourselves while we gawk at this unusual-looking family from the privacy of our living rooms." Simply, the show offers "voyeurism without the fear of being caught," Kennedy claims.[56] Such concerns extend beyond the Roloffs, raising questions about the basis for pop culture's minor obsession with little people today. Clearly, shows such as *Half-Pint Brawlers* fulfill these voyeuristic urges, organizing around the spectacle of little people's bodies engaged in kinetic stunts. But can the same be said of Dinklage's nuanced and engaging performances in the most complex roles ever written for little people? Despite the more nuanced roles, the pleasures of watching Dinklage on screen cannot so easily be wrested from the voyeuristic pleasures of viewing a body that deviates from cultural norms or the long history of sensationalizing non-normative bodies for the amusement of Western audiences.

The continuing discussion within entertainment journalism of Dinklage as a sex symbol reflects this thorny dilemma: does the discussion of Dinklage's hotness challenge stereotypes of little people that deny their sexuality, or does getting lost in his "soulful eyes" make dwarfism a fetish object for our voyeuristic urges? Does staring at Dinklage as a sex icon allow him a more complex individual identity than was offered to little people in the past, or is it simply a mechanism through which audiences feel more comfortable staring at bodily difference and the spectacle of a sexualized dwarf?

To answer these questions, Dinklage's sexiness must be understood as a discourse, a set of ideas, discussions, debates, and descriptions within the mass media that have come to define his public persona. This is not to deny the fact that Dinklage is an objectively handsome fellow whom many people are attracted to but rather to ask why a discussion of physical attractiveness has so often framed the media coverage of his career. Entertainment journalists often fawn over attractive stars, devising elaborate and clever ways of describing their physiques, but not all good-looking stars become sex symbols within the culture. So why has this discourse of sexiness and charm come to define Dinklage's fame? And how is it framed to code Dinklage as an acceptable model of cultural citizenship?

At least part of the prominence of the Dinklage-is-sexy discourse derives from today's imperative for cultural inclusion. Acknowledging Dinklage's sex appeal offers a certain cachet—it signifies an inclusive and accepting outlook. Images of people with disabilities and non-normative bodies often fulfill this function in contemporary capitalism, signaling a sentimental discourse of acceptance often deployed by advertisers to elicit sympathy.[57] While a discussion of Dinklage's sex appeal is not as emotionally exploitative as, say, including an adorable child with Down syndrome in a feel-good Nordstrom's ad, making note of his attractiveness still signifies a set of diverse values regarding bodily difference. Thus, most of the discussions of Dinklage's appeal frame him not just as "sexy," but as a new kind of sex icon. *Variety* dubbed Dinklage an emblem of the "new sexy," while the website *Hollywood Scoop* claims that he "redefines sexy."[58] Implicit in the "newness" of his appeal is the impact of diversity—he is the new "thinking person's" celebrity crush because swooning over him signals hip, inclusive taste in pop culture.[59] As I suggest in the introduction, public acknowledgment of Dinklage's attractiveness—for example, sharing those *Buzzfeed* images of him looking sexy on Facebook—becomes part of an individual project of self-construction and promotion in which Dinklage functions as diversity currency. The sharing of those images uses the diversity cachet of Dinklage to bolster and frame a narrative of personal tolerance and enlightenment.

Moreover, Dinklage is not defined by a vague notion of being good-looking, but rather embodies a specific vision of masculine sexiness. Embedded into the discussions of his good looks are a set of cultural referents that mark him as having a particular form of hip, urban, masculine coolness. He has become a regular figure in hipster-saturated Brooklyn but has urban credibility because he lived there as a starving artist well before it became gentrified. He looks good in a suit, but is most often photographed in jeans, hoodies, and beanies as he walks his dog (and more recently his young child) around his neighborhood. As one writer describes him, "He's wearing one of his James Perse hoodies ('I dress and eat like a fifth-grader, basically. I like sandwiches and cereals and hooded sweatshirts') over a pair of Varvatos blue-striped pants whose frayed bottoms suggest some aggressive amateur tailoring, possibly with a scissor, and his usual scuffed, Springsteen-esque leather boots."[60] This relaxed and casual (yet carefully crafted) fashion sense marks Dinklage as not only sexy but also undeniably hip.

Dinklage is also lauded with praise using a key currency of hipster appreciation: nostalgic allusions to the old guard of Hollywood leading men. His friends and colleagues always turn to nostalgic comparisons to describe Dinklage's charm and on-screen power. *The Station Agent* director Tom McCarthy likened Dinklage's ability to command an audience's attention to Gary Cooper's,[61] but in one-on-one flirtations, McCarthy says Dinklage is more like Warren Beatty: "he just locks in and the rest of the world goes away."[62] Jon Favreau, the director of *Elf*, thinks Dinklage "looks like a '70s movie star, an old style leading man,"[63] while one journalist's description of Dinklage's "darkly handsome" good looks includes a nod to his "sloping James Dean eyebrows."[64] (Dinklage himself, it seems, has more contemporary aspirations—he channels his inner Ryan Gosling from *Drive* while steering around his new neighborhood in upstate New York, according to one profile of the actor).[65]

Positioning Dinklage within this constellation of classic masculinities, the discourses explaining his sex appeal are almost excessive in their insistence on his masculine credibility. Not only is he a hip Brooklynite and an icon of trendy cultural tastes, but he is also apparently Gary Cooper, Warren Beatty, and James Dean all rolled into one. This insistence on his unassailable manhood is encapsulated in a 2011 *GQ* story under the simple headline, "Peter Dinklage: STUD." Referring to his hugely popular role on *Game of Thrones*, the story describes him as someone who "spends workdays bedding maidens on wolf pelts and plucking figs from between their perky breasts."[66]

The persistent emphasis on Dinklage's sex appeal and cool masculinity, then, offsets the challenge to normative body ideals that he represents. The rise of a little person as a true celebrity upsets traditional definitions of beauty, health, and individuality itself, a challenge that may be celebrated as a victory for diversity but nonetheless requires an accommodation in "normal" celebrity-hood. For Dinklage, this has meant assertions of hyper-masculinity to help "normalize" the place of a dwarf movie star.

Nowhere is this clearer than in several photo shoots of Dinklage in *GQ* during his rise to fame. Photographs of people with disabilities, Rosemarie Garland-Thomson suggests, have allowed the cultural practice of gazing at the non-normative body to persist past the spectacle of the sideshow. As such, they "organize our perceptions, shaping the objects as they depict them by using conventions or presentation that invoke cultural ideas and expecta-

FIGURE 3.5. *Peter Dinklage in* GQ, *December 2011*
(GQ.com).

tions."[67] The photographs of Dinklage, then, demonstrate a specific set of conventions that manage cultural expectations, namely the use of hypermasculine signifiers to make Dinklage a culturally acceptable vision of male stardom.

In his first shoot with *GQ* in 2004 after his indie-hit *The Station Agent*, Dinklage is photographed with thick stubble and wearing a "wife-beater" tank top. He plays with a set of dog tags dangling around his neck, and a half-smoked cigarette is perched precariously in his lips. Shot from the chest up, he is slouching slightly with his head tilted back in a pose of defiance and rebelliousness, channeling his inner James Dean. In 2011 after *Game of Thrones* became a hit, Dinklage was back in *GQ*, this time in a wrinkled shirt and loosely cocked tie with a black vest and slacks. In one shot he is seated, king-like, in a red velvet chaise longue while a nude woman, her back to the camera, is draped on the floor next to the chair, as if about to perform a sex act on the actor. In another shot, the naked woman is splayed across his lap as he sits in an armchair (this time in green velour) with her head turned so she remains anonymous. In both images Dinklage looks over the woman at the camera, expressionless.

These photos authorize gazing at Dinklage's body, allowing an uninterrupted opportunity to stare voyeuristically at physical difference. But more than that, they suggest that excessive markers of masculinity are necessary for Dinklage's fame. Disabled or non-normative bodies are often asexual in cultural representations, and male, non-normative bodies are often feminized, demonstrating the intersectional reliance of masculinity and ability in Western cultures. Thus the visual spectacle of disabled men provokes anxiety about American manhood (this is especially true following times of war when wounded and maimed men must occupy the contradictory position of war hero and seemingly emasculated man). In response, representations of disabled masculinity in popular culture revert to excessive markers of toughness or sexual potency to overcome the taint of femininity, a process seen in documentaries such as *Murderball* (about the viciously competitive world of men's quadriplegic rugby), or in news coverage of wounded soldiers that focus on uplifting stories of wounded men regaining their place as fathers and husbands.[68]

The markers of tough, working-class masculinity in the first shoot and the casual use of the woman as a prop in the second frame Dinklage as a "man's man," shoring up his masculinity against the possible threat of feminization. Like other photographs Garland-Thomson describes, these shots of Dinklage "completely rewrit[e] the cultural script of the emasculated invalid and the male who becomes feminized by disability."[69] If, under other circumstances, the spectacle of the dwarf body raises questions about sexuality and individualism—reflecting the anxieties of the able-bodied world about non-normative personhood—then these images keep those fears at bay through the spectacle of masculinity. Dinklage challenges conceptions of what a "leading man" might be, but the culture can accommodate this challenge if there is assurance that traditional values of masculinity are still in place within Dinklage's persona. The tough posturing and objectification of women in these photo shoots, then, suggest a sense of self-consciousness about Dinklage's manhood: the images resort to excessive markers of masculinity that mask a deep-seated anxiety about the feminization of disability.

Interestingly, Dinklage's cool masculine allure has also been drafted into popular discourses around geek masculinities, especially the ways that geekdom has authorized a kind of male victimization narrative. As Kom Kunyosying and Carter Soles argue in their compelling history of geeks in pop culture, the contemporary valorization of the geek has promulgated a narrative seeking to mask the typical whiteness and male privilege of geekdom. They write: "Confronted with his cultural centrality and white, masculine privi-

lege—geeks are most frequently represented as white males—the geek seeks
a simulated victimhood and even simulated ethnicity in order to justify his
existence as a protagonist in a world where an unmarked straight white male
protagonist is increasingly passé."[70] Embracing the rhetoric of cultural victimization that the diversity movement has made mainstream, such geek
narratives foreground their perceived victimization at the hands of "jocks"
(or other representatives of hegemonic masculinity) or the women who do
not take them seriously as romantic and sexual partners. This victim narrative, however, only further facilitates the misogyny and whiteness of stories
celebrating geekdom: constructing geeks as cultural victims only thinly veils
the ways such narratives simultaneously blame and exploit women as sexual
objects while expressing white anxieties about the loss of cultural prestige to
people of color.

Dinklage has found his way into a number of geekdom narratives, and
his inclusion lends credence to the "simulated ethnicity" claim constructing geeks as cultural victims. In films such as *Knights of Badassdom* or *Pixels*,
Dinklage pops up as part of a geek ensemble that proves the cultural value
of geekdom and in the process helps rejuvenate white masculinity. Given
the meritocratic narrative surrounding Dinklage's stardom (he is constructed
as the victim of cultural discrimination, even as his stardom suggests that
the talented will overcome such obstacles) it is not surprising that he appears in films constructing geeks as both hapless victims of cultural prejudice and yet heroic saviors thanks to their innate talent and skill. If straight
white male protagonists are increasingly passé, then making them geeks and
pairing them with Dinklage helps obscure their white, patriarchal privilege,
affirming their supposed status as cultural outsiders. In the process, this
"simulated ethnicity" authorizes their own misogyny as their masculinity is
rejuvenated thanks to the objectification of women. As with other stars with
non-normative bodies, Dinklage's roles in these films relies on his cultural
difference to assist those with cultural privilege in their own stories of personal triumph.

This trend is certainly at work in the horror comedy *Knights of Badassdom*,
where Dinklage plays a geeky LARPer (live-action role player). The film's protagonist, Joe (played by Ryan Kwanten), has just been dumped by his ambitious, classy girlfriend who disapproves of his dreams of death rock stardom
as well as his geeky friends Hung (Peter Dinklage) and Eric (Steve Zahn).
In order to get their buddy out of his post-breakup slump, Eric and Hung
convince the reluctant Joe to accompany them to a local LARP event at a
campground in the woods. But when Eric's prop spell book that he got on
eBay turns out to be a real demonic artifact, Joe and Eric accidentally sum-
mon an evil succubus from hell who takes the form of Joe's ex, Beth (Mar-

garita Levieva). With the help of Gwen (Summer Glau), Joe and the other LARPers are the only ones prepared to take on the demon, who is seducing and slaughtering people in the woods. Hung gets murdered by the succubus, but is briefly brought back by Joe's magic spell as a heroic swordsman who vanquishes the demon.

The film's geeks-save-the-world narrative celebrates geekdom (while gently mocking it) and helps Joe rejuvenate his manhood: his excursion into LARP-ing and geekdom help him stop wallowing in self-pity and get over Beth. In the end, Joe embraces his love of death rock (using one of his songs as a spell to defeat the demon) and asks Gwen out on a date; geekdom becomes the impetus for him to "man up," as it were. The discourse of geekdom, then, works to obscure the masculinist privileges of the narrative. The film deploys geekdom as a "simulated ethnicity" that marks Joe, Eric, and Hung as objects of cultural discrimination, especially as Beth dumps Joe because he won't leave his geeky friends and geeky dreams behind. Because she looks down on geeks, she gets refigured in the narrative as an evil, sexy succubus, threatening to use her feminine wiles to lure Joe and others to their deaths, a clear meta-phor for the real Beth trying to degeek Joe. Gwen by contrast is presented as a "cool-girl" geek fantasy: a sexy, LARPing geek who not only supports Joe's death rock dreams but plays the bass in his band at the film's end. Essen-tially, the film tells a misogynist story about rejecting the supposedly horrible women who hate geeks (and murdering their demonic doppelgangers) while indulging in fantasies about hot geek-girls who find men's geekdom sexy. But the film tries to bury this narrative under a geeks-as-victims discourse that figures the men as the real victims of antigeek sentiment (to hammer this message home, the film even includes violent rednecks that bully the LARPers, relying on stereotypes of social class to vilify poor whites and gar-ner sympathy for the geeks). Dinklage's role, then, helps shore up the male victimization narrative linking able-bodied white characters like Joe and Eric to the specter of cultural victimization.

Dinklage found himself in a similar role in the 2015 Adam Sandler com-edy *Pixels*, which again cast him as part of a geeky crew of misfits tasked with saving the world. In the film, Sandler plays Sam, an aging, former arcade game whiz who gets called into service when aliens challenge earthlings to a series of battles based on classic arcade games. Sam's best friend from child-hood, Will (Kevin James), now happens to be the president of the United States and needs Sam's expertise, along with that of Ludlow Lamonsoff (Josh Gad), another former arcade gamer, and Eddie Plant (Dinklage), a cocky arcade game champion (based on real-life arcade whiz Billy Mitchell) who happens to be Sam's former nemesis. As Sam and the crew take on the alien challenges, Sam finds the self-confidence to realize that he can make a contribution to the world (he has been working a dead-end job installing home theater systems, a clear disappointment considering his youthful talents). At the same time, Sam wins the heart of Violet Van Patten (Michelle Monaghan), a lieutenant colonel tasked with overseeing the geeks who is also a recently divorced single mom. Just as in *Knights of Badassdom*, the rejuvenation of the male protagonist aligns with his success in dating beautiful women.

The film also uses the same technique of masking its vision of masculine privilege by appealing to the narrative of geek victimization. The crew of geeks tasked with saving the world is at first mocked and bullied by the hypermasculine military personnel that want to take out the alien threats themselves before the geeks demonstrate their worth and are celebrated as heroes. And just as in *Knights of Badassdom*, the inclusion of Dinklage supports their depiction as outcasts and cultural outsiders. But by casting the white male geeks as sympathetic victims, the film only seems to want to distract its audience from a narrative in which white men play the heroes and highly sexualized women function as the trophies for male action. As Nico Lang puts it in an insightful takedown of Sandler's gender politics, "*Pixels* views women not as humans (or characters with their own arcs) but as prizes awarded to male heroes for acts of valor."[71] Nowhere is this clearer than when the aliens, after being bested by the earthlings, award Gad's character Ludlow with a real-life manifestation of "Lady Lisa," the sexy and sword-wielding video game character he has lusted after since childhood. Lisa has no lines nor seemingly any agency—she is simply an object traded between the aliens and the male heroes. But the misogynist tendencies in the film are supposed to be hidden behind the idea that the white male geeks are the real victims worthy of our sympathy.

Building off Dinklage's reputation as a sex symbol, the film also works hard to hypersexualize his character, turning him into a caricature of out-of-control geek masculinity. When we first meet Eddie as a child (played by Andrew Bambridge), he is flanked by anonymous, long-legged, busty-chested women to flatter his enormous ego. When we meet him again as an adult—he is in prison for tech crimes and has been divorced four times, we are told—he demands a threesome with Serena Williams and Martha Stewart in the Lincoln bedroom of the White House if they want his help, a ridiculous sexual demand that nonetheless comes true for him after he saves the world. He also constantly sexualizes Lieutenant Colonel Von Patten, referring to her sometimes as "sugar buns" or "Lieutenant Long Legs." While making Sandler's character seem downright gentlemanly, Dinklage's performance provides a foil for the rejuvenation of white manhood in the film, building sympathy for Sandler's geekdom by comparison.

The hypersexualization of Dinklage in the film also suggests the limi-

FIGURE 3.6. *Peter Dinklage as the outrageous video gamer Eddie Plant in* Pixels *(Happy Madison Productions, 2015).*

tations of his groundbreaking status as a dwarf sex symbol. Just as with his roles in the British and American versions of *Death at a Funeral*, in which he plays the secret gay lover of a family's deceased patriarch, *Pixels* is not really interested in Dinklage as a genuine object of (or possessor of) sexual desire. Rather, the film uses the supposedly ridiculous idea of a sexualized dwarf as a punchline, a set of comedic images and dialogue meant to highlight the dissonance between sexuality and non-normative bodies. The same is true of his role in the Melissa McCarthy comedy *The Boss*, in which he plays the McCarthy character's business rival and former lover; the intense sexual desire between the two characters is played for laughs as the supposedly humorous spectacle of a dwarf and an overweight woman making love. While *Game of Thrones* might take his sexuality seriously, when Dinklage is drafted into roles as quirky sidekicks who help people with cultural power reclaim or rehabilitate their place in the world (a trend for stars with non-normative bodies), his sexuality instead becomes a caricature, a means through which to ogle and laugh at the idea of "deviant" bodies and their "deviant" sexualities. Dinklage may be "the newest thinking person's sex symbol," but his position as a sex symbol is highly ambivalent as pop culture uses him to articulate traditional definitions of masculinity and male power.

CONCLUSION: COOL CONFIDENCE AND THE
PROMISE OF A POSTDISABILITY WORLD

Part of what makes Dinklage so alluring is the insistence on his cool self-confidence. After all, like any good sex symbol, Dinklage himself is often uncomfortable and self-deprecating about all the attention his good looks get him. When *GQ* asked him about his burgeoning reputation as a "ladies man" in 2004 (before he got married and became a dad), Dinklage turned "coy" and protested that the stories were exaggerated.[72] When asked if he and Vin Diesel, then his costar, would be competing for women after being named to *People*'s list of sexiest men alive, Dinklage dismissed the attention as "silly," insisting that he would not be "interested in somebody who is interested in something like that."[73] So when *GQ* proclaimed him a "stud" in 2011 and featured him draped in naked women, Dinklage was reportedly "oddly resistant to the term 'stud.'"[74] As this resistance suggests, he recognizes the insistence on his hypermasculinity as a façade, endearing him to us even more and showcasing his self-confidence.

Almost always tied to a discussion of his good looks is a celebration of his charm and self-assurance, mostly in the context of wooing women. His costars and coworkers are always touting his charming ability to flirt or command a conversation. His *Station Agent* costar Bobby Cannavale told *GQ*: "Pete's got this thing about him. You go into a bar with him, people just come up and start talking. And women—it's unbelievable! You turn your back for a second, he's talking to two, three girls."[75] *Game of Thrones* showrunner David Benioff affirms Dinklage's confident presence, noting that at one dinner party, "I looked around the table and realized that every woman there, including my wife, was hanging on his every word, enthralled."[76] And *Game of Thrones* costar Lena Headey has commented on his sex appeal and charm on more than one occasion: she told *Rolling Stone* in 2011 that Dinklage is "super attractive" and that "he totally knows he's got it,"[77] and then affirmed this notion in another piece on Dinklage in 2012, saying, "Pete is super-flirtatious, the most successful flirt I've ever met. . . . There's nothing about him that isn't anything but confident."[78]

Dinklage's self-confidence is also seen as offsetting his height, allowing him to overcome the stigma of his short stature. His close friend Sherman said in an interview with *People* that when Dinklage flirts with "tall blonde women" the actor "seems to be much taller than he is."[79] Likewise, a profile of the star in *Esquire* wallows in a detailed appreciation of his good looks as the writer conflates Dinklage's cool charm with the appearance of size: "Though at four feet six he is eleven inches shorter than me, he sits as if he were taller; I have to look up slightly to meet his blue-gray eyes, which seem more reflective of what's going on outside of himself than of what's happening within."[80] Linking self-assurance and height, such comments locate individual confidence as an appropriate strategy for overcoming the bias and discrimination that come with a non-normative body.

This is, in fact, an argument Dinklage has made himself, echoing the arguments made by Tyrion Lannister on *Game of Thrones*. "Any swagger is just defense," Dinklage says. "When you're reminded so much of who you are by people—not a fame thing, but with my size, constantly, growing up—you just either curl up in a corner in the dark or you wear it proudly, like armor or something. You can turn it on its head and use it yourself before anybody else gets a chance."[81] This insistence on facing adversity head-on means that "Dinklage comes off as more comfortable with himself than most humans of any size or shape," according to one writer.[82]

As I discuss in chapters 1 and 2, the discourses of self-confidence are deeply tied to a neoliberal worldview emphasizing individual self-actualization. In the face of structural inequalities, neoliberal culture encourages people to re-invent themselves or use their self-confidence to overcome the obstacles they face (rather than examine the structures that create inequality in the first place). Solutions to social inequality are to be found within, and inclusive icons such as the stars at the heart of this book suggest that self-confidence can be almost as successful as modifying your body when it comes to ensuring personal success. The emphasis on Dinklage's self-confidence exemplifies this trend, suggesting that in the face of a long history of stigma and stereotypes, the road to inclusion will not come from able-bodied culture changing attitudes or policies, but from talented folks with non-normative bodies who have the self-confidence to achieve fame and fortune.

This narrative of self-confidence also suggests the possibility of a problematic "postdisability" worldview. Feminist critics have long indicated the presence of "postfeminism," a pervasive worldview among privileged young women that recognizes the importance of the historical feminist movement but sees it as outdated and unnecessary in a world that embraces gender equity (despite evidence to the contrary).[83] Similarly, discourses of a "postracial" America intensified after the election of Barack Obama in 2008, particularly suggestions that the civil rights movement had finally reached its culmination and is no longer needed in a world capable of electing a black president. The rising fame of Peter Dinklage might indicate the possibilities of "postdisability," a worldview that embraces the cultural fronts of the disability rights movement (the rejection of stereotyping, the celebration of non-normative stars) but ignores the continuing structural inequalities facing people with disabilities. From within the worldview of postdisability, the stereotypes that have stigmatized little people are largely in the past or are the result of a few bigoted executives. The only barriers left are the internal holdups of those with non-normative bodies, who simply need to develop the self-confidence to assert themselves in an able-bodied world. Stars like Dinklage are the poster children of such a worldview, indicating that natural talent and hard work are always rewarded in an essentially fair society.

CHAPTER FOUR

Danny Trejo

LATINO ACTION STARDOM AND THE
SHIFTING BORDERS OF WHITENESS

In a 2014 segment on Jon Stewart's comedy news
show, *The Daily Show*, correspondent Al Madrigal heads to
Austin, Texas, to interview white citizens about their fears of Latino/a immigration. Middle-aged women worry about immigrants having too many
children, and a local sheriff is inexplicably concerned about the free com-
puters that he thinks are doled out to immigrants when they cross the border.
When Madrigal sets out to find the nefarious social mooches described by
the white interviewees (while "disguised" as a stereotypical *cholo*, circa 1992),
he predictably finds only hardworking Latinos/as trying to make a nice life
for themselves.

The segment ends by contrasting the hysterical fears of white Americans
against the mundane realities of middle-class Latinos. The segment shows
Danny Trejo—the muscled, tattooed, and weathered star of countless low-
budget action films—intruding upon scenes of white middle-class normalcy.
As Trejo steps menacingly out of a car, a mom playing with her kids in the
driveway looks apprehensive about his presence, but the kids run up to him
shouting "Daddy!" His wife then thanks him for bringing home Boston Market for dinner. In another scene, Trejo, shot from a low angle to emphasize
his strength, steps toward the camera with a bat, as if to beat a man to death,
but instead he hits a softball to a bevy of laughing children. Later, he douses
something off screen with gasoline and ignites it with the stumpy stogie on
which he has been chomping, before the camera pulls back to show that he is
lighting the barbeque as he asks his white wife to bring out the Boca Burgers.
In the kitchen, Trejo hacks at something on the counter with a machete, getting splattered with a blood-like substance, but the cut to a wider shot simply
shows him making salsa, all while the melodramatic narrator exclaims, "Latinos . . . they're not leaving until they get what they came for—a life as boring

as yours!" A split screen shot then shows Trejo enmeshed in middle-class life: getting the paper in a bathrobe, jogging in stylish exercise-wear, trimming the hedges at his house while waving to a neighbor, and helping an older woman carry her groceries.

The sketch skewers white hysteria about "dangerous" illegal immigrants, revealing the dissonance between the kinds of threatening Latino bodies that have been so popular in US entertainment media and the opening of the American dream to nonwhite bodies. Trejo, after all, has made a lucrative career for himself for the past thirty-five years by playing a range of hard-bodied baddies—often inmates—with penchants for gruesome violence. A former inmate with a violent past himself, Trejo has for years been the go-to character actor for Hollywood action and adventure films looking to cast a terrifying and menacing figure of fear. For much of his career, he has embodied American culture's worst fears and stereotypes about the dangers of Latino immigration with a persona that signifies violence, crime, and machismo. Integrating Trejo into scenes of middle-class bliss, the sketch on *The Daily Show* undercuts those stereotypes as the silly fantasies of US pop culture.

More accurately, the sketch explores the shifting boundaries of whiteness in the contemporary United States. The numerous references to middle-class white stereotypes—Boston Market, Boca Burgers, pristine suburban lawns, and an obsession with jogging—draw attention to whiteness as a cultural category and the process through which that category may expand to include certain traditionally nonwhite populations. Eduardo Bonilla-Silva describes this as a move toward a "tri-racial" system in which the social category of "white" is buffered from the "collective black" of African Americans, dark-skinned Latinos, and others by an emerging category of "honorary whites" that confers some of the privileges of whiteness on economically mobile, light-skinned racial and ethnic groups (for example, some Latinos/as, Japanese Americans, and Chinese Americans).[1] The central joke of the *Daily Show* sketch, then, is not that a Latino might be welcomed into the fold of whiteness, but that Danny Trejo, a Latino whose popular image affirms the place of Latinos in the "collective black" category, might aspire to honorary whiteness. After all, the cultural dissonance of a Latino cooking Boca Burgers with his white wife in the suburbs would evaporate if that Latino was, say, Gael García Bernal, the well-educated Mexican actor known for roles in art-house cinema. At the core of *The Daily Show*'s joke is the contested place of *some* working-class Latinos/as in the US racial imagination while others—for example, Jennifer Lopez, Jessica Alba, or John Leguizamo—are embraced as "honorary whites."

This chapter examines Trejo's journey from a B-movie bad guy to the (ar-

FIGURE 4.1. *Danny Trejo as Machete Cortez in* Machete *(Troublemaker Studios, 2010).*

guably) first Latino action hero in 2010's *Machete*, exploring how this journey parallels the shifting place of Latinos/as in the US cultural imagination. After years embodying US stereotypes about terrifying Latinos, Trejo has become a bona fide action hero in *Machete* and *Machete Kills* alongside his performances in the *Bad Ass* series, *Bullet*, *Dead in Tombstone*, and a host of other (often low-budget) genre films. His ascension to leading roles and action heroics is a remarkable feat given his physical appearance: he is a stocky, long-haired, often mustachioed, craggy-faced American of Mexican descent covered in prison tattoos from his previous life as a violent offender. While other Latinos/as in Hollywood have risen to fame through aspirations to honorary whiteness—often downplaying any ethnic identity or offering just a touch of "exotic" desirability—Trejo's body visibly marks him with the stereotypes that plague Latino men in the United States regarding violence, machismo, and criminality. For much of his career, moreover, Trejo unabashedly affirmed those stereotypes: he told *USA Today* that the film industry "still stereotypes me as this tough, Mexican criminal. . . . But that's OK. I was one."[2]

As Trejo's ambivalence about affirming stereotypes suggests, his rise to prominence as an icon of inclusivity in Hollywood has not been predicated on roles offering depth, nuance, and humanization for Latinos. Trejo remains an icon of hyperbolic, violent Latino manhood, but the meanings of his tough persona have changed in a neoliberal world purporting to value diversity and the need for self-transformation in order to secure cultural citizenship. Of course, the prevalence of color-blind, postracial rhetoric means that most Latino/a stars are brought into cultural citizenship much like the other stars discussed in this book: through appeals to normative gender roles to suggest "honorary whiteness" (for example, the allure of Eva Longoria in roles in which she is both "exotic" and aspires to domestic womanhood, or the hunky-yet-sensitive appeal of Guatemalan-born Oscar Isaac). But Trejo functions differently, offering an ironic caricature of Latino stereotypes that is often deployed with a wink and a nod, reveling in the excesses of those stereotypes while insisting that their use is just a joke. In a version of "hipster racism" in which people engage in racist speech or behavior, supposedly in an ironic way, to call attention to racism in general, Trejo's star persona since the mid-2000s has tried to be in on the joke of stereotypes and discrimination, offering an exaggerated vision of violent Latino manhood that is meant to ridicule popular assumptions about machismo.

Trejo's status as a postracial gag reinforces a neoliberal model of race relations in two key ways. First, his menacing, violent characters are often constructed as necessary figures in policing and reforming whiteness. As I note in the introduction, stars with non-normative bodies provide powerful images that demonstrate the magnanimous inclusion of "others" into the mainstream by the dominant group. The inclusion of stars such as Melissa McCarthy, Gabourey Sidibe, or Peter Dinklage shows that those with cultural power are able to accommodate the shifting demands of inclusivity and transform their own identities in a more diverse world (even if that transformation is purely individual and fails to address structural inequalities). At stake in the fame of stars with non-normative bodies is the implied reformation of the dominant group.

Reflecting and exaggerating this interest in reformation, Trejo's recent fame is predicated on roles in which he attacks bastions of white power and privilege. His latest roles use his violence to purge the world of the corruption and degradation of whiteness, or at least of a hyperbolic vision of white excess and villainy, or "hyperwhiteness," as Gretchen Bakke calls it.[3] In *Machete* and after, Trejo frequently finds himself in the role of a Latino avenger, rooting out the greed and depravity of white elites and other figures of white excess, especially white political corruption and hypocrisy. Such narratives, of course, are not really invested in social or political critique as much as they provide a melodramatic fantasy of "evil" whiteness that can be replaced by a more inclusive, diverse, and open-minded whiteness. In short, Trejo's ironic caricature of Latino masculinity can be easily pitted against a caricature of racist whiteness, affirming the transformation of white culture in the face of a more diverse world.

Second, Trejo's public persona affirms the place of Latinos/as as cultural citizens in the United States, but not because Trejo embodies a model of "honorary whiteness." Rather, Trejo's hypermacho violence on screen lovingly mocks outdated stereotypes, all while insisting that there is something appealing about the traditional gender roles on which those stereotypes are based. While Trejo's hypermasculine violence is constructed as an ironic joke, his machismo also suggests that cultural citizenship for Latinos/as and other nonwhite groups means embracing traditional models of gender and family. Reflecting the neoliberal tendency to place responsibility on individuals or communities to transform themselves (rather than to transform social or political systems), Trejo's violent persona on screen often asserts the need for individuals to reform and reclaim crime-ridden communities, replacing irresponsible criminal masculinities with (equally violent) masculinities devoted to middle-class family values. Trejo's characters can then make room for a new ethnic order that rethinks the borders of whiteness, imagining some hardworking Latinos/as as a vital part of middle-class values.

Such narratives are fueled by Trejo's own narrative of personal triumph. His stardom is often constructed as a reward for taking responsibility for his life: getting off drugs, starting a family, and devoting himself to helping other drug addicts (including Hollywood stars such as Dennis Hopper). While he has become a celebrated patriarch of the Latino/a community—especially in Los Angeles—his status rests on a neoliberal bootstrapping narrative that privileges the power of individuals to transform themselves and overcome discrimination.

As this suggests, central to Trejo's late-career resurgence is his age. He was sixty-six years old when his career opened up thanks to the success of *Machete* in 2010, and while some of his leading roles since avoid age—envisioning Trejo as an ageless icon of terror and violence—some films make explicit the nostalgia for older masculinities at the core of his contemporary persona. The *Bad Ass* films are perhaps the most explicit. In the films, almost everyone dismisses Trejo and his sidekicks as grumpy old men, especially since most of the time he is sporting a fanny pack and white sneakers, looking the part of a grandpa before bashing people's faces in. But even when the films make no mention of his age—for example, in the *Machete* films, in which he bounds from one sexual encounter to the next with women young enough to be his daughters—Trejo's age lingers as an important component of his persona. *Machete* and its sequels, after all, are nostalgia films, parodying yet embracing the pleasures of exploitation narratives from the 1970s. Trejo's sex appeal in the films, then, is partly a joke—he does not look the part of a Hollywood Romeo—but his allure also indicates a nostalgic yearning for an uncomplicated, violent manhood from the past.

As I will discuss in the next chapter, the anxieties of aging have become more prominent in US pop culture as the baby boomer generation approaches retirement and old age. Trejo's work in the *Bad Ass* films fits squarely into this recent trend, especially the increasing number of "geri-action" films: films exploring the continuing efficacy of aging male action bodies, typically the bodies of action icons from the 1970s and 1980s. Examples include *The Expendables* (2010) — an ensemble action film featuring Sylvester Stallone, Arnold Schwarzenegger, Bruce Willis, Mickey Rourke, Terry Crews, Dolph Lundgren, and others — or *R.E.D.* (2010), about retired secret agents getting back into action and starring Bruce Willis, Morgan Freeman, John Malkovich, Helen Mirren, and others. These narratives demonstrate the continuing vitality of aging action bodies — even if their bodies are not quite as able to perform feats of strength and violence as in their youth. The films acknowledge the vulnerabilities of age while nostalgically insisting that older male bodies, particularly but not exclusively white ones, can still prove their relevance in the contemporary world.[4]

The celebration of an aging but still muscled hero such as Trejo bolsters a neoliberal, postracial discourse suggesting that maybe the past was not as bad as activists and other critics think, that we should look to older models of traditional masculinity to restore individual responsibility in the United States. Trejo's popularity in the 2010s certainly taps into the same longing for the hard-bodied heroes of the 1970s and 1980s that keeps stars like Stallone and Schwarzenegger working into their sixties — a longing for violent masculinities that are not weighed down by the complexities of multiculturalism or political correctness. In the context of Latino/a cultural citizenship, then, Trejo's popularity rests on a nostalgia that is both ironic and genuine. Trejo offers a joke about how silly violent Latino machismo is while simultaneously expressing a deep longing for such masculinities. He can ironically lampoon the stereotypes that have plagued Latinos for hip, diversity-minded audiences, all while suggesting that cultural citizenship will only come through the individualist mantra of the macho action hero and the embrace of traditional gender roles.

LATINO CULTURAL CITIZENSHIP AND
THE IMMIGRATION DEBATE

Trejo's rise to stardom after 2010 coincided with increasingly intense public debate about Latino immigration in the United States and the role of Latinos — both legal citizens and otherwise — within US culture and society. The "problem" of Latino immigration has a long shelf life as a topic of public concern, from Mexican repatriation in the 1930s, to the controversies surrounding the bracero program in the 1940s–1960s, to the passing of Proposition 187 in California in the early 1990s. These long-standing tensions about Latino immigrants boiled over in the 2000s, especially in the wake of the 2008 election of Barack Obama, an advocate for immigration reform that would protect some illegal immigrants from deportation and create new paths toward citizenship for illegal immigrants in the United States. For example, in 2012, Obama initiated new federal policies to allow children who were brought to the United States illegally at a young age—dubbed "DREAMers" in reference to the long-debated DREAM Act—to remain in the country.[5] And in 2014, Obama indicated that he would use executive orders to change US immigration policy in the face of legislators' refusal to tackle comprehensive immigration reform.[6]

In response, conservatives in the United States have turned to increasingly draconian positions on immigration, seeking to undo any protections that Obama has initiated while advocating for tougher border security (maybe in the form of a wall along the US-Mexico border) or enforcement policies that target Latino Americans, such as Arizona's controversial SB 1070, which authorized local law enforcement agencies to demand identification from anyone they thought appeared to be an illegal alien, creating a fast track to racial profiling. In 2015 and 2016, presidential candidate Donald Trump took up the banner of these anti-immigrant sentiments, claiming that Mexican immigrants were rapists and suggesting a variety of radical policies to stem immigration from Latin America (and from Muslim-majority countries).

As the *Daily Show* sketch suggests, however, many of the anti-immigration political positions are less about law and policy and more about the social and cultural impact of Latinos/as in the United States. The prominent (and often spurious) arguments bandied about against Latino/a immigrants—that they are a drain on welfare and education systems, or bring crime and drugs across the border, or will not learn English and assimilate into US culture—express perceived threats to the power and stability of the white middle class. As Jenifer Wingard argues, contemporary debates about citizenship and immigration attempt to imagine a unifying idea of a "national citizenry" with shared economic and cultural interests, rather than simply defining national "rights" based on legal frameworks.[7] Legislation such as Arizona's much discussed SB 1070 normalizes a specific vision of a "citizen" based around whiteness and economic contributions by criminalizing the very appearance of those who look like poor Latinos/as. Such measures stem from a perceived threat to the imagined ideal of whiteness, seeing Latino/a bodies as intrinsically separate from the US cultural mainstream.

These concerns about immigrant bodies and their place within the culture are often predicated on demographic changes that seem troubling for the hegemony of white Americans. The number of Latinos/as in the United

States increased 50 percent between 2000 and 2012,[8] with an expansion in US-born Latinos/as surging while rates of immigration slowed during the 2008 economic downturn.[9] The US Latino/a population had already passed African Americans as the largest minority group in the country sometime around 2003 (at the time representing 13 percent of the US population compared to 12.5 percent for African Americans),[10] and at these rates, the US Latino/a population is projected to hit 129 million by 2060, around 31 percent of the expected US population.[11] This growth, along with the growth of other racial and ethnic groups, supports US census projections that whites will no longer represent the majority of the US population by the year 2043.[12]

While these looming demographic changes have cultural and political pundits anxious about the future of US whiteness, demographic changes do not always yield major shifts in political and social power. If Bonilla-Silva's prognostications are correct and the United States is heading toward a tripartite racial structure, then the emerging category of "honorary whites" will manage questions about whiteness and cultural belonging by buffering the tensions between whites and nonwhites. The inclusion of some Latinos/as and other typically nonwhite demographics under the umbrella of honorary whiteness will bolster postracial discourses of color-blindness by providing a bevy of multicultural success stories that seemingly demonstrate egalitarian opportunities. Meanwhile, the economic and social plight of the "collective black" is ignored in the face of this triumphant color-blindness, even as racial animosity increases between "honorary whites" and the "collective black," pitting different demographics of Latino/a Americans against others. In the process, the powers and privileges of whiteness are maintained, if negotiated.[13]

In the face of these demographic changes and the disruptions to the racial system that they bring, the popular media increasingly negotiate the shifting place of Latinos/as in the US popular imagination. The US entertainment media, of course, have a long history of stereotyping and stigmatizing Latinos/as on screen, a nuanced history that is well documented by scholars such as Charles Ramírez Berg, Chon Noriega, Clara Rodríguez, and others.[14] Ramírez Berg, in particular, has explicated the dominant on-screen stereotypes used to manage the social position of both US Latinos/as and Latinos/as as subjects of US imperialism: *el bandito*, the harlot, the male buffoon, the female clown, the Latin lover, and the dark lady. These roles build on and perpetuate assumptions about Latinos/as as violent, overly passionate, sexualized, and simplistic, traits that mark them as cultural "others" and deny them full cultural citizenship. Carefully demonstrating the history and complex contemporary usage of these stock character types, Ramírez Berg shows how these media stereotypes affirm systems of racial and ethnic inequality in the United States and abroad (and how some media makers have long challenged these assumptions about Latinos/as).

While these stereotypes persist in contemporary Hollywood, the growth of Latinos/as as an audience demographic has also facilitated more complex and negotiated representations in an attempt to woo this growing market.[15] The several television programs of comedian George Lopez—*George Lopez* (2002–2007), *Lopez Tonight* (2009–2011), and *Saint George* (2013–2014), in which Danny Trejo appeared—brought Latino/a faces and sometimes Latino issues to late-night comedy and prime time sitcoms. Comedian Cristela Alonzo, likewise, has taken up the mantle of the Latino/a sitcom with the success of her ABC show *Cristella* (2014–2015). The massive popularity of *Ugly Betty* (2006–2010), a US adaptation of a Colombian *telenovela* starring America Ferrera, brought a lovable, working-class Mexican American family to broadcast television, paving the way for the current success of *Jane the Virgin* (2015–), an adaptation of a Venezuelan *telenovela* about a pious virgin who is accidentally artificially inseminated thanks to a mix-up at her doctor's office. All the while, a spate of Latino/a actors have found success in film and television, including Jennifer Lopez, Eva Longoria, Michael Peña, Michelle Rodriguez, Salma Hayek, Selena Gomez, Cameron Diaz, Jessica Alba, Zoe Saldana, Sofia Vergara, Oscar Isaac, and many others.

At their best, programs and stars such as these help negotiate cultural citizenship, carving out a welcoming place for Latino/a Americans in the fold of US society. The celebration of Latino/a stars in mainstream entertainment media creates powerful models of Latino/a identity that reconcile cultural anxieties about the loss of white hegemony with images of likable, appealing, and largely unthreatening celebrity personas. Likewise, popular programs such as *Jane the Virgin* offer melodramatic narratives that help negotiate Latino/a identity and invite empathy from mainstream audiences. Anne Helen Petersen, in fact, argues that the emergence of nonwhite family melodramas such as *Jane the Virgin* not only challenges the whiteness of prime-time TV melodrama but also creates vibrant (if exaggerated) visions of various Latino/a identities, from the pious and traditional immigrant grandmother, to the rebellious first-generation Latina-American mother who rarely speaks Spanish and struggles with cooking traditional foods, to the assimilated second-generation Jane, who speaks without an accent and works to reconcile her grandmother's worldview with modern culture. While stereotypical, the melodramatic struggles of these characters and others—the wealthy Latino playboy, the dramatic *telenovela* star—invite emotional investments that explore the process of finding one's identity and place in the culture.[16]

At their worst, however, these contemporary images deploy Latino/a "exoticism" to add "spice" to film and television casting or broadcast lineups, an example of the postracial tendency to deny the social realities of racial oppression while insisting that racial or ethnic difference is a marketable commodity. As I discuss in chapter 2, one result of the postracial discourse becoming more resonant in US culture, and insisting that the culture has moved beyond the racial inequalities of its past and can embrace a color-blind worldview, is the perception of racial or ethnic identity as superficial markers that can be deployed for self-promotion or as a means of marketing to specific demographics. Stars such as Jennifer Lopez capitalize on the exoticism of being Latina (while tapping into historical stereotypes about Latina sexuality), but rarely do her songs or film roles address the material inequalities of life as an ethnic "other" in the United States. Similarly, the casting of Latino/a stars in film and television roles might help promote those products to the growing Latino/a market, but often those roles are devoid of cultural specificity, offering only a vacuous multiculturalism that avoids continuing racism and inequality.

As this suggests, the narrative of Hollywood's representation of Latinos and Latinas is not one of steady progress from bad stereotypes to nuanced roles, but rather one that is always fraught by the contradictions of particular historical moments. The work of Mary Beltrán and Priscilla Ovalle on the history of Latino and Latina stardom makes this clear, with each offering case studies of Latina and Latino bodies being constructed and consumed by mainstream culture in ways that negotiate various cultural demands on racial and ethnic "others." For Beltrán, stars such as Desi Arnaz, Freddie Prinze, Edward James Olmos, Jessica Alba, and others each helped reframe the very definitions of Latino/a identity in a shifting US historical context.[17] Likewise, for Ovalle, the image of the dancing Latina in particular—embodied by Dolores Del Rio, Carmen Miranda, Rita Hayworth, Rita Moreno, and Jennifer Lopez—has combined gendered and ethnic cultural assumptions to negotiate tensions around whiteness, race, sex, and national identity at various points in US history.[18]

Beltrán and Ovalle's work also indicates the crucial role of stars and celebrities in managing Latino cultural citizenship, providing powerful sites where the anxieties surrounding US whiteness and Latino immigration are both amplified and assuaged. The spate of popular Latino/a stars today, then, does not necessarily reflect a more nuanced and progressive place for Latinos/as in US culture, but rather shows how contested the idea of Latinos/as as cultural citizens or "honorary whites" actually is. US pop culture needs these varied images of Latino/a identity to address the vast contradictions of a shifting racial/ethnic landscape, one in which the Latino/a body is an object of desire, a threat to traditional values, a marketable commodity, and a vehicle for crime.

THE LATINO ACTION HERO: *MACHETE* AND
THE CHALLENGE TO "HYPERWHITENESS"

Trejo's long film career playing thugs and violent inmates in countless Hollywood films—from low-budget schlock to big-budget thrillers—
only came after a real career with crime and drugs in Southern California in
the 1950s and 1960s. Under the influence of his Uncle Gilbert, Trejo became a
drug addict at a young age and set out on an escalating series of crimes, from
armed robbery to violent assaults. He spent much of his youth in and out of
juvenile detention while building a local reputation as a tough hoodlum. He
eventually saw hard prison time after selling a bag of sugar to an undercover
federal officer, pretending it was heroin. He served time at a series of peni-
tentiaries in California, including Folsom, San Quentin, and Soledad; he became San Quentin's welterweight boxing champ while there. After helping to
incite a prison riot in the late 1960s, Trejo found himself in solitary confinement and decided that it was time to turn his life around. He decided to kick
his drug habit and make a new life for himself when he got out.[19]

When he was paroled in 1969, he kept himself out of trouble by helping
other addicts and ex-cons get off and stay off drugs, working for years as a
drug counselor and sponsor for struggling addicts. In the mid-1980s, when
one of these addicts asked him to come and visit the set of a film, Trejo's
muscled exterior and extensive prison tattoos landed him a job as an extra
on the jailbreak movie *Runaway Train*. On set, Trejo ran into Eddie Bunker,
a former inmate who had become a writer. Bunker was one of the screen-
writers on the film and recognized Trejo from his days as the San Quentin
boxing champ, so he secured Trejo a job training the film's star, Eric Roberts,
to box. Eventually Trejo made an appearance in the film as one of Roberts's
opponents in the ring.[20]

From there, Trejo found his way from smaller parts as inmates and criminals to larger parts, still mostly as inmates and criminals. In the 1990s he
earned bigger parts alongside Hollywood heavy hitters, such as his role as
a member of Robert De Niro's heist crew in Michael Mann's crime thriller
Heat (1995), also starring Al Pacino, Val Kilmer, and others. His character
in the film is simply named "Trejo," suggesting that Trejo is playing himself
when he takes on roles as career criminals. He also starred as the serial rapist
"Johnny 23" in the prison-airplane-escape adventure *Con Air* (1997) alongside
Nicholas Cage, John Malkovich, Steve Buscemi, John Cusack, Ving Rhames,
and others. In his biggest scene, he attempts to rape a female prison guard
before Nicholas Cage beats him up. In the mid-1990s he developed a relationship with the director Robert Rodriguez, taking on small, violent parts
in *Desperado* (1995) and *From Dusk till Dawn* (1996). Trejo became so asso-

ciated with roles as inmates or violent criminals that when he made a cameo in 2014's *Muppets Most Wanted* as a prisoner in a brutal Russian gulag run by Tina Fey, he was cast simply as himself, because what identity could be more hardened and tough than "Danny Trejo"?

These roles helped Trejo embody fears about Latino masculinity and, by extension, immigration. His muscled and tattooed frame earned him so much work in Hollywood because it so easily functions as shorthand for the culture's fears of racial violence, envisioning Latino men as hulking brutes who intimidate and bully. His body affirms cultural stereotypes envisioning Latino masculinity as hot-tempered and violent, with the prison tattoos also suggesting low social class. And then there is his distinctive face, which is often discussed as his trademark feature. A profile in *Entertainment Weekly* best captures the preoccupation with his face:

> chances are pretty good you remember [Trejo's] face. It's hard to shake. Pockmarked and weathered, more than anything Trejo's face resembles an old catchers mitt that's been left out in the rain. The pouches below his squinting green eyes have the consistency of used tea bags. The downward-turning corners of his steel-wool mustache radiate a sinister Fu Manchu vibe. The rest of his face—from his knotty forehead to his stubbled chin—is a relief map of scars. It's what happens to a pretty, young Mexican-American kid who grows up to be the welterweight boxing champion of San Quentin.[21]

The detailed fascination with the contours and textures of Trejo's face help construct Trejo as a caricature, an exaggerated and almost monstrous manifestation of how crime and violence transform Latino men.

Ironically, however, the same masculine attributes that made Trejo the embodiment of US racial fears—unemotional violence, a muscled exterior, a tendency toward sadistic brutality—would also facilitate his emergence as an action hero thanks to several cultural trends. The rise of a postracial perspective that increasingly sees race and ethnicity as marketable commodities, coupled with a tendency toward ironic nostalgia in US pop culture, helped transform Trejo from a menacing baddie to a lovable nostalgia object, a campy and ironic send-up of outdated stereotypes that could appeal to Latino/a markets. Instead of embodying US culture's fears about Latino immigration, Trejo's hardened persona now poked fun at those fears and the corrupt white elites who fueled them, making him an unlikely object of diversity and inclusion for media culture in the 2010s.

Trejo's star-making role in *Machete* in 2010 cemented this transition in his public persona. Originally imagined as a mock trailer by Robert Rodriguez

FIGURE 4.2. *A poster advertises* Machete *(Troublemaker Studios, 2010) by playing up Trejo's violent persona.*

and Quentin Tarantino for their B-movie double feature *Grindhouse, Machete* was developed as a full-length film after Trejo and others lobbied Rodriguez to flesh out the narrative of a tough former Mexican *federale* who finds himself enmeshed in the corrupt double dealings of US immigration politics. Dubbed "Mexploitation" by a variety of critics, the film adopts the style and sensibilities of 1970s exploitation films, grabbing contested political topics and weaving them into a ridiculous and over-the-top narrative with plenty of gratuitous sex and violence.[22]

Critics celebrated Trejo's emergence in the film as the "first Latino superhero"[23] as a sign of cultural progress and a long-overdue moment for Trejo's career. As one critic claimed, "*Machete* is the rarest of Hollywood products: a true blood Mexican superhero. . . . It's about time that Chicanos have a hero to call their own."[24] Trejo's promotion from a menacing figure terrorizing (typically white) action heroes to a full-blown action hero in his own right challenges the alignment of whiteness and heroism in the genre.

Reviewers of *Machete* and its sequel, *Machete Kills*, in fact frequently exploited the novelty of a Latino action star, describing Trejo's character through nostalgic references to classic action bodies. Scott Bowles of *USA Today* called Machete "Charles Bronson with a ponytail,"[25] a popular comparison, since another critic described Trejo's acting style as being "from the Charles Bronson school of deadpan minimalism."[26] For others, Trejo's performance was "equal parts Charles Bronson, Arnold Schwarzenegger and Jason Voorhees,"[27] situating Trejo's role in a constellation of nostalgic icons from the 1970s and 1980s. Robert Rodriguez validated these connections, comparing *Machete* and *Machete Kills* to the classic Sylvester Stallone action films *First Blood* and *Rambo*. Rodriguez said that Trejo in *Machete* is like the early Rambo—"He looks like a vagrant, but he's really a highly trained mercenary"—while *Machete Kills* raises the production values and allows the filmmaker to "go James Bond" with the character,[28] a comparison also made in *USA Today*, which called Machete "Bond with a bandolier."[29] While Trejo seems to embody all these classic, hard-bodied heroes rolled into a tattooed Latino frame, one reviewer claimed that he exceeded his heroic predecessors: "He manages to project an old fashioned kind of machismo that dudes like Stallone and Schwarzenegger can only fake."[30] Iconic white action bodies seemed to be the only cultural reference point to make sense of Trejo's new role, suggesting the importance of action-film masculinity as a standard against which Trejo's violent roles should be measured.

The action film, of course, has typically affirmed the white, muscled male body as a locus of national identity since the genre congealed into a set of conventions in the 1970s and 1980s. As Susan Jeffords, Yvonne Tasker, and other scholars have explored, action and adventure masculinities in popular cinema frequently negotiate the connections between gender and politics. For Jeffords, Hollywood tough guys and hard bodies in the 1980s and 1990s helped articulate the gendered appeal of Reagan's politics, exploring constructions of manhood, violence, and fatherhood that aligned with the masculine rhetoric of the "Reagan Revolution" and its continuation into the 1990s.[31] For Tasker, the spectacularly muscled bodies of stars such as Arnold Schwarzenegger and Sylvester Stallone mediated the national debate around US manhood in the 1980s and 1990s, especially in relation to the Vietnam War and other US foreign interventions. These hard bodies provided a sense of US triumph through a violent, individualistic, white hypermasculinity while also proving through their very excess the existence of a "crisis" in masculinity that no manner of bulging biceps can overcompensate for. Negotiating the shifts in US culture and politics, the muscled white body of the action star became a landscape upon which debates about national identity and the state of US manhood could play out.[32]

However, shifting audience demographics have yielded more diversity among action stars and narratives that valorize the importance of multiculturalism. As Mary Beltrán has demonstrated, films such as *Romeo Must Die* and *The Fast and the Furious* franchise illustrate a new trend in Hollywood action and adventure narratives that not only allow for nonwhite protagonists but actually valorize the importance of multiculturalism in navigating the violent and competitive world of the action film: "While brawn and courage continue to be valued qualities, what might be termed 'cultural competence' holds even more credence and power within the polyglot millennial environment, even when characters are written as white."[33] Within this cultural environment, action narratives have even allowed for images of nonwhite protagonists heroically exacting violence against white villains, taboo imagery for much of Hollywood's history. Gretchen Bakke, for example, has examined the emergence of black action heroes from out of the "buddy cop" ghetto of the 1980s and 1990s and into starring roles in which they kill off hordes of white men (whether zombies, robots, or actual evil white dudes). These roles—such as Wesley Snipes in the *Blade* series or Vin Diesel and later Ice Cube in the *xXx* series—dramatically overturn a century of Hollywood's racial politics, locating immorality and corruption within white masculinity and seeing the multicultural heroism of nonwhite men as a solution to the excesses of white corporate culture.

Of course, the new black action hero is not really providing the radical pleasures of eradicating white systems of power. Rather, such narratives create a fantasy in which a destructive, exaggerated model of "hyperwhiteness" is purged from society, leaving a presumably more enlightened and inclusive whiteness in its place. As Bakke's concern with zombies attests, the vision of white masculinity offered in these narratives draws out all the negative characteristics of whiteness in contemporary society; whiteness here is conformist, hive-minded, unsustainable, and driven by an insatiable, greedy hunger. Beyond zombies, even, white male villains in such narratives are evil corporate monsters, often tied to conspicuous consumption and megalomaniacal ambition. "Hyperwhite" antagonists, then, dramatize the need for white culture to reform itself and create new models of a more inclusive identity, reflecting the imperatives of neoliberal culture for constant self-transformation. Juxtaposed against nonwhite heroes, images of evil hyperwhiteness sensationalize the need for the dominant culture to adapt to the dictates of diversity and inclusion, or at least a highly individualized sense of inclusion. Not surprisingly, in this logic it is the responsibility of nonwhite heroes to spur such transformations in white culture.

Trejo's emergence as a Latino action star in *Machete* functions similarly, providing an over-the-top, ethnic assault on hyperwhiteness. In the film, Trejo plays the titular character, Isador "Machete" Cortez, whose wife and daughter are murdered in the opening minutes because his fellow agents double-crossed him to a Mexican drug kingpin (Steven Seagal). Years later, Machete is a day laborer in Texas who is pulled into an overly complex narrative about an anti-immigrant Texas senator (Robert De Niro) whose campaign manager (Jeff Fahey) plans to fake an attempted assassination of the senator in order to curry public favor for a border fence, which would allow the same Mexican drug kingpin that killed Machete's family to better control the flow of drugs into the United States. Along the way, Machete is assisted by "Shé," a taco truck vendor who runs a secret network for aiding new immigrants (Michelle Rodriguez); a Latina immigrations official who must learn to turn her back on the law to do what is right for her people (Jessica Alba); and his own brother, a priest who plays fast and loose with religion and the law (Cheech Marin). And as if there were not enough characters, he also has run-ins with the leader of a border vigilante group modeled on the Minutemen (Don Johnson) and the spoiled, promiscuous daughter of the senator's campaign manager (Lindsay Lohan), among others.

Given the film's focus on immigration from a Latino perspective, *Machete* immediately became marked as a political indictment of conservative politics, especially as its release coincided with the political debates surrounding Arizona's SB 1070, which was widely critiqued for encouraging racial profiling and legalizing police harassment of Latino Americans, whether legal citizens or not. Rodriguez, in fact, openly courted such controversy, releasing a fake trailer for the film with Trejo saying, "This is Machete with a special Cinco de Mayo message . . . for Arizona," followed by images from the film recut to look like an uprising of immigrants against the government. Conservative media took the bait, with Fox News posting (and then quickly removing) an online article saying that Rodriguez had declared war on Arizona. According to the *Hollywood Reporter*, other conservative blogs thought that the film would "glorify a race war" with its inflammatory images of corrupt politicians and frustrated, violent Latino immigrants.[34] The film's funding, moreover, became a source of local concern in Texas, with some conservative commentators seeking to block the film from receiving state subsidies for films produced in Texas on the grounds that it demeaned the state and the country.[35]

While the charges that the film would somehow incite a race war were clearly overblown, conservative commentators rightly recognized that the film offered a scathing critique of whiteness, or at least the exaggerated hyperwhiteness of the new multicultural action film. The sources of evil in the film are reprehensible stereotypes of white cultural power. De Niro's Senator McLaughlin parodies conservative politicians who spout xenophobic vitriol—his campaign commercials compare Mexican immigrants to cockroaches—and such rhetoric is tied to brutal violence: in one scene, McLaughlin murders a pregnant immigrant before she can cross the border so her baby cannot be born in the United States. McLaughlin's sleazy political adviser, Booth, is coded as extremely wealthy—from his mahogany-lined office to his sprawling estate—but in the film, wealth is synonymous with moral corruption. Booth actually works for the drug cartels and is attracted to his promiscuous daughter, who produces an incestuous porn video with her own mother and Machete. Von, the leader of the border vigilante group, enacts horrible violence on vulnerable immigrants and presides over a posse of rednecks sporting the Confederate flag. Even the main villain behind the scenes, the supposedly Mexican drug dealer Torrez, is played by the white action star Steven Seagal. This constellation of corrupt politicians, sleazy rich dudes, racist rednecks, and sexually debased brats locates the source of evil in the film not simply among white people but in the hyperbolic stereotypes of out-of-control white privilege.

The reliance on hyperwhiteness as a kind of immorality that only Machete's Latino masculinity can overcome is accentuated in the 2013 sequel, *Machete Kills*, which has Machete drafted into service by the US president to take down a Latin American revolutionary who has stolen a nuclear bomb. Just as in the first film, the events in *Machete Kills* are all being manipulated by a master villain, in this case Luther Voz (Mel Gibson), an arms dealer with precognition and a *Star Wars* fetish who has created a doomsday cult for the wealthy elite. Voz himself has initiated the nuclear crisis in order to lead his followers into space, and he hopes to bring Machete along with him so he can be cloned and made into an army of Machetes. The casting of Gibson as Voz only highlights the film's vision of corrupt hyperwhiteness, as Gibson's career has been in a tailspin since he was caught on tape shouting an anti-Semitic rant. These associations help align Voz with the racism of white elites.

This is not to suggest that *Machete* and other narratives of nonwhite action heroism should be read as radical political critiques, nor that they are the first set of films to exploit racial tensions with evil white villains being taken down by men of color. As most critics noted, *Machete*'s historical roots link it to exploitation genres—cheap, controversial films that transformed real political topics such as race relations into campy, melodramatic narratives

FIGURE 4.3. *Machete (Danny Trejo) wields a weed whacker, acknowledging stereotypes of Latinos as gardeners, in* Machete *(Troublemaker Studios, 2010).*

that titillated audiences with sex and violence. By linking the film to the history of exploitation cinema, most critics claimed that *Machete* is politically ambivalent, a silly, topical satire that delivers laughs but no real social commentary. After all, one of the most famous exploitation cycles—the blaxploitation films of the late 1960s and 1970s that featured strong black protagonists violently battling crime in US inner cities—often reinforced stereotypes about black masculinity and urban life as much as they challenged typical Hollywood representations of black men. Likewise, *Machete*'s action is as likely to indulge in stereotypes as challenge them, as in the scene when Machete dispatches a group of hired henchmen with pruning shears and a weed whacker after they mistake him for the gardener. Does the scene undermine the stereotypes of Latinos as low-wage gardeners, or simply offer a violent nightmare of Latino violence?

For Sean Brayton, however, the critics who dismissed the political impact of the film miss the point. Linking the film to the brief history of the "Mexican Avenger" exploitation films of the 1960s and 1970s, Brayton argues that exploitation cinema has the power to challenge audience expectations and highlight issues of social justice that are often invisible in US entertainment media. While silly, the humor in *Machete* uses "social satire to engage immigration politics and working class-struggle," Brayton contends.[36] Brayton offers a detailed analysis of the film's satire, exploring how the narrative and jokes invite the audience to see the importance of migrant workers and the need for collective action to protect them. Brayton might be overly optimistic about the social power of satire, but his astute breakdown of the film's politics shows how complex the "silly" genre parody in *Machete* is.

What narratives like *Machete* do accomplish is the reevaluation of whiteness and its relationship to ethnic communities in an age of diversity and inclusion. As Bakke illustrates in her discussion of the black action hero, the repudiation of hyperwhiteness in these narratives is not a challenge to white power as much as a reevaluation of the boundaries of whiteness and privilege. Films like *Machete*, after all, ask men of color to rehabilitate the concept of whiteness by attacking (literally) the stereotypical excesses of white masculinity. The cartoonish white bad guys are not genuine representations of whiteness in the United States (as Fox News assumed them to be in their knee-jerk condemnation of the film's stance on immigration) but rather loathsome caricatures of whiteness that everyone—regardless of ethnicity—can love to hate: immoral rich dudes or racist rednecks. Their destruction, then, yields not the destruction of white power and privilege, but rather a color-blind vision of whiteness that rejects the excesses of racism and embraces a flexible vision of identity and cultural citizenship. Whiteness is not killed off by a Latino avenger in the films; it is rejuvenated by being purged of overtly offensive elements, dramatizing the need for those with privilege to embrace diversity as a project of neoliberal self-improvement. In many ways, this is how nonwhite heroes have always functioned in Hollywood— making sacrifices of themselves and their bodies in order to save the white social order.

In the wake of this violent purge of hyperwhiteness, both *Machete* and *Machete Kills* imagine worlds where the boundaries between whiteness and Latin-ness are porous. Many of Rodriguez's casting choices reflect a playful toying with the boundaries of ethnicity. White action star Steven Seagal is cast as a Mexican drug czar without any explanation, while Daryl Sabara (from *Spy Kids*) plays a white, red-haired Latino ("I'm adopted!" he tells Machete). Later in the film, the Italian American Robert De Niro is easily mistaken for a Mexican immigrant when he disguises himself in a dirty plaid shirt, bandana, and cowboy hat. Biracial actress Jessica Alba, moreover, effectively used *Machete* to publicly "come out" as Latina after a career that largely cast her as white (in a narrative, moreover, in which she plays a traitor to Latinos/as as an immigration officer before eventually embracing the plight of her people). *Machete Kills* only ups the ante with this ethnic identity play. Charlie Sheen plays a (presumably white) version of the US president, but is billed under his birth name of Carlos Estevez, reminding the audience of the ethnic passing that he and his father (actor Martin Sheen) engage in to get better roles. Meanwhile, white actress Amber Heard plays a CIA opera-tive under cover as a beauty pageant contestant ambiguously named Blanca Vasquez. And in the film's most bizarre bit of casting, an assassin with a gift for disguises is played by white actor Walton Goggins, black actor Cuba Gooding Jr., Spanish actor Antonio Banderas, and white pop star Lady Gaga at different points in the movie. While the sources of evil and corruption in the film tend to align with whiteness, and sources of justice tend to be Latino/a, as a whole the films imagine a world where identity is playful and subject to interpretation.

These slippages between whiteness and Latin-ness in the films tap into US class politics in order to imagine poor, Latino/a immigrants as worthy, industrious, working-class citizens. After all, the repugnance of hyperwhiteness is reinforced through stereotypes of social class, casting horrible whiteness as the domain of either the extremely wealthy (corrupt figures such as Booth or Voz) or extremely trashy (the redneck border vigilantes in *Machete* or the racist small-town sheriff in *Machete Kills*, who tries to hang Machete when he thinks that Machete is an illegal immigrant). These are long-standing stereotypes in US popular culture that have historically managed the borders of whiteness, using the markers of "white trash" to suggest that poor whites are not quite fully white, or suggesting that wealthy whites become corrupt because they drift from middle-class values.[37] By deploying these tropes about whiteness and social class, the *Machete* films insert working-class Latinos/as into negotiations of whiteness, indicating that the valorization of the middle class (and those who aspire to it) in the United States should include poor Latinos/as. *Machete* in particular references the myriad Latino/a laborers, from gardeners to dishwashers to nurses, who keep the nation's economy running, imagining poor immigrants not as criminals or social mooches but as hardworking citizens who embody US cultural values more than the parodies of hyperwhiteness that oppose them. So as these poor Latinos/as organize into a makeshift army to fight the border vigilantes in a battle of stereotypes (*cholos* with low riders and gardeners with pruning shears versus dirty, plaid-wearing rednecks) in the film's ridiculous climactic action sequence, the film relies on the repugnance of "white trash" to demonstrate that some Latinos/as are more worthy of "honorary whiteness" than those who embody the excesses of hyperwhiteness.

Of course, this slippery ethnic order also depends on the hyper-Latino machismo of Machete/Trejo to enact this challenge to hyperwhiteness. If the films imagine a world where ethnic identity is fluid and poor Latinos/as might be better "whites" than rednecks or wealthy plutocrats, then this fluidity does not apply to Machete, who embodies an essential Latino machismo. From his penchant for black leather to his brutal violence with machetes and weed whackers, Machete represents an undiluted fantasy of violent and virile Latino manhood. Machete, for example, cannot seem to be killed. He gets riddled with bullets and always seems to recover. When a racist sheriff tries to hang him, his neck muscles are so thick that he does not die. The ability of his body to withstand these punishments reflects the typical hard bodied-ness of the action hero, whose endurance of pain usually dramatizes the perceived suffering of white, US masculinity in a world that seemingly devalues its violence and traditional values. For Machete, however, his toughness becomes an ambivalent joke, poking fun at seemingly outdated stereotypes about Latino violence while still yearning for tough, traditional manhood to save the social order.

Just as Voz needs the biological essence of Machete to build a super-weapon, the narratives of both films need Machete's potent Latino manhood to eradicate the evils of hyperwhiteness. Machete must counter hyperwhiteness with his "naturally" excessive Mexican manhood, which in the logic of the films is the only thing capable of destroying white corruption. As in other narratives of nonwhite heroics, the films affirm old stereotypes about the natural physicality of nonwhite bodies (in contrast to the intellectual ephemerality of whiteness) while demonstrating how the unique physicality of bodies of color can and should sacrifice themselves to reform the corruption of hyperwhiteness (as Will Smith's character does in *I Am Legend*, sacrificing himself to pass along his zombie-resistant blood and a possible cure for a new society). Thus, once Machete's machismo is triumphant, there is no longer a place for his essential Latino-ness in the social order, and he rides his motorcycle off into the sunset with his new girlfriend (Jessica Alba) at the end of the first film, content to right wrongs outside the confines of the legal system. As in the western genre and other action narratives, once violent manhood dispatches the threat to society, his brutality is no longer welcome in the community it helped create. There is no room in the multicultural future for a stereotypically violent Mexican.[38]

Like other heroes who take on "hyperwhiteness," Trejo's action persona is also well suited to tales of zombies and possession. He has had roles in a series of zombie films, including the 2012 made-for-TV movie *Rise of the Zombies*; *Zombie Hunter* (2013), in which he plays a zombie-slaying priest; and *The Burning Dead* (2015), in which he plays a Native American telling the story of a cursed volcano in the Sierra Nevadas that spews lava-filled, zombie-fied white pioneers from the 1840s. He plays another priest dealing with out-of-control white folks in 2013's *The Cloth*, a religious possession film, and he has a small role in 2014's *Voodoo Possession*.

These narratives are ideal for exploring the imagery of hyperwhiteness, as zombies and possessed souls often express an exaggerated vision of white corruption. Richard Dyer, for example, has argued that the zombies in *Night of the Living Dead* express anxieties about white stagnation that stand in contrast to the African American protagonist's physicality and competence, an argument central to Bakke's vision of hyperwhiteness in contemporary action films.[39] For both Dyer and Bakke, zombie imagery pulls together all the perceived pitfalls of whiteness—they are unemotional, single-minded, and intent on assimilation. As in *Machete*, Trejo's suitability as a zombie killer or demon vanquisher draws on the virility and strength of his ethnic identity to eradicate the scourge of hyperwhite infestation.

Trejo's eradication of hyperwhite privilege, however, is always tongue in cheek, suggesting that the racial dynamics of such narratives have more to do with a playful mockery of cultural identity than a genuine interrogation of power and privilege. After all, in the world of Trejo's films, Latino/a culture is subject to the same stereotyping as bastions of white corruption—*everyone* needs to loosen up and have a little fun in a multiracial and multiethnic America, according to the logic of the *Machete* films. This world of playful and fluid identities, where we laugh at send-ups of Latino stereotypes as much as caricatures of evil whites, suggests that everyone, regardless of social power and prestige, would become better cultural citizens if they developed a sense of humor about racial and ethnic inclusion. In this way, Trejo's ironic display of Latino violence against white power constructs humor as a project of neoliberal self-improvement. His persona demonstrates the power of whites laughing at caricatures of whiteness and Latinos/as laughing at stereotypes of Latino manhood to verify one's own diversity and progressive enlightenment. Such laughter, of course, does nothing to transform structural and economic inequalities, but the racial and ethnic humor that has become synonymous with Trejo's image since the late 2000s can provide a violent spectacle of postracial diversity.

THE MAYOR OF VENICE: REVITALIZING
DIVERSE COMMUNITIES

As I have noted, films such as *Machete* turn Trejo into a spectacle of Latino violence that secures a peaceful future for more equitable communities, but ultimately Trejo's characters cannot be part of the society he helped create, just as in the classic western genre. His 2013 action-western *Dead in Tombstone*, in fact, dramatizes this trend explicitly, with Trejo playing a double-crossed gunslinger brought back from the dead by Satan himself (Mickey Rourke) to slay his former gang and liberate an idyllic white community (appropriately named "Edendale") from the corruption of white tycoons. Trejo's action heroics, however, do not always lead to his characters being rejected from the communities they help to protect. In some cases, his violence against white corruption helps envision a future where urban, multi-ethnic communities epitomize US ideals of family and community, as long as a nostalgic, paternal figure such as Trejo can use violence to help people of color reclaim their communities and cultural citizenship.

In this way, Trejo's roles build upon his public persona as a local hero in his hometown community of Pacoima and a Los Angeles icon sometimes known as the "Mayor of Venice." Trejo is often a celebrity guest at Pacoima's annual holiday parade and festival, and served as the parade's grand marshal in 2010.[40] In 2012 a Los Angeles muralist painted a massive portrait of Trejo on the side of a building on Van Nuys Boulevard to honor the local hero.[41] And Trejo's role in the greater Los Angeles community grew even larger in 2015 when he opened his first restaurant, Trejo's Tacos, an industrial-looking taco shop near Hollywood with black leather seats that serves "bad ass tacos."[42] Trejo's status as a local icon and folk hero in parts of L.A. was also on display in a 2002 profile of the actor in *Entertainment Weekly* that depicted Trejo as a paternalistic dignitary in Venice:

> On the boulevards and boardwalks of this funky seaside community, the 57-year-old actor walks around with the smile and cocksure strut of a gladhanding alderman. Giddy Latino kids approach him for autographs. Buzzing needles whir to a halt when he waltzes into a tattoo parlor. And a young Mexican waitress fills him in on the husband whose life Trejo once helped turn around.[43]

Trejo is envisioned in the article as a benevolent authority figure: "the Mayor of Venice sits like a pasha atop a steep incline of cement steps that rise up from the boardwalk and overlook a pit of people working out on Muscle Beach." Trejo's individual success is linked to the revitalization of areas like Venice and Pacoima. "When he talks about his unlikely path from once-seedy sections of L.A. like this one to the glamour of Hollywood," the article continues, "you'd never guess that they're separated by just a matter of miles." Just as Trejo has transformed his life from a career criminal to a beloved movie star, the "once-seedy" multiethnic communities that revere him have transformed themselves into more vibrant neighborhoods.

On screen, Trejo's role in the revitalization of multiethnic communities is often made explicit as his action heroics make room for wholesome, multiethnic families in struggling neighborhoods. Nowhere is this clearer than in Trejo's popular movie *Bad Ass* (2012). In the film, Trejo plays Frank Vega, an aging Vietnam veteran who has watched life pass him by as he works a hot dog stand in Los Angeles. One day, Vega's life is changed forever when he gets into an altercation on a city bus with a couple of racist skinheads who are bothering an elderly black woman. He tries to avoid a conflict, but when pushed too far, he gives the skinheads a thorough beating. Bystanders on the bus record the incident, the video goes viral, and Vega becomes a local folk hero known as "Bad Ass." Vega begins to see life differently and wants to make a difference in his community, starting by opening his house to his old friend from his Vietnam days, Klondike. But when Klondike is murdered one evening, Vega decides to track down the killers, leaving a trail of violence in his wake.

The film is based on a real incident that was documented in the AC Transit bus fight video, which went viral in 2010 and inspired a host of memes around the man in the video, dubbed "Epic Beard Man." *Bad Ass*, however, provides a racial reimagining of the video's incident. In the real incident, Thomas Bruso, an older white gentleman with a snow-white beard, a fanny pack, and a tucked in T-shirt that reads "I Am a Motherfucker," punches out a black man who had accused him of making a racist remark about black people shining shoes. While the viral video delves into thorny issues of race and violence (is the video supposed to be pleasurable because the white grandpa punches out a menacing black "thug"?), the film makes the incident's racial politics unambiguous by replacing the black man with menacing white skinheads who target and bully people of color on the bus, only to be taught a gratifying lesson by a lovable Latino tough guy. Replacing "Epic Beard Man" (in reality a cantankerous white guy with a history of getting into altercations with the police) with the ethnic folk hero "Bad Ass," the film orients its narrative around working-class people of color taking back their communities from a few bad apples, here imagined as racist whites.

Vega's transformation from anonymous hot dog vendor to folk hero sets him on a path to reimagine his life and seek revenge on those tearing his community apart, a narrative that imagines how the unfulfilled promises of cultural citizenship for Latinos and others in the United States might finally be redeemed. Vega's life story in the film, after all, shows how worthy Vega is as an American citizen while also hinting at the history of oppression in the United States. Through flashback, the film shows pastoral images of Vega as a young man raised in California farmland. Vega lounges in the fields with his white sweetheart and explains that he is compelled to enlist to fight in Vietnam. After valiantly serving his country, Vega returns to find that his girlfriend has married someone else and no one will hire him, despite his exemplary service to his country. Although the film goes out of its way to deny the role of his ethnicity in Vega's stunted opportunities, the imagery of people of color dutifully serving their country in wartime only to find that

FIGURE 4.4. *Danny Trejo as Frank Vega in* Bad Ass *(Amber Lamps, LLC, 2012).*

they are second-class citizens during peacetime has been a familiar theme in US popular culture. So when the young Vega is denied entrance to the police academy to try to become a part of the Los Angeles Police Department because he does not have a college degree, that moment in his backstory articulates a history of ethnic oppression that is not explicitly named in the film, but is still clearly visible (especially if you are familiar with the racist history of the LAPD).

If the realities of ethnic discrimination laid the foundation for Vega's dreary, dead-end existence at the hot dog stand, then his emergence as a popular vigilante not only turns his life around but also reinvigorates life in his working-class, multiethnic community. His investigation into Klondike's death sees Vega crisscrossing the city as he works up the food chain of the criminal organization responsible for the murder, but along the way he also thwarts local crimes, such as a robbery at a convenience store, and helps his neighbor, Amber—a young black woman with a son in elementary school— rid herself of her abusive husband. In the process, Vega begins a relationship with Amber and starts to become a father to her son. The film might poke fun at the age difference between the new couple—Vega is old enough to be Amber's father and wears ridiculous, outdated, powder blue suits on their dates—but his old-fashioned chivalry (which includes protective violence) makes him an ideal candidate as a husband, regardless of age. When the vigilante narrative collides with the romance narrative as Panther, the leader of the criminal organization, tries to attack Amber and her son to punish Vega for his meddling, Vega's protective violence not only enables him to complete his revenge but ensures the safety of his new multicultural family as he beats Panther to a pulp. It takes an old-school Latino "Bad Ass," in other words, to make the community safe for hardworking multiethnic families.

In this way, *Bad Ass* realigns the cultural boundaries of whiteness through a nostalgic appeal to patriarchal, violent manhood. Latinos can articulate their place within the traditionally white middle-class value system by embracing violent patriarchs like Trejo, men whose violence in the past may have been figured as a threat to the white nuclear family, but who can become figures protecting a more diverse vision of nuclear family domesticity in today's media. After all, in *Bad Ass*, Vega leaves behind a trail of black and Latino hoodlums as he clears a violent path for multiracial families, tapping into conservative discourses about irresponsible nonwhite masculinities as the real scourge of poor, crime-ridden neighborhoods. And Vega is uniquely positioned to articulate this need for traditional masculinities because his story is so linked to individual responsibility: he is an ideal model of uncomplaining hard work who has patiently endured the racism and xenophobia of the past. It takes an apolitical and loving-yet-violent patriarch, in other words, to create a space for urban, nonwhite families within the category of "honorary whiteness."

If films like *Bad Ass* (and its sequel, *Bad Ass 2*, which follows a similar plot) imagine the possibilities of "honorary whiteness" for figures like Frank Vega, their vision of ethnic reimagining is based around individual solutions to systemic social problems. The films might locate an external source of corruption in figures such as the white mayor of Los Angeles—who, the film reveals, is pulling the strings behind the scenes—but the problems plaguing these neighborhoods seem to start and end with the megalomaniacal villains who simply need to be arrested or killed. And the only way to bring down these immoral figures is through the action heroics of tough father figures like Frank Vega. In this way, the social problems and injustices facing working-class, multiethnic communities—problems rooted in systematic economic inequalities such as mass incarceration or stifled educational opportunities— are displaced onto evil bad guys. The solution to innately evil individuals, then, can only be the heroic violence of figures like Frank Vega, suggesting that the inhabitants of struggling, multiethnic urban enclaves are responsible for reclaiming their own communities instead of exposing the complex systems of oppression that perpetuate racial and ethnic inequality in America. Perhaps this is why the black antagonist in *Bad Ass* is named Panther, an allusion to the black activist group the Black Panthers; in the world of *Bad Ass*, the kinds of politicized identity politics offered by groups like the Black Panthers are part of the corruption of the city, and only figures like Vega— heroes who do not "complain" about the discrimination they may have faced in the past—can carve out the possibility for "honorary whiteness" in the multiethnic city.

Most action narratives rely on this melodramatic narrative structure, casting complex social realities of manhood, crime, or national identity into pathos-laden narratives that articulate clear moral boundaries. The bad guys are always purely evil and intent on making others suffer, necessitating a hero whose violence can be celebrated, even if in other narrative circumstances the same violence would mark the hero as a destructive sociopath. The villains need to be extra-bad in order to authorize the vicarious pleasures of death and destruction the hero facilitates, legitimizing the hero's violence as necessary and morally pure.[44] In the world of Danny Trejo's action heroism, however, this moral polarity not only authorizes the hero's gruesome violence but also creates a space in which the violence of nonwhite bodies can become an acceptable vehicle for heroism and identification (rather than an icon of antisocial brutality). While the violent bodies of heroes of color might not be acceptable identities for "honorary whiteness" themselves, the emotional logic of such narratives suggests that the communities and identities for which the heroes fight can function as morally pure sites that can be brought into the fold of a seemingly inclusive model of whiteness. It takes a nostalgic, hyperviolent patriarch like Danny Trejo to facilitate these emotional logics.

In addition to his *Bad Ass* films, Trejo's other action hero antics exemplify these melodramatic tropes. For example, the 2014 film *Bullet* envisions Trejo as a tough L.A. cop who must take the law into his own hands to bring down a diabolical crime lord (Jonathan Banks) who is perpetually flanked by Kruger (Torsten Voges), a blond, lanky German killer. In the process of purging the film's vision of evil European whiteness, Trejo's character also revitalizes the Latino family, saving his grandson from the bad guys and his daughter from her drug addiction. Referencing Trejo's long history of work in drug and alcohol rehabilitation, his character in *Bullet* is a former addict whose daughter struggles with drug addiction. He serves as her sponsor in Narcotics Anonymous, but when her son is kidnapped, she returns to her habit and overdoses, nearly fatally. By rescuing his grandson, Trejo restores his family, and the film ends with the three of them happily walking on the beach.

This is not to suggest that Trejo has only taken on roles as heroic community saviors—the highly prolific actor still frequently plays menacing Latino figures. In the 2014 film *20 Feet Below*, for example, he plays a charismatic, homeless gang leader who dwells deep in the tunnels under New York City's subway. He plans to lead a violent revolt against the corruption of capitalism and consumerism, but his plans are foiled by a homeless former NYPD officer who wants to keep the tunnels safe for his "family" of homeless outcasts.

Additionally, the 2013 film *The Contractor* uses Trejo to explore white anxieties about Latino laborers working in one's home. In the film, Trejo plays a contractor named Javier Reyes who undertakes a small construction project for a rich Malibu couple. Reyes is charming at first, but starts terrorizing the family because the husband—a former prosecutor—was overzealous in the prosecution of Reyes's son years before. Just at the point where the audience's loyalty might pivot to Reyes and his condemnation of a racist justice system, the film lamely insists that the legal system is color-blind and paints Reyes as an ethnic monster attacking white families.

Trejo is also a go-to actor for independent productions about Los Angeles or Hollywood, whether they are serious films about the struggles of poor Latinos or satirical explorations of life in Hollywood. In films like *Strike One* (2014), Trejo plays a violent but charming uncle who provides a bad example for his young nephew who is growing up in a poor Latino neighborhood, a role that parallels Trejo's own history. In *Chavez, Cage of Glory* (2013), Trejo helps coach a poor Latino MMA fighter trying to make a better life for his family, including his ill son (played by Argentinean MMA fighter Hector Echavarría). In independent films such as *Smiley Face* (2007), *Amelia's 25th* (2013), and *L.A. Slasher* (2015), he takes on small roles parodying the surreal landscape of Los Angeles and the entertainment industry.

Trejo's close affiliations with Los Angeles both on screen and off help secure his status as an icon representing multiethnic cities in the popular imagination. Los Angeles is home to the largest population of Latinos/as in the United States, and is frequently used in pop culture as the center of the Latina/o experience. That Trejo's persona is so frequently grounded in L.A. both as his hometown and as a film setting positions him as not only the "mayor of Venice" but also a paternal figure symbolically overseeing all lower-middle-class ethnic enclaves. His presence insists that such communities can act as a locus of "honorary whiteness" and middle-class values surrounding gender and family—as long as a hardened patriarch like Trejo can enforce traditional masculinities.

CONCLUSION: IRONY AND POSTRACIAL HUMOR

Stoic, intense, violent, and chivalrous, Trejo's hyperbolic machismo has historically marked Latinos as "other"—"hot blooded" and prone to violence, according to typical Hollywood stereotypes. And when embodied by Trejo with his weathered face, muscled body, and prison tattoos, this machismo would seem to exemplify anxieties over immigrant bodies pouring across the border into the United States. But Trejo's recent popularity treats this nostalgic machismo as an object of irony, a joking reference to outdated stereotypes of Latino violence that are often set against the mockery of whiteness itself. On the big screen, this mockery often comes in the form of comically evil white elites, but his online presence often pokes fun at middle-class whiteness.

Examine, for example, his viral video "Breadanimals," in which Trejo uses an array of violent-looking knives and swords in a dark, industrial setting to carve goofy-looking animals out of bread loaves, a pastime befitting a white, suburban housewife. Just as with the *Daily Show* sketch, the video plays with the discrepancies between feminized, domestic white culture and Trejo's violent machismo, softening his image while making those domestic pursuits seem hardcore. The joke, then, exaggerates a cultural transaction between Latin-ness and whiteness, with each borrowing from the other to redefine their meanings: whiteness absorbs aspects of Latino/a culture to seem hip and relevant (as it has always historically done) while Latino/a culture pokes fun at itself (and whiteness) thanks to a more privileged cultural position.

These same dynamics characterize Trejo's performance in a Super Bowl commercial for the candy bar Snickers that went viral online. The commercial digitally inserts Trejo into the 1960s and 1970s sitcom *The Brady Bunch*, wearing a leather vest and wielding an ax as he plays the daughter Marcia in the classic episode in which she gets hit in the face with a football and cannot go to the school dance. Trejo-as-Marcia apparently gets a little hostile when hungry, vowing vengeance and exclaiming "an eye for an eye" as he sinks his ax into the family's coffee table (only to be restored to the real Marcia after eating a Snickers bar). The scene then shows Marcia's sister, Jan (played by Steve Buscemi), getting overly dramatic and storming off.

The humor is based on a couple of interlocking assumptions about race and ethnicity: (1) the idea that Trejo as a muscled Latino avenger is synonymous with hostility, and (2) that the comic potential of a menacing Latino like Trejo is maximized by setting him against icons of white, middle-class domesticity (essentially the same assumptions used by *The Daily Show*'s sketch discussed earlier). *The Brady Bunch* is a popular nostalgia object signifying the campy excesses of the white family sitcom, so the commercial builds on the dissonance between Trejo as exaggerated icon of ethnic violence and the Bradys as exaggerated icon of white domesticity. The commercial works, in short, because it mocks hyperbolic images of Latino violence at the same time that it mocks the culture's obsession with wholesome white families.

The Snickers commercial thus illustrates the larger role of Trejo in the culture as a figure who authorizes a stance on race and ethnicity that is ironic and playful, but that also helps occlude the harsh realities of continuing inequality. Trejo's popularity in the 2010s is predicated on his performance of violent Latino manhood being an ironic and reflexive joke, an exaggeration that we can clearly laugh at even as we revel in the pleasures such violent masculinity authorizes on screen. And yet how funny is a joke about menacing Latino men in an era when conservative politicians wail about the need for a border wall to keep Mexican criminals out? Trejo's public persona, however, assures us that this is indeed all an ironic joke, because whiteness is also gently mocked. It is okay to laugh at Trejo's exaggerated Latino violence because his persona also draws attention to and makes fun of whiteness instead of simply assuming whiteness is "normal." By poking fun at a stodgy white culture that needs to embrace diversity, Trejo's persona illustrates the trend in postracial discourse to treat race and ethnicity as playful and fluid categories, since the inequalities of the past are supposedly melting away. Exaggerated Latino stereotypes and send-ups of bourgeois whiteness can coexist in a seemingly egalitarian mash-up of racial and ethnic humor.

Trejo's hyperbolic image and its juxtaposition to images of racist or monotonous whiteness, then, provide the bookends to an emerging racial order in the United States. Some Latino/a subjectivities can be welcomed into the fold of "honorary whiteness" because they do not look or act like Danny Trejo. Meanwhile the category of whiteness is reformed and rejuvenated, demonstrating its adaptability to demands of diversity and inclusion, or at least a limited vision of inclusion of some "others" into the cultural fabric. And this transaction is ratified because both sides can mock themselves, allowing for a fun satire of both Latino stereotypes and white culture in a seemingly postracial world. But it should be clear that this transaction is not really equitable. At a historical moment when Latinos/as in the US media range from the Supreme Court justice Sonia Sotomayor to anonymous Mexican immigrants who, conservatives insist, are smuggling drugs across the border, the inclusion of some Latinos/as into the category of "honorary whiteness" is predicated on a set of white, middle-class, and deeply gendered values about who belongs and who does not. While the mockery of whiteness draws attention to the privileges and normalization of white culture, the "new and improved" whiteness that can poke fun at itself really only shores up its own privilege by deflecting discussion of the structural and economic foundations of white power in the United States. But the campy, tongue-in-cheek images of Trejo violently hacking away at bastions of white privilege assure us that this new era will offer humor and the pleasures of self-deprecating satire, unless you are Latino/a and happen to be beyond the border of "honorary whiteness," looking in.

CHAPTER FIVE

Betty White

BAWDY GRANDMAS, AGING IN AMERICA,
AND "PREFEMINIST" FANTASIES

*T*HE SPIKE IN POPULARITY OF COMEDIAN BETTY WHITE
starting in the mid-2000s is not a comeback. As White said
in *The Hollywood Reporter* in 2010, "I never went away!"[1] White, after all,
has been a mainstay of television comedy since there was such a thing. After
working in radio for years as a young woman in the 1930s and 1940s, White
landed her first regular TV role in 1949 cohosting a daily variety show called
Hollywood on Television, and she hosted the show solo starting in 1952. One
of her popular sketches on the show spawned her first sitcom, *Life with Elizabeth*, which ran from 1952 through 1955. White coproduced the show while
still in her late twenties, making her one of the first female TV producers in
history. She landed a daily talk show, *The Betty White Show*, in 1954 and was
a perennial TV personality through the 1960s and 1970s on popular game
shows (including *Password*, hosted by her husband, Allen Ludden) and as
the longtime host of NBC's coverage of the Tournament of Roses Parade.
In the 1970s she took on the iconic role of Sue Ann Nivens on *The Mary
Tyler Moore Show*, playing a TV personality who mirrored White's sweet and
innocent persona on screen but off screen was sharp-witted and hypersexual.
After landing another eponymous show—1977's short-lived *The Betty White
Show*—White brought to life another TV icon, the sweet and naïve Rose
Nylund on *The Golden Girls*, which ran from 1985 through 1992, securing
her status as a TV legend for another generation of fans. After *The Golden
Girls*, White continued to act, typically in guest spots on sitcoms and dra-
mas ranging from *The John Larroquette Show* to the WB drama *Everwood* to
NBC's *My Name Is Earl*. She also appeared in films such as *Hard Rain* (1998),
Lake Placid (1999), and the Steve Martin/Queen Latifah comedy *Bringing
Down the House* (2003).[2]

While White "never went away," she has been on a hot streak since the mid-2000s, especially for an actress in her eighties and nineties. She took on a role in the soap opera *The Bold and the Beautiful* in 2007 and 2008, and she had a recurring role on the primetime drama *Boston Legal* from 2005 to 2008. White costarred in the 2009 Sandra Bullock/Ryan Reynolds romance comedy *The Proposal*, garnering several MTV Movie Award nominations along the way, and a Facebook campaign to get White to host *Saturday Night Live* secured her a hosting job (which she had turned down in the past). In 2010 she also costarred in the multigenerational comedy *You Again* with Kristen Bell and Sigourney Weaver. She took on a recurring role on the TV Land sitcom *Hot in Cleveland*, which ran from 2010 to 2015, and she hosted an elder-themed hidden-camera prank show, *Betty White's Off Their Rockers*, which ran on NBC in 2012 and 2013 and was picked up by the cable network Lifetime in 2014. Her role in a Snickers candy bar commercial aired during the 2010 Super Bowl and quickly went viral online, as did a short sketch on the comedy site *Funny or Die*, which showed White behind the scenes on the set of *The Proposal* acting like a diva (she tells costar Ryan Reynolds, "When Betty White asks for a cup of coffee, you get her a f----ing cup of coffee!" to which he responds, "Go suck a hot c----!"). Reflecting her success and stature in contemporary pop culture, *Buzzfeed* has created not one but six of their trademark pop culture lists about her, ranging from "30 Reasons Betty White Is the Greatest" to "8 Surprising Things I Learned about Betty White in 15 Minutes" to "7 Ways that Betty White Is Better than Puppies."

Central to her late-career successes has been her ability to be witty and bawdy while still projecting a grandmotherly sensibility. While White's comedy has occasionally been marked by outrageous behavior and sexual innuendo, notably in the 1970s on *The Mary Tyler Moore Show* (and in her appearances on Johnny Carson's *The Tonight Show*), White's comic persona has most often been defined by traditional, polite femininity, but with a witty edge, as in the 1950s sitcom *Life with Elizabeth*, where she played a suburban housewife, or on *The Golden Girls*, where she portrayed an innocent midwestern grandmother whose naïve quips become inadvertently shocking. Since the year 2000, then, White's comedy has been built upon the discrepancy between her polite, beloved grandmotherly image and her frequent jokes about sex. In *The Proposal*, she cracks jokes about Sandra Bullock's boobs and enjoys the small town's male stripper, but she is still an old-fashioned grandma trying to keep her family happy. In one of her most popular sketches on *Saturday Night Live*, she plays an elderly woman famous for her baked goods who invites radio listeners to eat her "Dusty Muffin." While accepting her Screen Actors Guild Lifetime Achievement Award, she joked that throughout her long career, she got to know many people in the room and had many of them as lovers, too. And in *Hot in Cleveland* she plays a cantankerous woman who

FIGURE 5.1. *Gammy (Betty White) stuffs dollar bills down the pants of an exotic dancer in* The Proposal *(Touchstone Pictures, 2009).*

mocks her fifty-something neighbors for their sexual antics, but makes the rounds at the local senior center and frequently references her sexual prowess. For a generation of fans who remember her more as the sweet-hearted Rose Nylund than the lustful Sue Ann Nivens, the appeal of her late-career persona is rooted in the dissonance of looking and acting like America's favorite grandmother but cracking bawdy sex jokes or engaging in wild antics that we normally associate with youth.

Performances by women (or men performing as women) that combine aging femininity, a sharp wit, and shocking behavior have a long history in US pop culture beyond Betty White, ranging from the later career of Ruth Gordon (particularly in *Harold and Maude*), the other feisty women of the *Golden Girls* such as Bea Arthur and Estelle Getty, and the tradition of comics playing older women (such as drag queen Dame Edna, Vicki Lawrence as Thelma Harper, aka "Mama," and today with Tyler Perry's Madea performances, also in drag). Such comedy, of course, built on the success and shticks of women such as Sophie Tucker and Jackie "Moms" Mabley, especially their later careers cracking jokes about age and sex. Coinciding with the boom in Betty White's career, however, the popularity of older and outrageous female stars and characters has been on the rise. Ellen Albertini Dow performed "Rapper's Delight" in the 1998 comedy *The Wedding Singer* and went on to play kooky older women on TV and in films such as *54*. Estelle Harris (alongside Jerry Stiller in an equally quirky role) as the eccentric mother of George Costanza on the 1990s sitcom *Seinfeld* helped pave the way for a host of offbeat, aging mothers on TV such as Doris Roberts on *Everyone Loves Raymond*, Elaine Stritch as Collen Donaghy on *30 Rock*, Swoosie Kurtz on *Pushing Daisies* and *Mike & Molly*, and even Dame Maggie Smith as the sharp-witted matriarch on *Downton Abbey*. The popularity of comic Joan Rivers into her eighties brought her brand of mocking, acerbic wit to many new generations of fans, and the continuing popularity of Cloris Leachman playing wacky grandmothers almost rivals that of Betty White.

Men have also continued to make the most of older and outrageous characters: see, for example, William Shatner's TV career in the 2000s and beyond, which has been organized around curmudgeonly figures willing to make outrageous arguments (notably in the legal drama *Boston Legal* or the short-lived sitcom *Shit My Dad Says*). This trend can also be seen in the later careers of comedians Bill Murray and Chevy Chase in which they are cast in roles as old men doing wacky things (for example, Murray in *St. Vincent*, or Chase on the TV comedy *Community*). But wacky older women have become something of a trend in US pop culture, and Betty White remains the queen of the quirky elderly stars.

White's performances provide a fantasy of old age that tosses aside many of the social conventions regarding gender, sex, and age. As with Melissa McCarthy and other "unruly" female performers who turn social expectations about appropriate femininity on their heads, White's comedy flouts cultural norms concerning elderly women and gleefully challenges not only their general invisibility in pop culture but also what is expected of them once they pass the threshold of what men find desirable (their "last fuckable day," as Amy Schumer puts it in her satire of the narrowing role choices for aging actresses in Hollywood). Insisting on her own sexual desires and shrugging aside the notion that older women are simply mothers, grandmothers, or other women who sacrifice their own needs for others, White's comedy makes a mockery of the culture's dismissal of older women and the elderly more broadly. White's most recent popular roles hinge on this seeming contradiction between the irrelevance of old age and the vitality of women who insist on their desires: she can look the part of a "sweet" old lady—a woman whose commitment to politeness suggests traditional definitions of accommodating, naïve, and compliant femininity—but all the while she can swear and crack jokes about her sex life with a youthful sensibility. She can symbolize traditional values and old-fashioned commitment to family, but she does so while celebrating her sexual desires and exploits in a manner befitting a postfeminist twenty-something. She can celebrate the kind of vibrant, relevant future that baby boomers envision for themselves, but she insists that this future will come by embracing the values of the young, making her a favorite nostalgia object for the millennials who worship her on *Buzzfeed* and share her viral videos. Like other kooky elderly figures in the US media, she uses her position as an old woman—someone usually pushed to the margins of the culture—to undercut and mock social conventions, especially about women, aging, and sex.

Of course, much of the comedy is rooted in the perceived contradictions of aging women and sex—White's sex jokes are funny because the idea of an elderly woman enjoying an active sex life is so implausible in a youth-obsessed culture such as ours. In some ways, the joke is on older women themselves, turning the real issues of identity and desire for aging women into a punch line about senior center sluts, even as postfeminist culture reclaims "slut" as a less-stigmatizing term for younger women. But as it has done for most of her career, her comedy playfully undercuts the social expectations for women to be quiet, polite, and deferential.

Most often, however, such fantasies of a vibrant old age are not about the elderly themselves. Instead, performances of the old and outrageous dramatize the anxieties and preoccupations of the young and middle-aged: they pop up in narratives about middle-aged people contemplating their own aging or as irreverent nostalgia objects shared online. Moreover, such performances often help revitalize traditional gender values as hip and trendy today. Tyler Perry takes on the persona of the old black matriarch Madea to interject traditional Christian values (part of traditional black culture) back into black families and postfeminist culture. Old and outrageous men often function in similar ways. William Shatner dispenses shocking advice on *Shit My Dad Says* to help his sensitive, politically correct son revitalize his life and masculinity. Ignoring the stark inequities of the past, many of these figures suggest that elements of traditional gender roles can revitalize ideas about gender for the young and middle-aged today. Or, to be more accurate, the bawdy and sometimes bellicose elderly figures that punctuate pop culture demonstrate that traditional definitions of gender are actually compatible with youthful sensibilities about sex, humor, and relationships. The elderly are sometimes depicted as dowdy, prudish, or humorless—an indication of the irrelevance of their worldview on sex and relationships today. But the trope of the old and outrageous suggests that old-fashioned values can be hip, funny, and valuable to the young and to middle-aged people approaching old age.

In this way, White epitomizes what we might call the trope of "prefeminist" icons in contemporary popular culture: figures that predate second-wave feminism and provide a bookend to the "postfeminist" worldview that has become so prevalent in the US media since the 1990s. Such "prefeminist" icons authorize the dismissal of second-wave feminism and feminism as an ongoing political project because figures like White prove it never really was necessary. If the most pressing concerns facing women today are their ability to enjoy their femininity and the pleasures of sex—as postfeminist culture maintains—then prefeminist figures such as White, Joan Rivers, or Madea show us that women could have fun and be fun before, during, and after second-wave feminism. White's current popularity, then, affirms the postfeminist agenda of removing politics from the culture's understanding of sexuality and gender, promoting a notion of women's sexual enjoyment that can be removed from feminist discourses of social power, even as such a notion becomes deeply tied to the affirmation of traditional gender roles.

As this suggests, Betty White's fame and the general prominence of old and outrageous women in the media produces a revisionist historical narrative concerning women, sex, and power, a narrative largely ignoring the important cultural work of second-wave feminism. Second-wave feminism and the young baby boomers, of course, created the so-called sexual revolution of the 1960s and introduced the idea of "free love" to the American mainstream, among other cultural and political transformations. Before second-wave feminism and the women's rights movement of the 1960s and 1970s, women were held to a fierce double standard around sexuality, which celebrated their ability to cater to male sexual desires but enforced strict moral codes around their sexual purity, all while denying women rights over their bodies, including a lack of access to birth control and the inability to prosecute most rape cases, for example. Second-wave feminism helped change the cultural stigmas around women's sexuality, all while the advent of the birth control pill and the economic gains for women fostered by the women's rights movement liberated boomer women from the biological and ideological constraints concerning sex. The second wave's vision of sexual liberation, in short, was not simply about liberating women to enjoy sex, but rather liberating them from conventional ideas about femininity that were complicit in their sexual oppression.

However, the AIDS epidemic in the 1980s and the rise of conservative discourses about the decline of "family values" helped create a cultural backlash among many baby boomers against women's sexual liberation and the political project of second-wave feminism. This backlash paved the way for a postfeminist worldview in the 1990s that claimed to champion women's sexual pleasure, casting second-wave feminists as pleasureless obstacles to the fun of femininity. While still valorizing certain kinds of women's empowerment, this postfeminist ideology cast off the political projects of the second wave, insisting, now that the women's rights movement has altered the social landscape, that women can reject the supposed excesses of feminism and instead celebrate girlish femininity (makeup, fashion, shopping) and traditional notions of romance as women balance career and family.[3] Unlike during the sexual revolution, however, this celebration of femininity and women's sexuality in a postfeminist era largely situated the pleasures of sex within the dictates of patriarchal culture, valorizing women's ability to cater to male desires while positing that the "natural" purpose of women's sexuality is in the pursuit of heterosexual romance. Particularly in popular culture, these values have come to dominate in women-centric TV programs, romantic comedy films, and other "chick flicks" that valorize "a return to femininity, the primacy of romantic attachments, girlpower, a focus on female pleasure and pleasures, and the value of consumer culture and girlie goods," according to Suzanne Ferriss and Mallory Young.[4]

Just as postfeminist images and narratives try to imagine a world in which the restraints of feminist killjoys take all the pleasure out of femininity, sex, and traditional gender roles, "prefeminist" icons offer revisionist narratives that deny the harsh oppression of women's sexuality before second-wave feminism, celebrating the feisty and empowered women that remain culturally relevant in an attempt to rewrite the history of feminism and sexual politics in the United States.

Such historical revisions are most often obscured by the seemingly progressive challenge to stereotypes that old and outrageous figures provide. Performers like Betty White who remain popular into old age undermine the typical cultural position of the elderly in US society, where cultural citizenship often becomes tenuous in a culture that values youth and vitality. Especially for women, whose cultural worth is oppressively tied to beauty and male desire, aging can mean a loss of relevance, but White provides an idealized fantasy of maintaining hipness and vitality into old age. Heralded as an icon of Hollywood's inclusivity, White's recent fame makes it easy to simply celebrate the fact that the culture can accommodate stars who so visibly challenge the hegemony of youth and sexual allure for women. However, this narrative of inclusion reveals complex discourses surrounding women, sex, power, and age that should not be ignored.

This chapter, then, examines the star persona of Betty White as the most popular and pervasive prefeminist icon of the 2000s and 2010s. As the most ubiquitous figure combining old age and outrageous behavior, she provides a guidebook to both aging baby boomers and nostalgic millennials about the meanings of "successful aging" for women and the role that sexuality plays in the definitions of femininity across generations. Providing a fantasy of old age as a postfeminist haven where the elderly act young by swearing or sexting while celebrating the pleasures of romance, White's late-career persona shows how traditional gender roles from before the women's rights movement are easily compatible with a postfeminist worldview. Her stardom claims her as a strong role model who did not need second-wave feminism to be empowered, instead relishing her sexuality and the girly pleasures of traditional gender roles. While her visibility provides an important image of active and transgressive older women, that image is most often employed in popular narratives to help usher aging, second-wave feminists into a postfeminist old age and to provide a nostalgic assurance for postfeminist millennials that strong, vibrant, and, most importantly, sexual women exist outside of feminism as they understand it.

BABY BOOMERS, AGING ANXIETIES, AND EMBRACING POSTFEMINISM

It should not be surprising, of course, that performances of the old and outrageous are often found in narratives about middle-aged women rediscovering their sex lives and their capacity for romance. After all, for aging women, the possibilities of continued relevance and cultural belonging are intertwined with the ascendance of the postfeminist worldview in US culture. As Angela McRobbie explains in her seminal work on postfeminism, many young people since the 1990s have embraced a worldview that acknowledges the important victories of second-wave feminism, but sees the work of the feminist movement as largely finished.[5] In US media culture, then, aging baby boomers have often been seen as a hindrance to postfeminism, illustrating a generational conflict in which "older women, and the second wave feminism they stand for, tend to feature as outdated antagonists" to the younger generations.[6] Kathleen Rowe Karlyn explores these dynamics in detail in her book *Unruly Girls, Unrepentant Mothers*, which analyzes how generational conflicts between girls and mothers in pop culture dramatize young women's distant relationship with second-wave feminism.[7]

However, with the increasing prevalence of aging women in Hollywood, these older women frequently are brought into the fold of the postfeminist worldview. Romantic comedies featuring the dating dramas of older women imagine the possibilities for boomer women (and the second-wave feminism they signify) to soften up, accept the "girly" pleasures of dating, and revitalize their lives through romantic love. Ignoring the fact that these aging boomers were part of a massive sexual revolution that embraced women's sexual pleasures, such dramas show how, for aging baby boomer women, getting one's groove back means embracing postfeminist views of femininity and sexuality.

Betty White, of course, is no baby boomer, but these generational conflicts form the backdrop of her resurgence. White's later career popularity, after all, parallels the increasing focus on aging in Hollywood, especially for women, as the oldest of the baby boomer generation (and its pop culture icons) age into their sixties and seventies. While youth still reigns supreme in Tinseltown, an increasing number of films and TV shows are exploring the lives and anxieties of aging, providing a broader range of roles and narratives than has been available in the past. From aging-themed romance comedies such as 2009's *It's Complicated* to the 2012 British comic drama *The Best*

Exotic Marigold Hotel to Netflix's TV show *Grace & Frankie* (2015–) about two women in their seventies building a friendship and new lives for themselves after unexpected divorces, Hollywood has been more willing to cater to the aging baby boomer market with narratives focused on the perils and pleasures of women growing older (aging men have long been featured in the US entertainment media). Entertainment journalism, moreover, frequently condemns the gendered age inequalities of Hollywood, decrying the evaporating roles for aging women while aging men are matched with impossibly young ingénues. *Vulture* produced sleek infographics documenting the age hypocrisy of Hollywood in casting young women to play the love interests of aging men,[8] and the then thirty-seven-year-old Maggie Gyllenhaal told *The Wrap* in 2015 that producers deemed her too old to play the lover of a fifty-five-year-old character, sparking a series of discussions of aging women in Hollywood in entertainment journalism.[9] The tensions of aging women, their sexuality, and their desirability are working toward the cultural mainstream in pop culture in the 2010s.

White's fame and the increasing emphasis on aging in popular media, then, are intertwined more broadly with concerns about the cultural place of the elderly. As White's career heated up in the mid-2000s and Hollywood began to explore the dating lives of aging women, the United States faced the coming realities of an aging population. The oldest of the baby boomers—the massive generation of children born approximately between 1945 and 1964—turned sixty in 2005, the first tip of around 76 million baby boomers who would transition into the traditional realm of "old age" in America.

The coming waves of aging boomers yielded optimistic visions of aging, with catchphrases like "Fifty is the new thirty," but the prospect of one of the largest generations in US history pursuing retirement, drawing their Social Security benefits, and inundating the health care system with increasing rates of ailments and injuries also provoked (and continues to provoke) political and economic anxieties about the nation's future. In the 1999 book *Gray Dawn*, Peter G. Peterson casts the aging of the global population as a massive challenge to current systems of government and the global economy as a whole.[10] In 2005, Laurence Kotlikoff and Scott Burns predicted an impending crisis in labor and government in their book *The Coming Generational Storm*, which they revisited in 2012 with *The Clash of Generations*. Both books forecast future upheaval thanks to the irresponsible governing of older Americans willing to mortgage their children's economic future.[11]

As such prognostications suggest, it is not simply the size and age of the boomers that causes tension: older Americans will increasingly become a subject of political contention as resources are shifted away from the needs of younger Americans in order to sustain the baby boomers in their golden

Nick → ESPN

years.[12] As younger generations struggle with a stagnant economy for the middle class, massive spikes in educational costs, and weakened systems of government support for the poor, the political clout of the aging baby boomers will erode. Boomers may increasingly be seen as the generation that took full advantage of robust government services in their youth, only to pull the ladder to success up behind them when they attained political power.

Despite these political tensions, aging baby boomers remain a powerful demographic, and their journey into the twilight years brings with it a cultural reappraisal of old age. Baby boomers are pushing back their retirements (partly by choice, partly because of economic necessities thanks to the 2008 recession) and insisting on the continuing cultural relevance of people in their sixties and seventies. In popular culture and in advertisements, old age is increasingly envisioned as a time of leisure, fun, travel, and a healthy sex life, offering images of the old enjoying a vibrant, healthy existence.[13] As Stephen Katz and Barbara Marshall argue, "The advertising industry has chimed in with its portrayals of the new antiageist, positive senior as an independent, healthy, sexy, flexi-retired, 'citizen,' who bridges middle age and old age without suffering from the time-bound constraints of either."[14] And while aging men have long been lauded for their "experience" in their careers, thanks to the inroads of the feminist movement, we have more visible examples today of aging boomer women at the pinnacle of power, from Hillary Clinton to Oprah Winfrey to Arianna Huffington.

Of course, the celebratory possibilities of a vigorous and relevant old age often obscure the realities of aging for most people, which are much starker than these images suggest. As elder-care expert Dr. Muriel Gillick argues in her book *The Denial of Aging*, for a great many older Americans, the realities of life in old age will mean increasing health concerns and impairments coupled with decreasing mobility and independence. Even if medical advances stave off these realities further into one's sixties or seventies, such advances also mean longer life spans and a higher certainty that the elderly will be faced with serious health concerns. Rather than face these realities, however, Gillick points out that US culture prefers to ignore the challenges that old age creates: "We would prefer to believe that most people can skip old age altogether—proceeding directly from middle-age (itself an extension of youth) to death, preferably dying in one's sleep. We put our faith in exercise and diet as a means of assuring a healthy and vigorous old age, even though many of the principle scourges of old age cannot be prevented through exercise or diet."[15] The sobering realities of aging are a nagging anxiety that pop culture represses behind the imagery of the anti-aging industry, which promises youth and vitality.

As this suggests, aging—or, really, the denial of aging—demands increasing self-transformation from individuals in a world of neoliberal self-governance, especially for women who face steeper pressures to maintain standards of feminine beauty. Aging is yet another battlefront in the project of self-actualization today, prompting Americans to spend around $6 billion each year on pills, supplements, and serums that purportedly reverse at least the appearance of aging, if not aging itself. A library of self-help books offer guides to defy aging, while hair color dyes and Botox injections promise the veneer of youthfulness.[16] This massive anti-aging industry offers the promise of the "young old," the fun-loving, well-traveled, golf-playing sixty- to seventy-somethings touted in Viagra ads and by the AARP, but this vision of old age must be earned through self-regulation and the consumption of a bevy of anti-aging products.

As Su Holmes and Deborah Jermyn point out, the increasing presence of aging women within US celebrity culture helps articulate this discourse of neoliberal personal responsibility, providing models that can help market anti-aging products.[17] The increasingly prevalent images of the elderly and the near elderly in popular culture help model a vision of the "young old" as able to defy the normal processes of aging, whether through films and television shows in which aging protagonists rediscover some of the vitality of their youth, or through self-congratulatory profiles of female stars who are still sexy in their sixties and seventies, such as Helen Mirren or Raquel Welch (it is assumed that male stars would still be sexy in their sixties). These images and narratives provide models of "successful aging," outlining the kinds of self-actualization necessary to remain hip and relevant, whether through changes in attitudes or the manipulation of one's appearance to look younger. Of course, for women, working too hard to conceal one's age and appear young is also taboo—tabloids and Internet trolls excoriate aging women for too obviously manipulating their appearance, as happened to Kim Novak in 2014 when she presented at the 2014 Oscars at the age of eighty-one and was ridiculed for her plastic surgery.[18]

As this suggests, pop culture's fantasy of successful aging varies greatly between men and women. For men, the most prominent pop culture examples of reevaluating the meanings of aging have come in a cycle of "geri-action" films that dust off iconic action stars from the 1980s and 1990s (*The Expendables*, *R.E.D.*, and several remakes or sequels putting aging bodies back into action, such as *Rocky Balboa* [2006] or *Indiana Jones and the Kingdom of the Crystal Skull* [2008]). Aging stars such as Liam Neeson have also taken on action roles (in the *Taken* series, for example). These roles exploit nostalgia for the heroic bodies and films of the 1980s, but they also explore the changing contexts of masculinity in US culture, especially for aging baby boomers. Philippa Gates, for example, argues that the return to action roles for actors

[handwritten margin note: Can we stop saying we "feel like"]

such as Clint Eastwood, Sylvester Stallone, Bruce Willis, and Harrison Ford uses the aging body of the star as a signifier of vulnerability and sensitivity. Largely eschewing romance narratives, such roles see aging action stars rejuvenating relationships with their children or surrogate children while demonstrating their relevance through violent heroics, even if they struggle with the physical feats that came so easily in youth. Such narratives demonstrate the continuing relevance of aging men while suggesting that a younger generation can still learn something from older baby boomers.[19] Moreover, after the economic recession of 2008—which was popularly dubbed a "man-cession" because it impacted men's employment levels more than women's—these narratives of aging action stardom took on additional significance, exploring the worlds of men whose capacity to complete physical labor is reduced by age and changing social structures. For Boyle and Brayton, in fact, the aging action-star vehicle *The Expendables* explicitly dramatizes the labor politics of the postrecession world, interrogating the concept of "expendability" for aging men in labor markets.[20]

In contrast, for aging women, pop culture is mainly concerned with romance and sex, trying to imagine the previously unimaginable idea that older women might seek out romance past the point at which young men find them desirable. While the dominant aging male narratives grapple with the capacity of men to remain relevant through violent heroics, aging women in US pop culture must demonstrate their continuing relevance by insisting on their agency as romantic or sexual beings. Or, as Sadie Wearing argues, pop culture has become focused on the pleasures and impossibilities of "rejuvenating" older women, drawing them into the styles and outlooks of the young while still clinging to traditional forms of gender and policing.[21]

[handwritten margin note: memoir; women still sexy]

After all, one of the major shifts in the representation of older women in Hollywood is the expansion of youth into middle age, carving out space for (some) women in their forties and fifties to still be sex symbols instead of casting them into endless roles as mothers, who naturally cannot be seen as sexual in Hollywood cinema. Of course, men in their fifties in Hollywood continue to be cast as romantic leads paired with exceptionally young women, but actresses such as Julianne Moore, Julia Louis-Dreyfus, Courtney Cox, Cameron Diaz, Cate Blanchett, Sandra Bullock, Gwyneth Paltrow, Halle Berry, Jennifer Lopez, Jennifer Aniston, Monica Bellucci, Salma Hayek, Mary Louise Parker, and others have expanded the traditional shelf life of the Hollywood starlet as they continue to garner complex, sexy roles into their forties and fifties. While the inequalities between aging men and aging women in Hollywood are still stark, the idea of a fifty-something sex symbol is a dramatic change. Anne Bancroft was only thirty-six when she played the culture's most notorious "older woman" to then thirty-year-old

Dustin Hoffman in the 1967 movie *The Graduate*. Likewise, Rue McClanahan was only fifty-one when she took on her role as Blanche on *The Golden Girls* alongside Betty White; in the mid-1980s, fifty-one was already old for a woman (even if a feisty, sexual one). By contrast, White's *Hot in Cleveland* costar Wendie Malick was fifty-nine when the show started, and Malick's character is a glamorous soap opera star with a grudge against Susan Lucci (another sexy star in her sixties).

This trend is easy to celebrate as women are offered more complex roles as they age rather than just playing the mothers of younger actors, but the insistence on sexiness into their forties, fifties, and increasingly sixties and seventies also reflects the postfeminist "girling" of older women, as Deborah Jermyn puts it. Despite the celebration of aging actresses and their continuing sexuality, Jermyn argues that "we live in a culture where youth is still revered, envied, fought over." The prospect of aging, and in particular of aging women, remains "widely feared."[22] In response to this fear, the images of aging women in pop culture insist on their inherent girliness, drafting older women into a vision of postfeminist girl power that locates their strength in their continuing love lives (and their consumption of age-defying cosmetics). Enshrouded in empowering messages about the continued vitality and cultural relevance of older women, the images of aging sex symbols still insist that power is located in its proximity to youth, especially for women.

So while the boundaries of youth and desirability have expanded for stars like these, this trend reinforces the idea that women's value is tied to beauty and sex appeal, both of which are tied to youth. Women in Hollywood can keep their careers into their forties and beyond, but only if they can deny the aging process and prove desirable to the male gaze. Women are encouraged to constantly discipline and transform their bodies—whether through diet and exercise or through beauty creams and Botox—to aspire to the impossible ideal of Halle Berry, who was forty-eight in 2015 but looked much younger. In this way, expanding the expectation of sexy youthfulness into middle age only intensifies the pressures on women to conform to the same beauty standards they experienced in their twenties and thirties. Entertainment journalists might tout examples of aging stars as exemplars of inclusivity in Hollywood—for example, the self-congratulatory celebration of Helen Mirren's bikini body at the age of sixty-three when she was photographed on a beach in 2008—but such celebrations only work to incorporate a broader swath of women into patriarchal beauty standards, reducing Mirren's talent and career, for example, to her hot bikini bod.

The viral distribution of Mirren's bikini photo in fact drafted her into the discourses of postfeminist body politics, as suddenly Mirren was cast as an expert on aging well. Entertainment news sites wanted to know the secret diet and exercise routines that had facilitated her bikini body. The cultural relevance of one of the most revered and talented actresses on the British stage and screen became tied to how well she could teach other women to look hot in their sixties. Such discourses not only insist that aging can, in fact, be controlled if you just buy the same products that Mirren buys, but also that women's identities as they age are tied to their ability to still seem girly and attractive.

As the Mirren incident suggests, the spike in interest in aging women and their love lives in the 2000s saw a spate of iconic actresses who had long functioned as symbols of second-wave feminism being pulled into the orbit of postfeminist ideology. For example, Meryl Streep, one of the most respected serious actresses in Hollywood since the 1970s, acted in two romantic comedies centered on the dynamics of dating while middle-aged: the 2008 musical comedy *Mama Mia!* and 2009's *It's Complicated*. Goldie Hawn and Susan Sarandon played middle-aged women trying to resuscitate their youth in *The Banger Sisters* in 2002. And Diane Keaton starred in the Nancy Meyers 2003 aging-themed romantic comedy *Something's Gotta Give* with Jack Nicholson and the 2007 romantic comedy *Because I Said So* about a mother finding love herself while meddling in the love life of her daughter.

These stars bring a certain history to their more recent roles, either as explicit symbols of second-wave feminism or else as powerful women performers who attained stardom in the 1970s and 1980s and benefited from more complex roles thanks to the women's rights movement. But their roles in recent romantic comedies—a genre that epitomizes a postfeminist celebration of romance and the pleasures of consumption—dramatizes the process by which second-wave feminists negotiate and eventually embrace a postfeminist celebration of their sexuality and need for heteronormative romance. Depicting the aging process for women as synonymous with their capacity to find love in their fifties and sixties, these narratives show that aging women's self-fulfillment can only be accomplished through romance and a return to the girly pleasures of youthful femininity.

Examine, for example, the 2003 comedy *Something's Gotta Give*. In the film, Diane Keaton plays Erica, a wealthy, divorced, fifty-something playwright who finds herself drawn into an affair with Harry (Jack Nicholson), a sixty-something music producer with a history of dating only women under thirty, including Erica's daughter Marin (Amanda Peet). The film features the usual "will they or won't they?" drama of the romantic comedy, including a subplot in which Erica takes on a younger lover, a doctor played by Keanu Reeves. In the end, however, both Erica and Harry embrace their romance, forming one big happy family with Marin and her new husband and baby.

As Deborah Jermyn suggests, the casting of Keaton in *Something's Gotta*

Give brings historical weight to the role, as Keaton's fame from *The God-father* (1972) and the Woody Allen classic *Annie Hall* associates her with New Hollywood art cinema. Her work in *Annie Hall* in particular made her an icon of the new woman in the 1970s (and helped spur a fashion trend of women wearing men's ties and vests). Her stardom has long constructed her as an emblem of feminism and women's rights, a star who eschews the beauty and fashion politics of Hollywood. That Keaton earned an Oscar nomination for her role in *Something's Gotta Give*, Jermyn suggests, helped confer her his-torical weight onto the romantic comedy itself, "as if the genre and Keaton herself have matured together by the time of this film, with Keaton dem-onstrating to the genre's detractors once more how the rom-com can offer thought-provoking, intelligent roles for women, some two and a half decades after she won an Oscar for *Annie Hall*."[23]

While the film does offer more depth than others in the genre and ex-plores with some nuance the gendered implications of aging, much of this discussion is foisted onto Erica's sister in the film (Frances McDormand), a women's studies professor who can openly assert feminist positions, leaving Erica free to open herself to romance and heterosexual desires. When Erica and Harry first start their affair, in fact, their sex scene includes Harry using scissors to cut off Erica's white turtleneck. Erica's attire in the film parallels that of Keaton, who is famous for supposedly eccentric clothing choices that don't cater to the male gaze. When Harry cuts the turtleneck off, he "releases her from the constraints this sartorial motif has represented, marking and celebrating her re-entry into the active sexuality denied to her since her di-vorce."[24] He also symbolically frees Keaton herself from her feminist-inspired fashion choices, ushering her into a postfeminist celebration of her sexuality and the possibilities of girly romance. The central tensions in the film—and across the "older bird" romantic comedy in general—revolve around the pos-sibilities for aging second-wave feminists to adopt and embrace the postfemi-nist sensibilities of the younger generation.[25]

"PREFEMINIST" GUIDES TO THE POSTFEMINIST FUTURE

The resurgence of Betty White adds another dynamic to these gen-erational negotiations as aging boomers are brought into the fold of post-feminism. Offering a nostalgic longing for a prefeminist past coupled with a bawdy and sharp sense of humor, White's recent roles often see her navi-gating aging women into self-fulfillment and romance, offering a prefemi-nist fantasy of traditional values that, ironically, prove hip, rebellious, and relevant in old age. Betty White and other "prefeminist" figures, then, demonstrate what successful aging looks like in popular culture. For middle-aged women in particular, figures such as Betty White often show how aging women can look to the prefeminist past to chart their postfeminist future.

White's work in the 2009 romantic comedy *The Proposal* exemplifies the function of the prefeminist icon, with White serving as a comic sidekick facilitating the main character's embrace of romance and femininity. In the film, Sandra Bullock plays Margaret Tate, a high-powered publishing executive who bullies, belittles, and generally terrifies her subordinates, including her long-suffering personal assistant, Andrew, played by Ryan Reynolds. When Margaret risks losing her work visa (she's Canadian), she hornswoggles Andrew into a sham engagement, promising him the promotion to editor he has long sought. In order to convince skeptical immigration officials that the engagement is genuine, Margaret accompanies Andrew to his hometown of Sitka, Alaska, to meet his family, including his doting mother (played by Mary Steenburgen), his disapproving father (Craig T. Nelson), and his lovable grandmother Annie, aka "Gammy," played by Betty White. As Margaret and Andrew fumble their way through pretending to be a couple and Margaret gets to know Andrew's quirky family, they open up to one another and begin to fall in love. But when Andrew's family insists that the wedding take place right away during their visit, Margaret decides to call things off, leaving Andrew at the altar because she did not want him to get into too much trouble. Turning herself in to immigration officials, Margaret heads back to New York to pack up her life and return to Canada. Meanwhile, Gammy fakes a heart attack in order to help reconcile Andrew with his father. In the end, Andrew chases Margaret back to New York to profess his love, or at least to insist that they get married because he would really like to date her.

The Proposal does not bill itself as a film about the challenges facing aging women, but Margaret is a career-driven woman in her forties (Sandra Bullock was forty-four when the film came out, making her technically one of the youngest baby boomers). More importantly, Margaret's life has been centered on second-wave feminist goals, or at least a stereotype of second-wave feminist goals. When we first meet Margaret in the opening minutes of the film, she is abrasive, cold, and makes a point of emasculating the men around her. She calls Andrew pathetic for drinking the same kind of coffee as her (just in case hers spills) and insists when he accompanies her into a meeting that "you're just a prop in here." She also fires a pompous editor (Aasif Mandvi), calling him incompetent and entitled and threatening to have security toss him from the building. From a postfeminist perspective, she represents the worst excesses of female empowerment, aspiring for a masculine form of power and intimidation in the office, trading family and romance for career success, and abandoning her femininity. She wears all black in the opening scenes as the film openly compares her to a wicked witch—Andrew furtively messages the rest of the office that "THE WITCH IS ON HER BROOM" when Margaret is about to leave the office in a bad mood. In short, the film suggests that Margaret is a bitch who takes women's rights too far, a caricature of powerful women in their forties and fifties who turn their backs on all that can be playful, feminine, and self-fulfilling (presumably because they are feminist killjoys).

Given this logic, the film insists that Margaret needs to first be punished for her treatment of the men around her and then open herself emotionally, because apparently powerful women all harbor secret traumas that keep them from embracing their feminine side. As soon as Andrew has some power over Margaret, he uses it, forcing her to kneel before him on the city streets (but in a way that is supposed to be funny and charming!) and then generally treating her poorly when they arrive in Alaska. In scenes that are clearly meant to punish Margaret for being assertive and headstrong, Andrew insists to his family that Margaret will not accept help with her baggage—she's a feminist, he tells them—and then leaves her to struggle with her bag and inappropriate footwear in an extended slapstick sequence. Additionally, Margaret learns that Andrew's family is massively wealthy and owns most of the businesses in Sitka, inverting their power relations back in New York—he is an "Alaskan Kennedy," as Margaret puts it. Once Margaret is suitably punished for her gendered transgressions, though, she can open up to Andrew, confiding in him about the death of her parents when she was young and why she keeps people so distant. She also confesses to crying in the bathroom at work, revealing that her behavior in the office is a performance she uses in a misguided effort to garner respect. By the end of the film, the headstrong feminist who tries to wield masculine power in the corporate world is ready to embrace her feminine side and start a new relationship with Andrew.

During Margaret's transformation, White's character Gammy plays a key role in facilitating Margaret's embrace of romance by offering her the family connections she lost when Margaret's parents died. But Gammy does so not by simply being a mouthpiece for traditional family values, but by bridging old-fashioned gender ideas with a risqué, contemporary sense of humor. She wants Margaret and Andrew to have kids, so she suggests they share a bed under a blanket she has dubbed "the babymaker," offering a wink and nudge about the bedroom antics they will presumably engage in. She wants Margaret to feel welcomed and integrated into the family, so she takes her to the local exotic dancer, tucks a wad of cash down his pants, and encourages Margaret to "smack his ass" when she gets a lap dance. She offers to let Margaret

FIGURE 5.2. *Gammy (Betty White) shares a heartfelt moment with Margaret (Sandra Bullock) in* The Proposal *(Touchstone Pictures, 2009).*

wear her wedding dress that she wore in 1929, but when the dress is a little baggy, she mocks how small Margaret's breasts are, noting, "I'm a bit chesty to begin with and I happened to be knocked up when I wore this."

Gammy, then, exemplifies the traits of "prefeminist" characters, blending frank assertions of old-fashioned values with a postfeminist celebration of "girly" femininity and the pleasures of sex. She is an emblem of old-fashioned family values, but she makes those values seem hip and relevant, especially by acknowledging the sexual pleasures of the good old days. In the process, Gammy's role in the film downplays the realities of gender oppression that existed before second-wave feminism and persist today. The old-fashioned values within which a character like Gammy *actually* came of age were harsh and misogynistic, predicated on women's subordination to men and an obsession with women's purity. A strong, feisty, yet somewhat traditional woman, Gammy's very existence suggests that empowered women can thrive under oppressive conditions, but her character also indicates that maybe the oppressive past was not as bad as we think. As Gammy ushers Margaret into an acceptance of the power of love and family, those values do not feel incompatible with the pleasures of male strippers or the open acknowledgement of female desire, even though Gammy represents a generation for whom "family values" were even more openly tied to the stifling of women's opportunities and the policing of women's sexuality. In short, for Margaret— a woman mocked for being a feminist earlier in the film—the world before second-wave feminism can provide role models of empowered, feisty women.

This historical reevaluation is made clear in one of the film's more poignant scenes when Gammy gives Margaret a turquoise necklace, an old family heirloom that her great-grandfather gave to her great-grandmother on their wedding day:

GAMMY: They were quite a scandal, you know. He was Russian, and she was Tlingit. Back then, you had to get approval from every member of the tribe before you got married. Almost broke them up.

MARGARET: How did they stay together?

GAMMY: She was a lot like you: tough, wouldn't take no for an answer. She was good for him.

The scene illustrates the film's troubling use of Native American imagery and identity to aid white people's quest for self-fulfillment (earlier in the film, Gammy does a comic Native American ritual in the woods). But it also provides a powerful, cross-generational narrative of sisterhood celebrating feisty women overcoming adversity. As Kathleen Rowe Karlyn has argued, the romantic comedy genre has the ability to disrupt patriarchal social hierarchies and create more inclusive communities, especially through the comedic antics of "unruly" women.[26] This scene is one of those moments, linking the great-grandmother, Gammy, and now Margaret to a long line of formidable women who persevere against the challenges that women face, fostering a community of strong, disruptive women.

At the same time, in the context of a larger narrative mocking Margaret's brand of career success, this historical narrative points her toward strong women who existed before second-wave feminism. In a film that openly denigrates Margaret's urban and assertive vision of women's power tied to a life of loneliness, Gammy offers an alternative: women who did not need second-wave feminism to be strong because they came of age before that form of feminism transformed the country (and, the film suggests, might even be the worse for it because it supposedly denied women the pleasures of preliberated femininity). Women like Gammy and her great-grandmother help teach Margaret models of strength that do not involve abandoning family and romance—essentially, she can look to a prefeminist past to find her postfeminist future.

White functions similarly on her TV Land sitcom, *Hot in Cleveland* (2010–2015), playing a grumpy and sharp-witted elderly woman who becomes involved in the lives of three middle-aged women living in Cleveland, Ohio. Played by famous sitcom actresses Valerie Bertinelli (star of the 1970s sitcom *One Day at a Time*), Jane Leeves (famous for her role as Daphne in the 1990s sitcom *Frasier*), and Wendie Malick (who starred in the 1990s sitcoms *Dream On* and *Just Shoot Me!*), the women at the heart of *Hot in Cleveland* are a pack of friends from Los Angeles who end up spending the night in Cleveland when their flight to Paris is grounded because of mechanical troubles. Horrified at first by the midwestern city, they discover to their delight that the men in Cleveland find them irresistible. In L.A., they were past

FIGURE 5.3. *Betty White as Elka Ostrovsky with Valerie Bertinelli as Melanie Moretti in* Hot in Cleveland *(TV Land, 2010–2015).*

their prime, competing with aspiring actresses in their twenties and thirties, but in Cleveland, they are hot (thus the title). Spurred on by the recently divorced Melanie (Bertinelli), the three women rent a sprawling home that comes with an elderly caretaker, Elka Ostrovsky, played by Betty White.

Shot as a traditional three-camera sitcom, the show takes a mostly light-hearted look at the women's challenges in finding fulfilling love lives while getting older, keeping the characters focused on the postfeminist goals of girly romance and looking pretty, even as those goals are complicated by their age. In the first season, for example, Victoria (Malick), a soap star whose show has been canceled, tries to rekindle a hot and heavy romance from her past with a rock star, only to discover that neither of them are up to the physical feats of lovemaking they were accustomed to in their youth. Meanwhile, Joy (Leeves), a beautician, starts a romance with a younger man, only to become concerned that he might be the son she had when she was fifteen and gave up for adoption. Throughout the show's six seasons, the women grapple with the challenges of aging—from starting new careers to managing their relationships with their grown children—but the core narrative for all the women centers on their quest for romance in middle age.

Just as in *The Proposal*, Betty White plays an old-fashioned yet hip side-kick to the adventurous middle-aged women, providing an assuring model of "successful aging" organized around the continuing appeal of sex and romance into one's eighties and nineties. As Elka, she is constantly belittling Joy, frequently for the never-married woman's inability to land a man and for her promiscuous behavior. But meanwhile Elka dates two men from the senior center simultaneously and is clearly turned on when they consider fighting one another over her. It is also implied that she is constantly smoking pot in her basement, and she spends some time in jail when it is revealed that her late husband was a fence for the mob and she has been hoarding a basement full of stolen goods (her husband, it turns out, actually faked his death, and he turns up just as she is going to remarry, making her love life a central part of the show's comedy).

While the humor plays up the unexpectedly sharp wit and romantic antics of Elka, White's performance of elderly relevance exists in relation to the middle-aged women and their quest for self-fulfillment. For example, in an episode in season 4, Joy, who has recently returned to college to reinvent herself and her career, laments that she does not fit in with her twenty-something classmates, despite her best efforts to look and act young. But Elka, who is also taking classes, is immediately popular with the college students (a sly nod to White's popularity with young people in the 2010s). According to Joy, Elka quickly fell in with the popular "mean girls" clique (Elka says she is simply "naturally cool") while the style-conscious college women ignore or belittle Joy. When Elka tells Joy to stop trying too hard to be young, however, Joy finally connects with the cool girls, dispensing essential romantic advice based on her years on the dating scene to the naïve young women.

Joy discovers in this moment that her relevance to the younger women is tied to her mastery of the postfeminist dating scene—like a self-help guru, she can teach the young women how to effectively manage their romantic relationships with the men in their lives. Even though she ran a massively successful business as a beautician to the stars back in L.A., Joy is only interesting to the young women inasmuch as she can help them master their love lives. When one of the young women sounds excited that a guy she is interested in is finally texting her back late at night to see if she wants to come over, Joy explains to the naïve coed that the text message is simply a booty call. Joy then uses the theories from their economics class to illustrate why the young woman should withhold sex in order to increase its value and get what she wants in return, presumably actual romance and commitment from the young man in question. Seeing sex as an economic exchange, Joy's explanation endorses a postfeminist worldview in which women's power is tied to their desirability and identity is chained to the possibilities of romance, exactly the kind of sexual economy second-wave feminism tried to overturn. As the scene fades out, Joy continues to dole out expert tidbits of wisdom that celebrate the cross-generational bond between the women, as long as they are bonding over how to manage their relationships with men.

Betty White's Elka, of course, is the catalyst for this cross-generational bonding; while Elka dismisses her popularity by claiming to be a ninety-year-old novelty with the young women, it is her feisty persona that brings Joy and the young millennials together over their shared interest in sex and romance. White's role as a "prefeminist" guide, in other words, can help the aging boomer find her relevance to the hip, young, white heterosexual women who are so central to the culture's definition of "normal" femininity.

OLD AGE AND MILLENNIAL NOSTALGIA

It is not just aging baby boomers who benefit from White's guidance in the romantic comedy genre, though. Her 2010 romance comedy *You Again* shows her multigenerational appeal. In the film, Kristen Bell plays Marnie, a dorky, bullied high school student who perseveres to become by her twenties a beautiful and successful PR executive with a promising career. But when her kindhearted brother gets engaged to Joanna (Odette Yustman), the Queen Bee mean girl who tormented her in high school, Marnie's confidence is shaken as she is pulled back into the petty insecurities of her school years. Meanwhile Joanna's aunt, Ramona (Sigourney Weaver), turns out to be the high school friend-turned-rival of Marnie's mother, Gail (Jamie Lee Curtis), who herself was a bit of a Queen Bee in high school. Ramona and Gail engage in fairly standard tensions about middle-aged women and romance (Ramona is rich and successful, but her failed marriages leave her jealous of Gail's middle-class family life), and the younger generation also gets drawn into the same tensions, with Joanna's popular friends being unable to relate to the single-woman career path of Marnie, and Joanna wanting to simply start popping out babies after the wedding.

As both generations grapple with the rivalries of the past, White plays Grandma Bunny, a sweet and flirty grandmother who reminds everyone that the struggles of the past are what made them all the people they are today. She also becomes an object of competition between Marnie and Joanna, who both try to be the better granddaughter as White glides through the film tossing out charming one-liners about her sex life (in one scene, she has Marnie help secure her dentures so she will be ready to make out at a party later that day).

As this suggests, White's popularity rests not just with aging baby boomers contemplating life in their eighties and beyond. Her resurgence is also tied to her popularity with younger millennials who have made her an Internet star and fetishized the image of the feisty and flirty grandmother figure. In addition to her roles on film and television, White has crafted a vibrant online presence, frequently starring in or producing outrageous viral videos about her youthful antics. White's online presence has become so popular, in fact,

FIGURE 5.4. *Betty White flanked by young, well-muscled men in her music video with Luciana Caporaso, "I'm Still Hot" (2012).*

that a report by Intel Security listed Betty White alongside the music icons Britney Spears and Usher as the celebrities whose names formed the most dangerous Internet searches, since hackers use their allure to attract unwary fans to dangerous links full of viruses and malware.[27]

Much of White's online persona focuses on the humor of the elderly acting young. In 2011, for example, White starred in singer Luciana Caporaso's music video for "I'm Still Hot" as part of a promotion benefiting the Los Angeles Zoo. In the video, White sits atop a golden throne while surrounded by muscled beefcake models as she raps, and in one scene a body double makes it appear as though White breakdances on the dance floor. In a 2013 promo for *Off Their Rockers*, White rides atop a swinging wrecking ball (fully clothed) in a parody of the popular Miley Cyrus video in which Cyrus straddles a wrecking ball in the nude. It is no wonder, then, that the AARP used White in their 2011 campaign promoting the idea that old age can be youthful and fun. In one online video, White makes a series of silly prank phone calls. In another, she lustfully watches on as a hunky, shirtless young man washes her sports car and gets splashed by White wielding a hose. Both videos circulated widely online.

Part of the Internet's fascination with White clearly centers on images of the elderly mastering youth culture. In one scene in *You Again*, for example, White's Grandma Bunny hits on a younger gentleman on the street, offering her phone number before declaring that she is also on Facebook and Twitter, if he wants to get a date with her. The dissonance of the old acting young suggests not only that aging individuals can remain relevant within youth culture, but that the elderly can help younger people loosen up and actually enjoy the modern world. These are the pleasures at the heart of the elder-themed prank show White hosted, *Off Their Rockers*, in which elderly comedians play pranks on the young. Most of the hidden-camera gags surprise unsuspecting young people with the wild and youthful antics of the elderly. The comedians in one gag gleefully race their scooters down a sidewalk on the beach to the amusement of onlookers. In another, an elderly gentleman asks a stranger to help him type a text message, playing on assumptions that old people are not good at using technology, but then the elderly man dictates a graphic "sext" message, much to the surprise of the stranger. Toying with people's expectations about the elderly as polite and old-fashioned, the show demonstrates that the values of aging Americans are not always opposed to the pleasures of youth culture. White herself is too recognizable to participate in the gags, but she serves as a host, introducing each segment with scripted gags usually about her having younger male lovers.

Being old while acting young, however, only accounts for part of the youthful appeal of Betty White and other old and outrageous figures in pop culture. While she shows how the elderly can master youth culture, her popularity also shows how youth culture can learn from previous generations, tapping into a certain nostalgia for some of the values of an earlier time. Like other performers playing old and outrageous characters, White's comedy suggests that the elderly bring a frank outlook on the foibles of youth culture—while she can master youth culture, she can also ridicule the trends of the present because her characters have seen it all, remaining vibrant, sharp-witted, and spirited in the face of massive social and cultural changes. The commentary of quirky elderly figures such as White, then, reveals a longing, if not for the actual past itself, then for the perceived lessons of the past to inform the present and the future. Of course, as White's portrayal of Elka on *Hot in Cleveland* or her role in *The Proposal* suggest, the "past" as constructed by such figures is not so much an actual engagement with the struggles of women throughout the twentieth century in America, but rather a nostalgic fantasy of women who could both embody traditional gender values about women's subservience to men and still be seen as strong, empowered, and sexy.

White's opening monologue as host of *Saturday Night Live* in 2010 exploits this nostalgia coupled with the insistence on her sex drive. From the start, her jokes remind the audience of her past in classic television while playfully ridiculing *SNL*: "You know, I'm not new to live TV. In 1952 I starred in my first live sitcom, which was *Life of Elizabeth*. And of course, back then, we didn't want to do it live, we just didn't know how to tape things. So I don't know what this show's excuse is." Like other old and outrageous figures, she quickly mocks the contemporary world, starting with *SNL* and then moving on to Facebook: "When I first heard about the campaign to get me to host Saturday Night Live, I didn't know what Facebook was. And now that I do know what it is, I have to say, it sounds like a huge waste of time. I would never say the people on it were losers, but that's only because I'm polite." Her playful mockery of Facebook, however, does not stop at ridiculing the habits of the young—she also suggests that in her time, young people had more fun, and maybe more sex, providing a fantasy of prefeminist sexual pleasures that existed before AIDS and widespread concerns about other STDs: "Needless to say, we didn't have Facebook when I was growing up. . . . Yes, we had 'poking,' but it wasn't something you did on a computer. It was something you did on a hayride, under a blanket . . ." And then she drifts off while presumably contemplating some romantic encounter from the past. By the monologue's end, she thanks the crowd for being there, saying, "If I could, I would take you all on a big hayride. Starting with you, sir," as she indicates a man she finds handsome in the audience.

The crux of the monologue is a nostalgic celebration of a simpler time, before Facebook and online dating and social technologies, when romance was characterized by youthful romps on hayrides. Rather than simply valorizing the "good old days," however, the monologue draws out the contemporary allure of this vision of the past: in the logic of the joke, almost everyone today would choose the hayride over Facebook. In this way, the monologue actually suggests continuity between its vision of the past and the present. The culture may change along with the rituals of modern life, but the values of romance and the pleasures of sex remain central to identity and social life. The joke unifies the audience in its celebration of carefree sex, imagining the past as a nostalgic space of innocent sexual encounters that contemporary audiences should aspire to in the present. Lost in the mix, of course, are the historical realities—for women like White growing up in the 1930s, the possible consequences of having sex on a hayride were much more severe than they are today. But that is inconsequential for the joke, which imagines a fantasy of romance in a mythic past that should inform the pleasures of femininity today. The "prefeminist" moment of the hayride becomes an argument for the postfeminist future valorizing girly romance and women's sexual pleasures.

White's popularity with young people today, then, participates in contemporary pop culture's fetish for nostalgia and the reimagining of the past. From historically themed TV dramas such as *Mad Men*, *Pan-Am* (2011–2012), or *Boardwalk Empire* (2010–2014) to Hollywood's obsession with rebooting classic films and television series from the 1970s and 1980s—including horror remakes such as *Halloween* (2007), *A Nightmare on Elm Street* (2010), and

Poltergeist (2015), or film adaptations of cult classic television shows like *The Dukes of Hazard* (2005) and *21 Jump Street* (2012)—US popular culture has been cashing in on the nostalgia craze, mining the past to lure both young and old audiences.

While this trend toward nostalgia in entertainment media certainly reflects the marketing assumptions of the various industries involved (as producers seek to capitalize on the trend's profitability), the obsession with the past in contemporary pop culture also taps into cultural assumptions about time and social change. As Katharina Niemeyer argues in her volume on media and nostalgia, "nostalgia is not only a fashion or a trend. Rather, it very often expresses or hints at something more profound, as it deals with positive or negative relations to time and space. It is related to a way of living, imagining, and sometimes exploiting or (re)inventing the past, present and future."[28] US popular media looks to the past, in other words, not simply to appropriate and rework the styles and fashions of eras gone by, but to position the present and future in relation to a particular, often fictitious construction of the "past." Such exercises in nostalgia mine the past for perspectives on the present and ideas about the future.

It is not surprising, then, that White's popularity also coincides with a burgeoning online fashion trend among young women valorizing the no-nonsense styles of sandals with socks and "granny panties" along with the appeal of gray hair. Granny fashion images circulated on social networks and fashion blogs so much that in 2015 a panel of cultural critics at *Buzzfeed* suggested that we have reached "peak granny."[29] As the panel discussed, this trend offers some intriguing possibilities for women to experiment with styles of dress that are not organized around the male gaze, styles that might be interpreted as a backlash against the hyperfeminine fashions of postfeminist culture. Of course, as the panel noted, this trend consists mostly of young, white women putting on a stylized vision of older, feisty women—there is not yet any indication that the trend might empower women who are actually going gray to challenge male-centric fashion standards. But set against the increasing presence of strong, complicated older women in pop culture, the "granny" trend and the popularity of Betty White raise important questions about the penchant for feisty grandmas among young people today and the bout of nostalgia gripping pop culture. Is this nostalgic appreciation of older women and their styles an indication of real engagement with issues of aging, or just a kind of postmodern irony that fetishizes a caricature of the past?

White's viral video promoting HoodieBuddie.com suggests the latter. In 2010, White partnered with the makers of a popular hoodie that includes built-in ear buds on a line of products featuring images of the star on a series of hoodies and T-shirts. To help promote the line, the company released a "Built by Betty" video showing White running amok at their factory. Among other antics, White yells at the workers ("I'm Betty f----ing White!" she tells them), mocks the creative staff, grabs a quickie with a young intern in the break room, and chides one man for staring at her breasts (her "golden girls," she calls them). Much like her backstage video with Ryan Reynolds promoting *The Proposal*, the humor rests on the discrepancy between her image as a polite grandmother and her diva-esque bad behavior and foul mouth.

That the video promotes a line of hokey clothing featuring retro images of Betty White only underscores how much White's old-as-outrageous shtick is itself a commercial commodity. The clothing features White's face set into retro, 1980s imagery; one T-shirt, for example, shows White in sunglasses next to a palm tree and over the words "White Heat" in neon blues and pinks that make it look like an advertisement for *Miami Vice*. Another has White's face repeated over and over against multicolored squares, as in Andy Warhol's much parodied pop art. In short, the products are kitschy objects of camp, meant to be worn with a sense of hip irony. Against that backdrop, it is difficult to read White's routine in the video as anything but the same: a well-worn routine meant to invoke nostalgic irony, a joke about the continuing presence of out-of-date commercial products. The young women profiled in the *Buzzfeed* piece about making granny style fashionable might be tapping into a cultural moment fascinated with aging women, but how far removed is their professed love of granny panties from the 2015 release of campy *Golden Girls* granny panties featuring the faces of White and the other cast members across their large backsides?[30] Each trend purports to celebrate icons of aging femininity, but ultimately turns older women into fetish objects for the young and nostalgic.

Importantly, this fetishizing of White as a fun object of retro consumption tries to cover up the video's mockery of women as bosses. The release of the Betty White line of clothes in 2010 came on the heels of her success in *The Proposal*, a film about the supposed horrors of having a strong, assertive career woman as a boss. So the video's presentation of White as a cruel taskmaster ("She's the devil!" the seamstresses exclaim in Spanish as she walks through the factory) reference Sandra Bullock's role in the film and envision White as a mean-spirited diva who would be a train wreck as a boss. The joke is not just about depicting a sweet grandmother as a domineering team leader, but also illustrating the horrible excesses of domineering women in leadership positions. But we are not supposed to indulge in this level of scrutiny, because the fun images of Betty White being outrageous online are just ironic, kitschy clickbait, empty objects of nostalgia like those hoodies and T-shirts.

CONCLUSION: SEX AND CITIZENSHIP FOR AGING WOMEN

During an appearance on the Ellen DeGeneres Show, Betty White gets a surprise from Ellen when a muscled exotic dancer sneaks up behind her and suddenly gives her a lap dance. Without missing a beat, White starts grooving to the dance and enjoying the sex appeal of the dancer, finally asking Ellen, "Do I get to take him home?" In many ways the moment is charming and fun: given the ostracism of the old in US culture and their removal from full cultural citizenship, the image of young folks celebrating the work of an icon like Betty White is gratifying, especially since it is not a historical appreciation ("she used to be funny") but a recognition that she is still witty and sharp. Her overt enjoyment of the male form also allows her a kind of sexuality and agency that is often denied to older performers, who are tracked into roles as mothers and others who must sacrifice for younger characters. In short, it is hard not to love Betty White's ribald humor.

But the ways White can be brought into the fold of cultural relevance insist upon women's heterosexual desire as central to the idea of empowerment and cultural belonging, aligning with a broader cultural movement to see sexuality—almost always of the hetero variety—as the benchmark for a "healthy" aging process. As Stephen Katz and Barbara Marshall argue, sexuality has become a standard means of measuring health and vitality in old age, spurred by the profitability of "cures" for the "disease" of sexual dysfunction: "The commercial successes of pharmaceutical and mechanical remedies for sexual dysfunction rest on a recent cultural-scientific conviction that lifelong sexual function is a primary component of achieving successful aging in general. The discourses of positive aging have created the sexy ageless consumer as a personally and socially responsible citizen."[31] Aligned with a neoliberal worldview organized around self-improvement and self-maintenance as vital to consumer citizenship and cultural belonging, the fantasies of youthful aging in advertising and popular media draw from a shifting medical discourse that links sexual activity with health in old age (in contrast to the long-standing position that a declining sex drive is a natural part of aging). Responsible, healthy citizens, according to this logic, must actively work to maintain robust sex drives, even well into old age. "It is through sexual functionality and the anxieties provoked around its maintenance," Katz and Marshall claim, "that the aging subject is connected to the wondrous, interlocking, and illimitable worlds of cosmetic, prosthetic, virtual, informational, and consumerist technology."[32]

The dominance of this worldview has now paved the way for the first pharmaceutical treatment for female sexual dysfunction, providing more pressures for women to seek consumer remedies for the perceived problem of a

low libido. In 2015, advisers to the US Food and Drug Administration rec-
ommended the approval of flibanserin, a controversial drug that is claimed to
increase a woman's sex drive. Supporters of the drug heralded the recommen-
dation as a victory for equality, especially since science has expended far more
resources on male erectile dysfunction as part of a general cultural dismissal
of the importance of female desire. Critics, on the other hand, claim that the
drug is ineffective but is being pushed through the FDA approval process so
that big companies can profit on women's sexual insecurities. Cindy Pearson
of the National Women's Health Network said, "pharmaceutical executives
hype the prospect of a 'pink Viagra' because the potential market is estimated
to exceed $2 billion annually."[33] The assumption that low libido is a "prob-
lem," moreover, might encourage women to overlook other health issues they
might be experiencing or avoid considering other reasons why they might not
be interested in sex.

The public celebration of Betty White's seemingly expansive libido places
her stardom in the middle of these public debates, reveling in the disruptive
pleasures of older women insisting on their own desires while still maintaining that a vigorous heterosexuality is healthy and necessary for women's cultural citizenship. But White's popularity tells us much more about younger
generations than about our attitudes toward the elderly: she offers a set of historical lessons for the young and middle-aged about the impossible fantasy of
the "young old," suggesting a set of values that people should embrace today
so that they, too, can be like White when they get older. Some of these lessons
are surely about notions of health and sex. As Katz and Marshall point out,
advertising images of the elderly seeking youthful romance and sex carry lessons for those younger: embrace the consumerist management of your health
today in order to have a "healthy" sex life down the road.[34] Some of these lessons are about the past and what it teaches us. Evading the politics of second-
wave feminism, figures like White suggest that women's empowerment and
sexual freedom are not incompatible with traditional notions of gender roles,
romance, and marriage. But all of these lessons place a robust sexuality at the
center of aging women's relevance and citizenship in a neoliberal age.

CHAPTER SIX

Conclusion

LAVERNE COX, TRANS WOMEN, AND THE LIMITS OF NEOLIBERAL CITIZENSHIP

TRANSGENDER INDIVIDUALS (AND TRANS WOMEN IN PAR-
ticular) have been increasingly visible in US pop culture since
the turn of the millennium. The critical success of the 1999 film *Boys Don't
Cry* (along with the news coverage of the real-life 1993 transphobic murder on
which the film is based) helped raise public awareness of issues of transgender
identity in the US public imagination, ushering in a series of high-profile
media productions about transgender people. The 2005 film *Transamerica*
won critical acclaim for its portrayal of a transgender woman's journey of
self-discovery on the verge of her sex-reassignment surgery. The public transition of Chaz Bono in 2008–2010 (followed by his stint on *Dancing with
the Stars* in 2011) provided a well-known public face for transgender identity,
and *America's Next Top Model* included trans woman Isis King in the competition in 2008. Meanwhile, transgender actress and choreographer Candis
Cayne took on recurring roles on ABC's *Dirty Sexy Money* in 2007–2008
and on the FX show *Nip/Tuck*, while season 3 of the drag-themed reality TV
show *RuPaul's Drag Race* helped launch the public profile of reality TV personality and model Carmen Carrera in 2011. The 2014–2015 Amazon original
series *Transparent* has garnered a slew of awards for its portrayal of a transgender woman's shifting relationship with her children as she transitions into
womanhood, and in 2015 the public coming out of former Olympic athlete-
turned-reality-TV-star Caitlyn Jenner made her a new, high-profile icon for
the transgender rights movement. Such images of transgender people are
often fraught with troubling stereotypes, but the transgender body—always
a source of fascination and stigma—has increasingly become an object of diversity and inclusion in popular culture.[1]

In the midst of this increasing media exploration of transgender identity, actress and activist Laverne Cox has earned her spot as one of the most

public faces of the transgender rights movement. Cox was the first trans woman of color to appear on a US reality TV program (VH1's *I Want to Work for Diddy*), and in 2010 she went on to produce her own reality make-over show on VH1 called *TRANSform Me*. But she has become best known for her Emmy-nominated performance on Netflix's *Orange Is the New Black* (2013–present), which has propelled her acting and her activism. She has become a de facto spokesperson for the transgender rights movement in her interviews and in her producing (she produced a documentary for MTV and LogoTV on transgender teenagers called *Laverne Cox Presents: The T Word* in 2014 and is currently producing another documentary about inequalities in the US justice system for transgender people). She even became the first transgender woman to get her own wax statue at Madame Tussauds. It is no wonder, then, that when *Time* published an issue around the theme of the "transgender tipping point," the burgeoning acceptance of transgender identity as a legitimate site of civil rights struggle, Laverne Cox stood alone on the magazine's cover, as she did again on the cover of *Entertainment Weekly* when it devoted an issue to LGBTQ performers.

Like the other case studies examined here, Cox has emerged as a source of feel-good, tolerance-themed entertainment news coverage, a heroic crusader against Hollywood bigotry and discrimination. Hers is a body that raises a host of cultural anxieties about gender identity, sexuality, and the transformation of cultural body norms, but her popularity and cultural resonance has provided a powerful and humanizing image for a particularly vulnerable population. She has also become a site upon which media can publicly demonstrate their tolerance and inclusivity. However, unlike well-established performers such as Melissa McCarthy, Peter Dinklage, Gabourey Sidibe, Danny Trejo, and Betty White, Cox's star persona is still new and developing, so it remains to be seen whether the anxieties surrounding transgender bodies can be fully managed and assuaged by the culture, and whether Cox can truly become a Hollywood star instead of a multicultural gimmick.

By means of conclusion, this chapter looks to Cox as a case study of the possibilities and limitations of neoliberal citizenship for those with non-normative bodies. More than other stars examined here, Cox offers the most politicized and activism-oriented star persona—she frequently uses her fame to ask challenging questions or to critique the neoliberal media culture. And yet the political nature of her stardom faces pressure as she is more often drafted into postfeminist ideals of consumerist pleasure and neoliberal mantras of constant self-discipline. The popular media increasingly frame her identity around the feminine pleasures of makeup and fashion and the individualistic power of self-confidence, supporting the idea that transgender identity is simply a superficial embrace of self-actualization and self-

FIGURE 6.1. *Laverne Cox on the cover of* Time, *June 2014.*

promotion (rather than a fundamental rejection of Western gender norms). Especially as the transgender rights movement becomes more visible in the United States, the very definitions of transgender identity for the culture at large are at stake in Cox's fame: can identities that are fundamentally disruptive to normative gender ideologies be made palatable to neoliberal culture? In other words, the meaning attached to Cox's stardom indicates the extent to which the media's vision of transgender identity radically challenges the patriarchal gender binary, or whether transgender identity can become a superficial site of consumerism and self-actualization in neoliberal capitalism.

For the other stars I examine here, these questions have largely been an-

[handwritten: early stages as of 2017]

swered, and their fame provides a model for imagining bodily difference as a site of neoliberal self-improvement. But these questions remain at issue for Cox, whose mainstream career is still in its early stages. As her career unfolds, it will become clear how much transgression neoliberal citizenship can tolerate. Are there discourses and narratives powerful enough to accommodate the kinds of gendered transgressions at the core of the transgender experience? After all, as this book demonstrates, normative gender behavior often functions as a master category that helps assuage the anxieties of non-normative bodies. So can transgender bodies—bodies that question patriarchal gender norms by definition—ever be brought into alignment with neoliberal gender roles? These tensions form the foundation of Cox's star persona as her political advocacy is balanced with a vision of trans womanhood organized around consumerist feminine performance and normative female beauty. Only time will tell how this balancing act will play out, indicating the power (or lack thereof) of neoliberal citizenship to draw non-normative identities into its orbit.

[handwritten right margin: claim of entire book]

[handwritten: I think he is s a full of himself]

TRANS WOMEN, MEDIA, AND THE NEOLIBERAL SUBJECT

John Phillips's 2006 book *Transgender on Screen* offers a detailed and analytical exploration of the history of transgender images in popular film, television, and now the Internet, ranging from cross-dressing comedies such as *Victor/Victoria* to gender-bending thrillers such as *Psycho* and *Dressed to Kill* to the increasing market for transgender pornography online. Phillips's psychoanalytic account is far too detailed and varied to summarize here, except to point out his general assessment of transgender cinema between 1950 and 1990:

[handwritten left margin: John Phillip]

> The intelligently written comedies of this period have been shown to contain a residual normativity that neutralized their more progressive features. The mixed-genre productions exhibit a greater ambivalence: ostensibly aiming to educate their audiences into adopting more tolerant attitudes to transgender, these films have nevertheless been shown to reinforce the same stereotypes at unconscious levels, while the thriller genre has found an easy scapegoat in the ostensible strangeness of the transgendered.[2]

[handwritten: What is this saying?]

[handwritten right margin: It is the job of the films + in turn the stars body to take on burden of explaining]

The proliferation of transgender pornography on the Internet leads Phillips to some provocative conclusions about a more fluid future of identity and sexuality, but in mainstream cinema even the thoughtful attempts to explore

[handwritten: why do they only talk about porn in this chapter.]

transgender identity tend to fall back on the stereotypes and assumptions of the cis-gendered world. Most often, such films use the transgender body as an object to explore the boundaries of gender and subjectivity in a postmodern world rather than embracing the perspectives or realties of transgender people.

As Phillips's examples attest, the popular media have been far more interested in trans women than trans men, especially since mediated images of trans women often serve as objects of cisgender anxiety and reflection. This is especially true in popular cinema, which fulfills patriarchal desires to define, interrogate, and objectify femininity and women's bodies. Within the visual regime of cinema, the bodies of trans women are subject to the same objectifying gaze as all women, except that trans women's bodies become sites upon which the definitions of femininity and personhood are worked out. As E. Jessica Groothis explains:

> Trans women and other gender variant people are not merely visual objects to be looked at, but their gender variance—transfemininity most of all—is a source of reevaluation, and a site of meaning creation beyond the mere erotic. Although the issue is frequently a pull between the attractive and the repulsive—framed as a question of whether or not she is a valid source of attraction to heterosexual (cisgender) men—trans women's bodies are a site of discourse on something much more fundamental. Where film theorist Laura Mulvey hypothesized that women "tended to bring the story to a stop and capture the spectator's gaze in excess," trans bodies interrupt the spectator's look similarly, although with an entirely different effect: with a perceived incongruity in socially constructed understandings of sex and gender. That interruption, when materialized in cinema, turns her into something beyond object of the look: object of the (symbolic) touch, a form of nonconsensual redefinition which designates trans women as, above all, the Other, a canvas on which the rules of gender are carved.[3]

For Groothis, the cinematic gaze interrogates trans women's bodies as a site of feminine façade hiding a dark, visual truth, often using the sudden revelation of trans women's genitalia and the perceived gender incongruity of such images to undermine trans personhood. The "shocking" exposure of trans women's anatomy in films such as the campy horror *Sleepaway Camp* (1983), the thriller *The Silence of the Lambs* (1991), or the comedy *Ace Ventura: Pet Detective* (1994) explicitly links disruptions in gendered expectations with violence, crime, and insanity.[4]

ask ? about trans gaze

The increase in media images of trans women in pop culture since the mid-2000s is often aimed at challenging this history of representation, carving out more nuanced narratives and images around transgender identity (although, as Groothis shows, the transgender gaze equally defines a seemingly more progressive-minded film such as *Transamerica*). However, much of this media discourse continues to use the images and stories of trans women to negotiate the meanings and definitions of normative femininity rather than to create alternative narratives of gender and identity. Especially in the news media and entertainment journalism, the stories and images of certain (white, privileged) trans women who articulate the pleasures of normative femininity tend to become the public face of transgender identity in public discourse, often at the expense of discourse that highlights the severe obstacles that face trans women of color. *Why? Pacify people w/ comfortable rep.*

This tendency to privilege the narratives of white trans women at the expense of trans women of color is nothing new. As Emily Skidmore points out, media coverage of trans women who underwent sex-reassignment surgery (SRS) in the 1950s and 1960s made whiteness a defining characteristic of "authentic" trans womanhood in US culture. White trans women such as Christine Jorgensen, Charlotte McLeod, and Tamara Rees all became subjects of fascination for the mainstream press in the 1950s, linking the discourses of scientific achievement with normative definitions of white femininity. SRS could be celebrated as an object of medical progress as long as the subjects reproduced the values of white womanhood, such as domesticity and heterosexuality. Meanwhile, trans women of color in the 1950s and 1960s such as Marta Olmos Ramiro, Laverne Peterson, and Delisa Newton were relegated to the pages of the African American press or constructed as objects of ridicule in the tabloids, where the authenticity of their womanhood was often questioned. As Skidmore explains, the intersection of whiteness and normative femininity were requirements for trans women as acceptable citizens.[5]

Half a century later, these same dynamics often characterize the dominant images of trans womanhood in the media. Examine, for example, the media frenzy over the coming out of Caitlyn Jenner. After months of media speculation, the former Olympic decathlete Jenner came out as a transgender person in a lengthy primetime interview on *20/20* with Diane Sawyer in April 2015. In July, Jenner appeared on the cover of *Vanity Fair* with a profile by Buzz Bissinger accompanied by glamorous photos taken by Annie Leibovitz, and later that month she was presented with the Arthur Ashe Courage Award at ESPN's annual award show, the ESPYs. The coverage of Jenner's transition became a major media event for not only Jenner and the transgender rights community but also celebrity culture in general as stars and celebrities rushed to show public support for Jenner, often by remarking on how beautiful she looked in the *Vanity Fair* profile. At the same time, negative responses to Jenner's story quickly evoked public ire. Former Nickelodeon and Disney star Drake Bell tweeted that he preferred to keep calling Jenner "Bruce," prompting a wave of criticism that resulted in a public apology from Bell.[6] And when director Peter Berg criticized ESPN for giving a courage award to Jenner instead of honoring veterans, his comments also sparked media outrage (as well as a wave of support from those critical of ESPN's perspective on bravery).[7] Jenner's coming out, in short, quickly became a litmus test for transgender tolerance, an opportunity for the mainstream media to acknowledge their acceptance of transgender individuals while drawing out and calling out transphobic responses.

Like other trans women in the media, Jenner's narrative also spurred public debate about the nature and meanings of femininity and women's identity. In a *New York Times* op-ed titled "What Makes a Woman," academic-turned-journalist Elinor Burkett lambasted the public celebration of Jenner for promoting a narrow and normative view of femininity. As articulated in her interview with Sawyer and her *Vanity Fair* profile, Jenner's vision of being a woman, according to Burkett, is defined by "a cleavage-boosting corset, sultry poses, thick mascara and the prospect of regular 'girls' nights' of banter about hair and makeup."[8] For Burkett, the "born this way" rhetoric often used in the transgender rights movement signals an old-fashioned notion of gender essentialism linking womanhood to the external markers of femininity (fashion, makeup, breasts, etc.). Being a woman, Burkett concludes, is about experiencing the oppressions of womanhood your whole life, leaving trans women out of the picture.

Burkett's article did not go over well. Condemned as the "angry" rant of an aging TERF (trans-exclusive radical feminist), Burkett's piece elicited a flurry of denunciations for her critique of transgender identity at this pivotal juncture in the public's perception of transgender individuals. Of these voices, longtime feminist and transgender activist Dana Beyer offered the most detailed and thoughtful response, clearly laying out the feminist imperative to embrace a variety of lived experiences of gender.[9]

The real core of this public debate, however, largely went unexamined: the role of the media in shaping the images of trans women and, by extension, the image of the transgender rights movement. Burkett's real discomfort with the public images of transgender identity circulating around Caitlyn Jenner is not with the transgender community in general, but with the processes by which transgender identity is brought into the fold of neoliberal citizenship thanks to the mass media. Among other failures, Burkett mistook the public celebration of Jenner as a direct stand-in for the transgender community and

*[margin: as far as activism goes.
and is terrible
Show Dylan tweet + ask if this is
all you saw what would you think]*

transgender activism, rather than seeing Jenner's narrative as the mainstream media's necessarily limited perspective on transgender identity. Jenner might be one of the new faces of transgender identity in the US public imagination, but hers is a face (and a body) chosen and shaped by neoliberal media culture. *[boo hiss bad conclusion]*

After all, Burkett does raise an important question concerning gender essentialism and normative gender performances with respect to transgender identity; she just fails to recognize the way these questions are shaped by media culture. As Ann Friedman points out, the "born this way" rhetoric is largely fostered by media discourse on transgender identity that tends to reduce complex issues of identity into oversimplified concepts. "If you only read magazine cover lines and watch heavily edited cable-news interviews," Friedman explains, "you hear binary-enforcing phrases like 'born in the wrong body' or 'nature made a mistake.' Listen a little closer, though, and it's clear that such descriptions of what it's like to be trans are merely a media-friendly shorthand."[10] Delving deeper into the stories of being trans yields a much more diverse range of identities that trouble the gender essentialism of "born in the wrong body" rhetoric, as evidenced in the writings of Thomas Page McBee,[11] Kai Cheng Thom,[12] and others. As this suggests, there are many nonbinary trans people who do not identify as either a man or a woman, as well as many nonbinary public figures: celebrities such as Tilda Swinton, Ruby Rose, Richard O'Brien (who wrote *The Rocky Horror Show*), and Kate Bornstein who reject the gender binary as it relates to their identity. These examples trouble the very idea of gender and are not easily contained in media discourses about being "born in the wrong body." Part of Caitlyn Jenner's resonance in the mainstream media, then, is the fact that her experiences align with the culture's assumptions about transgender identity as a "simple" inverse of biological expectations, not a messy repudiation of that gender binary itself.

Moreover, Jenner's prominent place as a celebrated transgender icon comes as a result of her whiteness and normative gender performance. For Burkett, Jenner's conflation of femininity with fashion and nail polish serves as a stand-in for her own discomfort with the transgender performance of gender norms in general, but Jenner became a media darling not because she was proffered up by the transgender community as a leader and unifying image, but rather because her story resonates with the assumptions about transgender identity for those working in media industries. It should not be surprising that the media would be much more comfortable with the images of a white, slender Jenner draped across a sofa in a little black dress in *Vanity Fair* than with images of trans women of color or transgender individuals who challenge the very notion of womanhood.

[margin: not palatable]

That Caitlyn Jenner has been so thoroughly adopted by the US media as the public face of transgender identity, then, indicates the attempts of media discourse to bring transgender identity into alignment with neoliberal and white, postfeminist individualism. Examples such as Jenner provide easy affirmations that transgender identity can still be grounded in the dominant, normative models of gender in Western patriarchy, that being a woman does, in fact, all boil down to makeup and pretty dresses and external attempts to meet the culture's beauty standards. This model of femininity, after all, is explicitly consumerist and highly privileged—the primary means through which one expresses femininity is through the presumably feminine pursuit of shopping and maintaining one's external beauty, either through expensive fashion choices or even more expensive surgeries (a common theme in defining womanhood in a postfeminist era). The elevation of Jenner to heroic status in media discourse, then, helps affirm the idea that transgender identity is the ultimate form of neoliberal self-actualization: remaking oneself, disciplining and shaping one's body and appearance, in order to be a "better you" and to fit into dominant notions of gender and personhood.

This is not a critique of Jenner's personal decision to craft her own identity according to whatever notions of femininity that she sees fit. Rather, this is to suggest that media discourses made Jenner a focal point in the public debate around transgender identity because hers is a fairly safe and comfortable model of white, trans womanhood that affirms the "freedom" to craft one's own identity—as long as that identity aligns with dominant norms about gender and social class. After all, trans people of color and with few economic opportunities are the most vulnerable and in need of public support, so while Jenner should be celebrated and might help change the public perception of transgender people, we should not lose sight of the big picture. But the media are much more comfortable lauding the transition of a wealthy, white trans woman who looks great in a dress on the cover of *Vanity Fair*. (For that matter, academics too are often more comfortable with this image of white, trans womanhood, as trans women of color have been underrepresented as both subjects and authors in the scholarship of transgender studies.)[13]

Benny LeMaster makes a similar argument concerning the drag performances on *RuPaul's Drag U* about the role that genderqueer individuals play in neoliberal media culture. Although discussing drag and not transgender identity, LeMaster's argument suggests broader trends. *Drag U* was a short-lived reality television program in which cisgender women who are apparently struggling to look good by contemporary standards of beauty are given style lessons by drag queens. According to the logic of the show, only by "dragging" themselves in an overt performance of femininity can the women learn how to express their "natural" femininity. The drag queens (as most of the "professors" on the show identified themselves) serve as guides to the world of femininity, people whose knowledge of gender performance makes them experts on femininity itself. Just as in the "makeover TV" described by Brenda Weber, *Drag U* affirms the centrality of self-transformation for responsible citizenship, especially for women who need to "improve" their performance of femininity. For LeMaster, the show adopts the postfeminist mantras of femininity-as-consumption, indicating that true womanhood comes from having the "freedom" to craft one's own gender identity, but in a world in which women must compete to master the norms and behaviors of appropriate femininity. The drag queen professors, then, are merely presented as men in costumes who can usher "natural" women toward practices of postfeminist self-making.[14]

As LeMaster suggests, *Drag U* falls into the trend toward "homonormativity" in public discourse as described by Lisa Duggan. For Duggan, "homonormativity" represents a neoliberal trend in gay and lesbian politics toward a consumerist, apolitical model of individualism. This shift reflects "a politics that does not contest dominant heteronormative assumptions and institutions but upholds and sustains them while promising the possibility of a demobilized gay constituency and a privatized, depoliticized gay culture anchored in domesticity and consumption."[15] Rejecting both the bigotry of the conservative right and the supposed extremism of leftist queer theory, the politics of homonormativity drafts gay and lesbian populations into conservative institutions like marriage, sees oppression as an individual issue to be remedied by self-transformation and consumption, and insists on the normative domesticity of gay and lesbian private lives. Part of this trend toward homonormativity is the exclusion of bisexual, trans, and genderqueer folks as too radical for homonormative gay and lesbian identities. But LeMaster suggests that the same tendencies toward apolitical, neoliberal identities increasingly inform media representations of trans and genderqueer individuals. A show such as *Drag U*, then, shows how an apolitical, "homonormative" depiction of genderqueer folks can interpolate cisgender women into consumerist models of fashion and identity. At stake are not the issues of poverty or discrimination facing LGBT populations, but rather how gender play can help individuals achieve self-actualization.[16]

The myriad discourses around transgender identity in the media in the 2010s—from the coming out of Caitlyn Jenner to the critical success of *Transparent* to Laverne Cox's wax statue at Madame Tussauds—all suggest that trans women are the next major subject of homonormative politics. These discourses negotiate the possible meanings of transgender femininity in the public imagination, drawing certain aspects of the transgender experience into neoliberal narratives about individual self-determination and the power of normative gender roles, obscuring the complex and often stark realities of transgender populations. Just as the prominent images of gays and lesbians in popular culture in the 2010s have gravitated toward homonormative models of privileged and domestic queerness—see, for example, the critically acclaimed depiction of gay men in the ABC sitcom *Modern Family*— the emerging model of transgender tolerance in the US public imagination is increasingly centered on privileged, gender-normative trans women who affirm the postfeminist imperatives to achieve self-actualization through fashion, makeup, and the power of "girly" femininity. Trans women, more than trans men it would seem, make for more acceptable objects of cultural tolerance and representation, perhaps because they affirm the power of consumerist self-transformation as a guiding force in contemporary femininity.

How, then, do these trends impact the meanings of Laverne Cox's fame, especially given that Cox often pushes back against the media's representation of transgender people (especially trans people of color) in her role as an activist as well as a performer? In what ways does her fame draw her into homonormative politics, and when does she push media discourse to acknowledge realities about transgender identity that challenge neoliberal gender politics?

MEDIATING COX

Given the complex media landscape for trans women (and transgender people in general), Laverne Cox's star persona is often pulled in different directions. Occasionally, she is the subject of scorn in the mainstream media, such as in Kevin Williamson's editorial for the *National Review* online arguing that "Laverne Cox is not a woman."[17] Largely, however, the popular press constructs Cox as a progressive heroine who illustrates media tolerance and acts as an honorable role model for an underrepresented minority. The meanings of her fame within this coverage, however, can vary, as she is sometimes a deeply political trans activist who interrogates the intersections of race, gender, and media, while at other times she is a feel-good fashion icon who only advocates for body positivity and self-actualization. There is no doubt that her public narrative has helped humanize and raise awareness of the inequalities faced by transgender people, but her political advocacy is often drawn into the neoliberal model of homonormativity exemplified by the coverage of Caitlyn Jenner, shoehorning the cultural challenges of transgender identity into a celebration of postfeminist self-making.

In this way, Cox's fame makes her different from the celebrities in the other case studies examined here. As the previous chapters demonstrate, the fame of McCarthy, Sidibe, Dinklage, Trejo, and White tends to depoliticize their non-normative identities, rejecting identity politics in favor of narratives of individual talent, charm, or hard work. While each is heralded as a trailblazer or progressive icon who defies the history of Hollywood stereotyping, their trailblazing efforts must be balanced with an assertion that their fame is not political, that they simply want to be artists and performers. These dynamics are most at play in my discussion of Dinklage, whose story is often framed in ways similar to that of Cox: as a pioneer creating a new history for an underrepresented and stereotyped group. But in his interviews, Dinklage explicitly works to undercut this political narrative, casting himself as a regular actor looking for good roles, just like everyone else. This is a good career move for Dinklage, opening up roles beyond those that want to make a political statement about little people, but this tendency also illustrates a cultural need for such role models to disavow politics as part of mainstream success.

Laverne Cox offers no such disavowal. Rather, she consistently articulates a deeply political, challenging commentary about the failures and inequalities of US culture. She spends as much time speaking at colleges and universities about her life and transgender identity as she spends working as an actress and budding media mogul. She looks for nuanced roles for herself, but she also works as an activist, producing documentaries such as *The T Word* for MTV about the experiences of young transgender people as well as her forthcoming documentary *Free CeCe!* about CeCe McDonald, a black, transgender woman who was sentenced to jail time for fighting back when she was assaulted in a hate crime. While the other stars examined in this book have sought more traditional models of stardom organized around talent and charisma, Cox from the start has explicitly seen her stardom as a vehicle for social change.

Her personal backstory, for example, allows her to articulate the challenges facing transgender individuals in a gender-normative world. She often speaks frankly about being bullied as a child growing up in Alabama and about her suicide attempt at the age of eleven. In linking her struggles with her single mother's poverty and a black southern culture that put so much pressure on young boys to rejuvenate black masculinity, her story chronicles the harrowing cultural pressures facing young transgender people.[18] Moreover, she often describes the continuing daily stigmas she faces living in New York. "I've experienced so much street harassment living in New York," Cox told the LGBTQ magazine *The Advocate*. "There have been so many moments I've walked down the street and been called a man, called the f-word. I was kicked on the street before my finale for [the reality TV show] *I Want to Work for Diddy*." Speaking of her anger and how close she came to lashing out against such aggression, she says, "I could have easily been CeCe [McDonald]."[19]

Of course, as I argue in my discussion of Peter Dinklage, such narratives can also serve as the backdrop for tales about overcoming personal adversity, affirmations that individual perseverance and dedication are the solutions to the challenges of inequality rather than cultural and structural change. Such is the case with Dinklage and Gabourey Sidibe in particular, who are both celebrated by media discourse for the personal coping skills that paved their way to success—Dinklage for crafting a cool, detached persona that is sexy and insulates him from the gawking of passersby, and Sidibe for a superhuman self-confidence that keeps her "girly" and fun. In these cases, harrowing tales of bigotry are only the rationale for self-improvement and self-actualization, placing responsibility on individuals to reshape themselves instead of the world around them.

While this model of an overcoming narrative sometimes appears in Cox's persona, it is often undercut by her activism and her insistence that the culture understand and adapt to the challenges of including transgender people as good cultural citizens. Cox repeatedly speaks to the need for cultural change, not just individual change, and often teaches mainstream US culture about the meanings of transgender identity. As she told *Time*:

> There is not just one trans story. There's not just one trans experience. And I think what they [the people of America] need to understand is that not everybody who is born feels that their gender identity is in alignment with what they're assigned at birth, based on their genitalia. If someone needs to express their gender in a way that is different, that is okay, and they should not be denied healthcare. They should not be bullied. They don't deserve to be victims of violence.[20]

She echoed this sentiment in the Canadian fashion magazine *Flare*, in which she advocated for an end to the gender binary: "I want the lives of trans people to be treated as though they have intrinsic value, and I want to see a more complicated understanding of gender. We have to move beyond this system of thinking in binary ways."[21]

Moreover, while these assertions of the dignity of trans people are fairly generic multicultural assertions, Cox never seems to let these feel-good claims about tolerance overshadow the real dangers and tragedies facing trans people. In relation to several states considering so-called bathroom bills, which criminalize trans people who use the bathrooms that align with their gender identity rather than their gender assigned at birth, Cox called out the hypocrisy of constructing transgender people as a threat when they are so vulnerable to violence. "It's a way to sort of scapegoat us," she said. "We are the ones that are really unsafe. The first eight weeks of 2015, seven trans people were murdered, almost one a week. So we're the ones whose lives are in danger. So to portray us as potential predators is unfortunate."[22] And when asked about the increasing media visibility of transgender people, Cox urged caution, turning the conversation toward the material realities of the trans experience that might get obscured by self-congratulatory media coverage. "I would say that 2014 was a watershed moment for visibility," she claimed, "but the record unemployment rates, homicide rates, and discrimination that we experience, that has not changed. So we need more of what's happening in the media in terms of visibility to affect policies and how we treat transgender folks."[23]

When speaking with an openly political magazine like *The Advocate*, moreover, Cox even addresses the complex intersections of race and transgender experience, questions often ignored in more mainstream publications. Notably, she spoke about the tendency for black communities to engage in gender policing as part of systems of racial discrimination:

> When I was perceived as a black man I became a threat to public safety. When I dressed as myself, it was my safety that was threatened. It was usually other black people who policed my gender, called me out, or made fun of me on subways, street corners, and delicatessens. I believe it is because I am also black that I became their target. These same folks would often ignore white trans and gender nonconforming folks in the same spaces, even those who passed even less than I did at the time. Systemic racism not only encourages the state and non-black individuals to police and monitor black bodies, white supremacy encourages other black folks to do so as well.[24]

Cox also spoke about the dangers to black bodies in relation to the trials of CeCe McDonald and George Zimmerman, who both used a self-defense claim when charged with the murder of unarmed black teenagers. "Certain people in certain bodies are able to claim self-defense, and other bodies aren't," Cox said. "When CeCe's trial was in the pretrial stage, the [George] Zimmerman trial was going on and [there was] all this conversation about 'stand your ground.' But 'stand your ground' is not for black people. It's not for black trans women."[25] According to the *New Yorker*, Cox has even struck up a friendship with radical black academic bell hooks,[26] and she may very well be the only Hollywood star to cite hooks's definition of "imperialist white supremacist capitalist patriarchy."[27]

Of course with Cox being an actress, these cultural critiques are often channeled by media discourse into questions of Hollywood stereotyping and media representations, much as in the other case studies discussed in the book. Cox's fame has prompted a larger discussion about how transgender people are depicted, as it did in a *Newsweek* profile on the actress, which noted,

> scripted roles for transgender actors are few and far between. More often than not they are limited to bit parts where they deliver a single sassy line, solicit someone for sex in a sordid alley, or die brutally during the opening credits of a police procedural. Cox is all too familiar with these roles, having played them before, as deeply and richly as their problematic scripts would allow.[28]

As with the media coverage of Peter Dinklage, this dearth of roles is blamed on bigoted casting agents and executives who refuse to change their attitudes about transgender identity. In the same *Newsweek* profile, Cox claimed that decision makers in the entertainment industry continue to see trans women as "fake women," keeping them from being cast in nontransspecific roles. A prominent director also reportedly once told Cox that as a trans woman, "all she could do was glamour."[29]

[handwritten margin note: Limited Roles for trans women]

In this way, while Cox remains an important trailblazer and cultural icon, her position in the industry is still fraught with challenges. In a particularly astute analysis for *Entertainment Weekly*, one reporter described the lingering stigma against transgender people as a series of compromises:

> It means Cox has made history as the first transgender actress to earn an Emmy nomination for her role on *Orange is the New Black*, but she has to play a prostitute seven times before she got there. It means she gets Christmas cards from Beyoncé and takes selfies with Jane Fonda, yet still has to compete for the few transgender roles that exist, as if she were a Hollywood outsider.[30]

Cox assures readers, however, that this is changing, particularly because of social media. "We've had years of being at the end of the bad jokes and getting our bodies sensationalized," says Cox, "but we have since learned to speak up. Transgender people in social media began standing up and saying 'This is not me and this is not acceptable.'"[31]

Cox's most famous moment of trans advocacy exemplifies this power of social media. In a 2014 interview with Cox and transgender model Carmen Carrera, Katie Couric repeatedly pressed the women to discuss the private matter of any surgeries—namely genital surgeries—they have had as part of their transition. Rather than simply deflect the question, Cox eloquently called Couric out on her complicity in objectifying transgender bodies:

> The preoccupation with transition and surgery objectifies trans people. And then we don't get to really deal with the real lived experiences. The reality of trans people's lives is that so often we are targets of violence. We experience discrimination disproportionately to the rest of the community. Our unemployment rate is twice the national average; if you are a trans person of color, that rate is four times the national average. The homicide rate is highest among trans women. If we focus on transition, we don't actually get to talk about those things.

clip

Video of the interview quickly went viral in a slew of stories condemning Couric's line of questioning. The incident became so well known that John Oliver made it the centerpiece of a segment about the media's treatment of transgender people on his show *Last Week Tonight*.

as we become more visible as we experience more violence

While Cox has worked diligently to channel her stardom toward the very real issues of discrimination that face transgender people in the United States and elsewhere, she often must do so in the face of a media culture that seeks to make her into an icon of postfeminist empowerment, a figure affirming the transformative power of fashion, makeup, and normative beauty standards. After all, as Cox has admitted, part of the reason she has become such a prominent figure for the transgender community is her appearance—like Caitlyn Jenner, she is glamorous and conforms to typical standards of feminine beauty. On magazine covers, Cox is presented using the same styles and techniques of cisgender femininity, offering her up as a figure who affirms normative ideas of feminine beauty. Her nude photo in *Allure* highlights her movie-star feminine figure, and indeed one reporter noted, "She speaks and moves with the grace of a movie star from a bygone era."[32] As such, she is becoming a frequent fixture in fashion discourse. A writer for *Marie Claire* reported on her turn as a guest judge for the reality show *Project Runway* at New York's fashion week,[33] while an article in *InStyle* gushes over her "luscious, leggy look" that suggests "elegance, flair, power."[34]

In keeping with her political commitments, Cox at times confronts the way that the media drafts her into the discourses of normative beauty standards. After being celebrated for her beauty after her appearance on *Time*'s cover, Cox pointed out:

> . . . in certain lighting, at certain angles, [I] am able to embody certain cisnormative beauty standards. . . . There are many trans folks

She happens to conform [handwritten]

[who], because of genetics and/or lack of material access, will never be able to embody those standards. More important, many trans folks don't want to embody them, and we shouldn't [have to conform] to be seen and respected as ourselves.[35]

And in response to the media furor over Caitlyn Jenner's *Vanity Fair* cover, Cox used the media attention to suggest the need for images of beauty that do not align with "cisnormative beauty standards" as hers and Jenner's do, signaling the need for more diverse images of transgender identity.[36]

But many of Cox's primary opportunities in the entertainment media have come in programs organized around the transformative power of fashion and normative feminine style, using her, like the "professors" in *RuPaul's Drag U*, as an expert on feminine performance. One of her first big breaks after her run on *I Want to Work with Diddy* was as a host and producer for VH1's *TRANSform Me*, a makeover reality TV show in which a team of *It's like queer eye* [handwritten] trans women "rescue" cis-gendered women who are not living up to their style potential. Affirming the trends analyzed by Brenda Weber in *Makeover TV* (discussed in more detail in my Introduction), the show suggests that appropriate femininity and good consumer citizenship are projects of self-discipline. Those who cannot live up to the normative identity standards of the culture must turn themselves over to experts who will guide them not only to a "better" external appearance, but to a more confident inner sense of self that can be reflected in their new sense of style.[37] For example, in episode 4 of *TRANSform Me*, Cox and trans women Jamie Clayton and Nina Poon surprise a struggling black single mother from Buffalo, New York, with

FIGURE 6.2. *Laverne Cox posing for* Allure, *April 2015 (Allure.com).*

[handwritten: literally queer eye]

a fashion intervention. Rather than simply drape her in new clothes and makeup, however, Cox has an intimate sit-down with the subject, Marlece, about being bullied and having low self-esteem. Cox's narrative affirms the power of being "fabulous" as the most appropriate response to social stigma, inviting Marlece to find a more empowered sense of self through normative beauty standards. Equipped with this new self-actualization, Marlece is depicted as better able to make a more fulfilling life for herself. *[handwritten: need to use the "other" to formows self-coaching]*

The show's use of transgender life coaches offers a quirky twist to the many makeover shows on cable television, but it also draws transgender identity into a model of tolerance and identity similar to "homonormativity." Illustrating the neoliberal mantras of constant self-improvement and flexibility as imperative to citizenship and upward mobility, *TRANSform Me* presents the transgender experience as simply another form of self-transformation organized around consumption and the postfeminist pleasures of "girly" femininity. Cox, in fact, says as much in the program, explaining that as transgender women who have worked hard to discover the women they are inside, they are "uniquely qualified" to help the show's subjects discover their inner women. Not surprisingly, the inner woman each of them discovers must find self-fulfillment by disciplining her appearance to meet normative feminine beauty standards. By extension, the program suggests that appropriate transgender identity boils down to fashion, makeup, and looking "fabulous," proffering a neoliberal model of trans women as ideal consumers. *[handwritten: it isn't addressing] [handwritten: Poor paid]*

Cox found a similar role as the host of an online video series sponsored by the cosmetics company Revlon as part of their #GoBold campaign in 2014. In the show, contestants take on challenges related to fashion, makeup, and creating their own individual brand, with a $10,000 prize on the line. Just as with *TRANSform Me*, Cox is celebrated for her abilities at self-transformation and self-branding, aligning the personal transformation of transgender identity with the kinds of competitive, neoliberal self-promotion that are part of marketing oneself on the job market or in the world of media. It is no wonder, then, that Cox was celebrated by *Seventeen* magazine for helping young readers discover "the possibility of being unabashedly who you are,"[38] but this feel-good model of self-fulfillment only barely obscures the neoliberal logics of constant self-promotion and transformation. In the process, the cultural tolerance of transgender individuals becomes tied to a narrow model of transgender citizenship based on consumption and self-branding.

Cox's stardom, therefore, is caught between divergent discourses on the place of transgender people in US culture, offering the kinds of political rhetoric that other stars with non-normative bodies shy away from. Cox expresses the need for structural and policy changes to address inequality while

FIGURE 6.3. *Laverne Cox as Sophia Burset in* Orange Is the New Black *(Lionsgate, 2013–present)*.

still being drawn into narratives about the power of individual merit and self-actualization to overcome social adversity. She gives voice to challenging political positions, but her allure in pop culture is increasingly tied to the idea that personal style and self-confidence is all trans women need to stop being victims (provided they have the "luscious, leggy look" of Laverne Cox).

These tensions manifest themselves in the role for which Cox is best known: Sophia Burset, a transgender inmate in a federal prison on *Orange Is the New Black*. Through flashbacks, we learn that before her character's transition, Burset was a New York City firefighter who had stolen the credit card information from fire victims in order to pay for her sex-reassignment surgeries. In prison, Sophia's storyline centers on her relationship with her ex-wife and son, both of whom struggle with Burset's new identity and her imprisonment. It is one of the most complex and fully formed roles for a transgender woman in popular media, depicting Burset as funny, smart, and complicated, a real person trying to make hard decisions, not a victim whose transgender identity is a result of past trauma.

Even so, the show at times sees her as an object of curiosity or as an example of the power of feminine self-confidence. The first time we meet Burset, she is topless in the bathroom getting ready for the day, an object of voyeuristic curiosity for both the audience and the main character, Piper Chapman, as she gets to know the prison's cast of characters. Like other trans women, Burset's body is offered up as a source of scrutiny and reflection on the nature of femininity—the scene asks us to contemplate whether this is the body of a woman. Moreover, Burset is a kind of de facto expert on all things feminine in the prison: she runs one of the prison's salons and helps the women with hair and makeup when they want to look nice. In one episode, she even offers a detailed lesson on the female anatomy to a group of largely cis-gendered women when a debate breaks out in the prison about the nuances of the vagina. Because of her past, she is seen as an expert on normative feminine performance, helping other women strive for feminine beauty norms, much as Cox herself did in *TRANSform Me*. Burset's self-confident and sassy persona, then, gets her through the struggles of prison life.

The show, however, also catalogs the structural challenges facing trans women in the justice system and in general. In the first season, prison cost-cutting measures deprive her of hormone treatments, prompting an exploration of the biases in the health care system and in prison bureaucracy. And in the third season, Burset is exposed again to the cultural and structural discrimination that transgender people face. In the show, Burset gets into a tiff with Mendoza, the Latina prisoner who runs the kitchen at the prison and whose son had been hanging out with Burset's son back in the city, leading Burset to become fed up and push Mendoza in the bathroom. Mendoza hits her head as a result of the shove, and a prison feud begins. Mendoza and the other Latina prisoners spread rumors that Burset still has her penis, resulting in another set of prisoners attacking Burset. When the undertrained guards (thanks to the prison's recent transition to corporate management) cannot keep her safe, prison officials punish Burset, placing her in solitary confinement rather than trying to prepare guards to handle the situation. The inhumane treatment of transgender prisoners and the profit-driven policies of the corporate world align and lead to her persecution.

That Cox rose to fame in a show willing to explore the complexities of transgender identity and discrimination should not be surprising. For all the case studies analyzed in this book, stars with non-normative bodies became prominent performers (or redefined their fame) in films or TV shows that were touted as progressive challenges to the status quo. *Orange Is the New Black* performs the same function for Cox, providing a star-making role that openly politicizes her fame and challenges the typical narratives about transgender people. For the other performers I analyze, their more political breakouts often paved the way for far more ambivalent roles, many of which simply used them as quirky sidekicks for projects of normative self-affirmation. But for Cox, this narrative is still in progress, as her insistence on political activism must be negotiated alongside her role in mainstream media as a feel-good, homonormative guide to cisgender self-improvement.

THE LIMITS OF TOLERANCE

In her illuminating study of contemporary tolerance discourse, Wendy Brown stresses the importance of separating equality from tolerance. Equality concerns the historical consequences of discrimination through policy and structural changes, but tolerance is focused instead on individual transformation, becoming yet another marketable skill or area of self-help in a world of constant self-discipline. In this way, the discourses of tolerance ironically often work to depoliticize issues of social justice rather than to effect social change, making tolerance a characteristic of "good" individual citizenship rather than a social commitment to equity. Working to publicly demonstrate one's own tolerance becomes a more important goal than addressing systematic discrimination.[39]

Currently, Laverne Cox's star persona hovers tentatively between tolerance and equality. As an activist as well as a performer, Cox has worked admirably to use her fame as a vehicle of equality, drawing attention to the stark realities of transgender existence such as high rates of victimization and suicide, especially for trans people of color. And yet US pop culture seems intent on making her an icon of tolerance, a figure who can be deployed to signify a model of inclusivity stripped of the more radical political challenges that non-normative bodies bring. The contemporary entertainment media seem more comfortable sharing feel-good viral videos of Cox giving inspirational advice to young children, or seeing her help cis-gendered women discipline themselves into conformity with postfeminist gender norms. These images might help demonstrate a sense of individual tolerance and multicultural enlightenment, but how far do they go to address the structural and political bigotry facing transgender people?

This is not to suggest that the cultural and the structural are not linked. As Isaac West analyzes in his book on transgender identity in legal discourses, a host of cultural assumptions about bodies, sexuality, and public visibility constrain the possibilities of full cultural citizenship for transgender individuals in the United States. As a result, the rights and responsibilities of transgender citizens are frequently denied, questioned, or negotiated according to the dominant cultural assumptions about gender and sexual deviance.[40] In this way, the legal and political challenges faced by transgender people are deeply tied to cultural stigmas, making nuanced and humanizing media images about transgender identity potentially important sites for the articulation of transgender citizenship. Tolerance discourses, in other words, can sometimes become an effective vehicle for projects of equality, and the powerful images of Laverne Cox as a complex, likable individual can play a part in this process.

These possibilities may be contained, however, as the popular media draw Cox and other trans women celebrities into superficial narratives about the power of self-actualization and the pleasures of feminine performance. In the eyes of the media, navigating a successful gender transition becomes a marker of individual grit and determination, an obstacle that effective citizens will overcome in their pursuit of a more fulfilling (and still externally normative) identity, rather than an obstacle that needs to be mitigated through cultural and structural changes.

The role of transgender celebrities and performers in the popular media, then, may increasingly be to punctuate narratives of self-awareness, not just for themselves but also for others with more normative identities. After all, like the other stars discussed in this book, Cox's recent roles use her to help other folks attain self-awareness. There is certainly a trace of this tendency in *Orange Is the New Black*, which centers on the struggles of Piper Chapman, an affluent white woman trying to understand herself through her harrowing prison experience. Although the show often resists this narrative by exploring the lives and complexities of its diverse ensemble cast, or by critiquing the white woman at the center of the show, at times the eccentric characters surrounding Piper serve as inspiration or as props to her own self-actualization. This trend is much more explicit in Cox's role in the 2015 "dramedy" *Grandma*, starring Lily Tomlin. Depicting a frantic day in the life of a caustic, seventy-something feminist radical trying to quickly raise some cash for her estranged granddaughter's abortion, the film explores the intergenerational tensions (and humor) of the aging and the young as the two women rekindle a relationship. Meanwhile, Tomlin's character learns to come to terms with the pain of the past. In their adventures, Cox plays a sharp-witted tattoo artist who cannot help her old friend raise cash, but does give her some fresh ink along the way. In this way, Cox serves as another eccentric decoration in a white woman's journey of personal change.

Cox seemed poised, then, to follow other stars with non-normative bodies and become an icon of inclusivity, a figure that can self-consciously demonstrate how enlightened entertainment media has become, even if their personas circumscribe a very narrow vision of non-normative subjectivity within neoliberal citizenship. Enshrining the seeming power of individuals to control their lives and their success through self-discipline, self-transformation, or self-confidence, such figures imagine a form of citizenship ostensibly free and open to all. But such citizenship is contingent upon internalizing the values of consumerism and normative gender roles as the keys to a "better" you.

For Cox and the other stars discussed in this book, however, there remain possibilities for resistance. As Richard Dyer explains in *Heavenly Bodies*, stars such as Paul Robeson and Judy Garland, while still operating within the limitations of dominant ideological systems, provide powerful images and narratives that can resist prevailing cultural assumptions about race, gender, or sexuality.[41] While media celebrities are the products of a capitalist media system that spurs consumerism and compliance with definitions of "acceptable" identities, stars and celebrities can also act as icons of social change, figures who inspire audiences and fans to reconsider their perspectives on the world. Stars like those at the core of this book can foster powerful counternarratives about who belongs, or about the struggles of those who deviate from social norms. Stars like Melissa McCarthy, Gabourey Sidibe, Peter Dinklage, Danny Trejo, Betty White, and Laverne Cox can act as emotional sites of identification that provide lines of flight from the troubling discrimination and stigma faced by so many in the United States and elsewhere. For many, these stars are vibrant beacons illuminating a range of previously unimaginable possibilities.

While respecting these possibilities, this book suggests that we should also be wary of such narratives, especially when put forward by popular media discourses that commodify the spectacle of cultural tolerance. The empowering meanings of stars with non-normative bodies can be both personally empowering and an object of neoliberal consumption. The stars in this book challenge our assumptions about a "normal" body, but they are also held up in a self-congratulatory exhibition of the culture's newfound tolerance, all while carefully managing the kinds of bodies that can warrant such tolerance. In the face of the media's often loud and melodramatic insistence that it embraces diversity, we should be constantly questioning if equality and justice remain nagging absences in our supposedly more tolerant world.

Notes

INTRODUCTION

1. Jessica Coen, "We're Offering $10,000 for Unretouched Images of Lena Dunham in *Vogue*," *Jezebel*, January 16, 2014, http://jezebel.com/were-offering-10-000-for-unretouched-images-of-lena-d-1502000514.

2. Jessica Coen, "Here Are the Unretouched Images from Lena Dunham's *Vogue* Shoot," *Jezebel*, January 17, 2014, http://jezebel.com/here-are-the-unretouched-images-from-lena-dunhams-vogu-1503336657.

3. Eliana Dockterman, "Lena Dunham Slams *Jezebel* for Publishing Her Un-Retouched *Vogue* Photos," *Time* online, February 20, 2014, http://time.com/9227/lena-dunham-on-jezebel-and-the-vogue-photos/.

4. Sami K. Martin, "Lena Dunham: 'Hollywood Has to Change, and I'm Trying,' Actress Says," *Christian Post*, March 13, 2014, http://www.christianpost.com/news/lena-dunham-hollywood-has-to-change-and-im-trying-actress-says-116112/.

5. Isha Aran, "Lena Dunham's Stint on *SNL* Was a Feminist Extravaganza," *Jezebel*, March 9, 2014, http://jezebel.com/lena-dunhams-stint-on-snl-was-a-feminist-extravaganza-1539842686.

6. Cavan Sieczkowski, "Joan Rivers Slams Lena Dunham's Weight, Says Her Message Is: 'Stay Fat. Get Diabetes,'" *Huffington Post*, March 27, 2014, http://www.huffingtonpost.com/2014/03/27/joan-rivers-lena-dunham-weight_n_5041256.html.

7. Emma Woolf, "Why 'Girls' Is Bad for Women," *Daily Beast*, March 31, 2014, http://www.thedailybeast.com/articles/2014/03/31/emma-woolf-on-losing-her-girls-virginity.html.

8. Amy Zimmerman, "The Right-Wing War on Lena Dunham," *Daily Beast*, May 27, 2015, http://www.thedailybeast.com/articles/2015/05/27/the-right-wing-war-on-lena-dunham.html.

9. This argument is deeply influenced by Robert McRuer's writings on the intersections of homonormativity and what he calls "compulsory able-bodied-ness." For McRuer, contemporary culture requires highly visible examples of mainstream cul-

ture's accommodation and tolerance of both queer and disabled bodies—such examples affirm the flexibility of homonormative, able-bodied identities in a neoliberal age. I would extend this argument to other categories of oppression: contemporary culture requires highly visible manifestations of tolerance as an individual skill in the neoliberal economy. See Robert McRuer, *Crip Theory: Cultural Signs of Queerness and Disability* (New York: New York University Press, 2006).

10. The concept of cultural citizenship looks beyond the basic legal questions of belonging—who has a legal right to live and to work in a particular community—to ask how complex questions of cultural identity inform community membership and, in turn, full participation in that community. As Nick Stevenson explains, "Cultural understandings of citizenship are concerned not only with 'formal' processes, such as who is entitled to vote and the maintenance of an active civil society, but crucially with whose cultural practices are disrespected, marginalized, stereotyped and rendered invisible" (Stevenson, *Cultural Citizenship: Cosmopolitan Questions* [Berkshire, UK: Open University Press, 2003], 23). If older conceptions of citizenship have been organized around land ownership and economic participation as requisites for the duties and obligations of citizenship, then how are those requisites different in a "symbolic" society in which cultural participation and political participation are so often intertwined? This question is especially relevant in a historical moment when the processes of globalization and multiculturalism have challenged the status of those typically at the cultural center of citizenship and privilege (ibid., 7–9). In short, questions of cultural citizenship revolve around inclusion or exclusion from shared cultural practices and how these dynamics shape ideas about entitlement, obligations, and rights in the political and legal sense. For the case studies discussed in this book, then, questions of cultural citizenship ask how certain kinds of identities and bodies can be included in our conceptions of civil society—who belongs and can demand rights?

11. A good example of this process is the dramatic change in higher education funding in the United States. For decades, state and federal governments have steadily chipped away at budgets for higher education, leaving most state colleges and universities to dramatically increase tuition with the expectation that students will seek out loans (both private and government sponsored) to cover those costs. Shifting the responsibility of funding higher education from the state to individual students (while creating a massive and profitable market for student loans), these changes increasingly restrict access to higher education for the economically disadvantaged and saddle students with more and more debt as they start their careers. This transformation has also helped promote a model of students as consumers that has university administrators investing in cushy recreation centers instead of, say, faculty salaries. For more on neoliberalism in education, see Henry Giroux, "Neoliberalism, Corporate Culture, and the Promise of Higher Education: The University as a Democratic Public Sphere," *Harvard Educational Review* 72, no. 4 (2002): 425–463.

12. Sarah Ahmed, *Strange Encounters: Embodied Others in Post-Coloniality* (New York: Routledge, 2000).

13. Elizabeth A. Povinelli, *Economies of Abandonment: Social Belonging and Endurance in Late Liberalism* (Durham, NC: Duke University Press, 2011).

14. Jennifer Wingard, *Branded Bodies, Rhetoric, and the Neoliberal Nation-State* (Lanham, MD: Lexington Books, 2013).

15. Ibid., 57.

16. Ibid., ix.

17. As this suggests, in the United States the cultural dimensions of citizenship are intertwined with tangible issues of access, inclusion, and individual rights, even if national citizenship is not literally at stake. For some groups, such as Latino/a immigrants, their place within US culture is directly tied to legal citizenship status: policies governing their citizenship are informed by white stereotypes about Latino/a identity, crime, and labor. For others within US culture, though, the cultural construction of their identities impacts not just issues of media representation but also their civic rights and ability to fully participate in the community. The cultural stigmas surrounding obesity, for instance, not only influence personal attitudes and beliefs but also lead to policies that medicalize and govern the "problem" of overweight bodies. New medical guidelines published in 2015, for example, extol doctors to treat obesity first in all overweight patients before addressing any other symptoms, insisting that patients demonstrate a commitment to weight loss before other health conditions are taken seriously ("Horrible New Medical Guidelines for Fat Patients," *Dances with Fat*, January 2015, https://danceswithfat.wordpress.com/2015/01/21/horrible-new-medical-guidelines-for-fat-patients/). Similarly, cultural assumptions about the capacity of people with disabilities to work or the accommodations necessary to foster inclusion help keep them out of gainful employment, all while government support services for this population have been gutted in recent decades. African Americans, especially those with low incomes, continue to have their right to participate in civil society curtailed thanks to cultural assumptions about blackness and poverty, which encourage, for example, disenfranchisement tactics like voter ID laws and redistricting, or law enforcement practices that disproportionately target black populations. As baby boomers age, their access to Social Security and subsidized health care is increasingly contested thanks to cultural assumptions about their drain on the economy. Likewise, for transgender individuals, cultural assumptions about sexuality and deviance are a foundational impediment to legislation that might expand transgender rights or curtail the epidemic of violence against transgender individuals.

18. Wendy Brown, *Regulating Aversion: Tolerance in the Age of Identity and Empire* (Princeton, NJ: Princeton University Press, 2006), 5.

19. Ibid., 15.

20. Brown's discussion of tolerance discourse within neoliberal politics echoes a number of other scholars who explore issues of diversity and neoliberalism. For example, Lisa Duggan's *Twilight of Equality? Neoliberalism, Cultural Politics, and the Attack on Democracy* (Boston: Beacon, 2003) explores the "stripped-down, nonredistributive form of 'equality' designed for global consumption" (xii) that emerged in the cultural politics of the 1990s. Likewise, Henry Giroux's *Against the Terror of*

Neoliberalism: Politics beyond the Age of Greed (New York: Routledge, 2008) explores the "privatization" of equality discourse—especially discourse on race—that centered discussions of equality on individualism instead of social structures or economics. And Povinelli's *Economies of Abandonment* offers a detailed discussion of the uneven cultural power of neoliberalism and what she refers to as "late liberalism," a contemporary governmental orientation that manages the "crisis of how to allow cultures a space within liberalism without rupturing the core frameworks of liberal justice" (26).

21. Toby Miller, *Cultural Citizenship: Cosmopolitanism, Consumerism and Television in a Neoliberal Age* (Philadelphia: Temple University Press, 2006).

22. Richard Dyer, *Stars* (London: British Film Institute, 1979).

23. Richard Dyer, *Heavenly Bodies: Film Stars and Society* (London: Routledge, 1986).

24. For a detailed overview of the theories on stardom and celebrity, see Graeme Turner, *Understanding Celebrity* (Los Angeles: Sage, 2004).

25. Ellis Cashmore, *Beyond Black: Celebrity and Race in Obama's America* (New York: Bloomsbury Academic, 2012).

26. Sike Alaine Dagbovie, "Star-Light, Star-Bright, Star Damn Near White: Mixed-Race Superstars," *Journal of Popular Culture* 40, no. 2 (2007): 217–237.

27. Jamie Skerski, "From Prime-Time to Daytime: The Domestication of Ellen DeGeneres," *Communication and Critical/Cultural Studies* 4, no. 4 (2007): 363–381.

28. Chris Holmlund, *Impossible Bodies: Femininity and Masculinity at the Movies* (New York: Routledge, 2001).

29. Sam Stoloff, "Normalizing Stars: Roscoe "Fatty" Arbuckle and Hollywood Consolidation," in *American Silent Film: Discovering Marginalized Voices*, ed. Gregg Bachman and Thomas J. Slater (Carbondale: Southern Illinois University Press, 2002), 148–175.

30. Ramona Curry, *Too Much of a Good Thing: Mae West as Cultural Icon* (Minneapolis: University of Minnesota Press, 1996), 28.

31. Ibid., 29.

32. Anne Helen Petersen, *Scandals of Classic Hollywood: Sex, Deviance, and Drama from the Golden Age of American Cinema* (New York: Plume, 2014), 95.

33. This massive body of research is too large to summarize or cite here, but for general overviews of such research on diversity, multiculturalism, and the media, see, for example, Clint C. Wilson II, Félix Gutiérrez, and Lena M. Chao, *Racism, Sexism, and the Media: The Rise of Class Communication in Multicultural America* (Thousand Oaks, CA: Sage, 2003) or Catherine A. Luther, Carolyn Ringer Lepre, and Naeemah Clark, *Diversity in U.S. Mass Media* (Malden, MA: Wiley-Blackwell, 2012).

34. "Gibson: 'I Am Not an Anti-Semite,'" CNN.com, August 1, 2006, http://www.cnn.com/2006/SHOWBIZ/Movies/07/31/gibson.dui/.

35. For a detailed discussion of the role of scandal in shaping star meanings, see Petersen, *Scandals of Classic Hollywood*.

36. The phenomenon of online public shaming has grown so pervasive that its

morality became a topic of public conversation surrounding the publication of Jon Ronson's *So You've Been Publicly Shamed* (New York: Penguin, 2015).

37. Eliana Dockerman, "TV's Strongest Female Characters Share One Stupid Flaw," *Time* online, October 10, 2013, http://entertainment.time.com/2013/10/10/tvs -strongest-female-characters-share-one-stupid-flaw/.

38. Rhonda Richford, "MIPTV: Kim Cattrall Talks 'Sensitive Skin,' Hollywood's Sidelining of Older Women," *Hollywood Reporter* online, April 8, 2014, http://www .hollywoodreporter.com/news/miptv-kim-cattrall-talks-sensitive-694429. See also Kyle Buchanan, "Leading Men Age, but Their Love Interests Don't," *Vulture*, April 18, 2013, http://www.vulture.com/2013/04/leading-men-age-but-their-love-interests -dont.html.

39. Molly Freeman, "Is the Bechdel Test Out of Date?" Hollywood.com, April 11, 2014, http://www.hollywood.com/news/movies/56856832/is-the-bechdel-test-out-of -date. See also Noah Berlatsky, "It's Time to Retire the Bechdel Test," *Salon*, May 9, 2014, http://www.salon.com/2014/05/09/its_time_to_retire_the_bechdel_test/.

40. Cynthia Littleton, "TV's Diversity Dilemma: A Candid Conversation with Fox Execs," *Variety*, January 15, 2014, http://variety.com/2014/tv/news/fox-meets-diver sity-dilemma-head-on-1201056056/.

41. Lily Rothman, "The Hidden Factor in Hollywood's Racial Diversity Prob- lem," *Time* online, February 13, 2014, http://time.com/7278/agencies-hollywood -racial-diversity/.

42. "Mental Disability Groups Protest 'Tropic Thunder,'" FoxNews.com, August 12, 2008, http://www.foxnews.com/story/2008/08/12/mental-disability-groups-protest -tropic-thunder/. See also Anthony Breznican, "Disability Groups vs. 'Tropic Thun- der,'" *USA Today* online, August 12, 2008, http://usatoday30.usatoday.com/life/movies /news/2008-08-11-tropic-thunder-premiere_N.htm?csp=DailyBriefing. See also "Dis- abled Group Calls for 'Tropic Thunder' Boycott," NPR.com, August 12, 2008, http:// www.npr.org/templates/story/story.php?storyId=93540773.

43. Shawn Adler, "'Tropic Thunder' Director/Star Stiller Says Disability Advo- cates' Planned Boycott Is Unwarranted," MTV.com, August 11, 2008, http://www .mtv.com/news/1592544/tropic-thunder-directorstar-ben-stiller-says-disability-advo cates-planned-boycott-is-unwarranted/.

44. Drew Magary, "What the Duck?" *GQ* online, January 2014, http://www .gq.com/entertainment/television/201401/duck-dynasty-phil-robertson; Holly Yan and Dana Ford, "'Duck Dynasty' Family Stands by Suspended Patriarch," CNN .com, December 20, 2013, http://www.cnn.com/2013/12/19/showbiz/duck-dynasty -suspension/.

45. Jose Delreal, "Bobby Jindal Hits 'Duck Dynasty' Backlash," *Politico* online, December 19, 2013, http://www.politico.com/story/2013/12/bobby-jindal-duck-dy nasty-101330.html; Cavan Sieczkowski, "Sarah Palin Defends 'Duck Dynasty' Star's Anti-Gay Comments as Free Speech," *Huffington Post*, December 19, 2013, http:// www.huffingtonpost.com/2013/12/19/sarah-palin-duck-dynasty-anti-gay-n_4472178 .html.

46. Monica Heisey, "Amy Schumer: Comedy's Viral Queen," *The Guardian* online, June 28, 2015, http://www.theguardian.com/tv-and-radio/2015/jun/28/amy-schumer-comedys-viral-queen.

47. Teo Bugbee, "The Persecution of Amy Schumer: Political Correctness and Comedy," *Daily Beast*, July 5, 2015, http://www.thedailybeast.com/articles/2015/07/05/the-persecution-of-amy-schumer-political-correctness-and-comedy.html.

48. Jonathan Chait, "How the Language Police Are Perverting Liberalism," *New York* online, January 27, 2015, http://nymag.com/daily/intelligencer/2015/01/not-a-very-pc-thing-to-say.html.

49. Greg Braxton, "On Diversity, Mindy Kaling Finds Herself Held to a Higher Standard," *Los Angeles Times* online, March 29, 2014, http://www.latimes.com/entertainment/tv/showtracker/la-et-st-mindy-project-diversity-20140329-story.html#axzz2ybZXyJrD.

50. Aaron A. Schiller, "Stephen Colbert Should Apologize," CNN.com, April 2, 2014, http://us.cnn.com/2014/04/02/opinion/schiller-colbert-report/?obWgt=articlefooter&iref=obnetwork.

51. Andrew O'Hehir, "Why We Fight about Colbert and Lena Dunham: Twitter Politics Is All We Have Left," *Salon*, March 29, 2014, http://www.salon.com/2014/03/29/colbert_gate_and_our_failed_pseudo_democracy/.

52. Karen Sternheimer, *Celebrity Culture and the American Dream: Stardom and Social Mobility* (New York: Routledge, 2011), 3.

53. P. David Marshall, *Celebrity and Power: Fame in Contemporary Culture* (Minneapolis: University of Minnesota Press, 1997).

54. Gilbert Chin and Elizabeth Culotta, "The Science of Inequality: What the Numbers Tell Us," *Science* 23 (May 2014): 818–821, available online at http://www.sciencemag.org/content/344/6186/818.

55. Jason DeParle, "Harder for Americans to Rise from Lower Rungs," *New York Times* online, January 4, 2012, http://www.nytimes.com/2012/01/05/us/harder-for-americans-to-rise-from-lower-rungs.html?pagewanted=all&_r=0.

56. David Leonhardt, "Upward Mobility Has Not Declined, Study Says," *New York Times* online, January 23, 2014, http://www.nytimes.com/2014/01/23/business/upward-mobility-has-not-declined-study-says.html.

57. While fighting for social and economic mobility has long been emphasized by liberals and Democrats, even some conservative leaders are speaking out against the scope of these inequalities. As cited in DeParle, "Harder for Americans to Rise from Lower Rungs," the former Republican senator Rick Santorum has spoken out against stifling levels of immobility in the United States, as has the *National Review* and the Republican congressman Paul Ryan.

58. Duggan's *The Twilight of Equality?* explores the cultural politics of neoliberalism in detail, demonstrating how issues of race, gender, class, and sexuality inform neoliberal regimes of individualism.

59. Jayne Raisborough, *Lifestyle Media and the Formation of the Self* (New York: Palgrave MacMillan, 2011), 7.

60. Ibid.

61. Brenda Weber, *Makeover TV: Selfhood, Citizenship, and Celebrity* (Durham, NC: Duke University Press, 2009), 5.

62. Ibid., 13.

63. Ibid., 38–39.

64. P. David Marshall, "The Promotion and Presentation of the Self: Celebrity as Marker of Presentational Media," *Celebrity Studies* 1, no. 1 (2010): 36. This article continues Marshall's foundational work in *Celebrity and Power*, which demonstrates how stars and celebrities govern acceptable forms of subjectivity in the modern world.

65. Chris Rojek, *Celebrity* (London: Reaktion Books, 2001).

66. Jo Littler, "Celebrity and Meritocracy," *Soundings* 26 (2004): 118–130.

67. Marshall, "The Promotion and Presentation of the Self," 35.

68. Ibid., 39.

69. For a more detailed definition of postfeminism, see Angela McRobbie, "Post-Feminism and Popular Culture," *Feminist Media Studies* 4, no. 3 (2004): 255–264. For a wide-ranging examination of the politics of postfeminism, see Yvonne Tasker and Diane Negra, eds., *Interrogating Postfeminism: Gender and the Politics of Popular Culture* (Durham, NC: Duke University Press, 2007).

70. For a more detailed discussion of postracial media discourse, see Catherine Squires, *The Post-Racial Mystique: Media and Race in the Twenty-First Century* (New York: New York University Press, 2014).

71. Suzanne Smythe, "The Good Mother: A Critical Discourse Analysis of Literacy Advice to Mothers in the 20th Century" (PhD diss., University of British Columbia, 2006), 23.

72. Joshua Gamson, *Claims to Fame: Celebrity in Contemporary America* (Berkeley: University of California Press, 1994).

CHAPTER 1: MELISSA MCCARTHY

Portions of this chapter previously appeared as "Class, Corpulence, and Neoliberal Citizenship: Melissa McCarthy on Saturday Night Live," *Celebrity Studies*, June 2, 2015, used by permission of Taylor & Francis Ltd., www.tandfonline.com.

1. Rex Reed, "Declined: In *Identity Thief*, Bateman's Bankable Billing Can't Lift This Flick Out of the Red," *New York Observer* online, February 5, 2013, http://observer.com/2013/02/declined-in-identity-thief-batemans-bankable-billing-cant-lift-this-flick-out-of-the-red/.

2. Joyce Chen, "Rex Reed Refuses to Apologize for Melissa McCarthy Comments," *Us Weekly* online, June 21, 2013, http://www.usmagazine.com/celebrity-news/news/rex-reed-refuses-to-apologize-for-melissa-mccarthy-comments-i-stand-by-all-of-my-original-remarks-2013216.

3. Ibid.

4. Reed, "Declined."

5. Karen Valby, "The New Queen of Comedy," *Entertainment Weekly*, November 4, 2011, 30–34.

6. Sonia Harmon, "Melissa McCarthy," *Ladies' Home Journal*, June 2011, 20.

7. Judith Newman, "Funny Girl," *Ladies' Home Journal*, May 2012, 84.

8. David Keeps, "Funny Girl," *Good Housekeeping*, December 2012, 134–147.

9. Michelle Tauber, Oliver Jones, Elizabeth Leonard, and Paul Chi, "Melissa's Magic," *People*, July 15, 2013, 78.

10. Sara Vilkomerson, "Melissa McCarthy on Hollywood Sexism: 'It's an Intense Sickness,'" *Entertainment Weekly* online, May 15, 2015, http://www.ew.com/article/2015/05/14/melissa-mccarthy-spy-sexism.

11. Margy Rochin, "You're Perfect, Melissa," *Redbook*, July 2014, 92–97.

12. June Thomas, "*Elle* Put Melissa McCarthy on Its Cover, and Then Covered Her Up," *Slate*, October 15, 2013, http://www.slate.com/blogs/xx_factor/2013/10/15/melissa_mccarthy_in_elle_the_magazine_put_the_plus_size_comedian_on_its.html.

13. Rochin, "You're Perfect, Melissa."

14. Thomas, "Elle Put Melissa McCarthy on Its Cover."

15. Natalie Boero, "All the News That's Fat to Print: The American 'Obesity Epidemic' and the Media," *Qualitative Sociology* 30, no. 1 (March 2007): 41–60.

16. Katherine Sender and Margaret Sullivan, "Epidemics of Will, Failures of Self-Esteem: Responding to Fat Bodies in *The Biggest Loser* and *What Not to Wear*," *Continuum: Journal of Media and Cultural Studies* 22, no. 4 (2008): 573–584. See also Rebecca M. Puhl et al., "Headless, Hungry, and Unhealthy: A Video Content Analysis of Obese Persons Portrayed in Online News," *Journal of Health Communication* 18, no. 6 (2013): 686–702; and Chelsea A. Heuer, Kimberly J. McClure, and Rebecca M. Puhl, "Obesity Stigma in Online News: A Visual Content Analysis," *Journal of Health Communication* 16, no. 9 (2011): 976–987.

17. Francis Ray White, "'We're Kind of Devolving': Visual Tropes of Evolution in Obesity Discourse," *Critical Public Health* 23, no. 3 (2013): 320–330.

18. Natalie Boero, *Killer Fat: Media, Medicine, and Morals in the American Obesity Epidemic* (New Brunswick, NJ: Rutgers University Press, 2012).

19. For an overview of public health policy and consumerism, see Pat Lyons, "Prescription for Harm: Diet Industry Influence, Public Health Policy, and the 'Obesity Epidemic,'" in *The Fat Studies Reader*, ed. Esther Rothblum and Sondra Solovay (New York: New York University Press, 2009), 75–87.

20. Boero, "All the News That's Fat to Print."

21. Puhl et al., "Headless, Hungry, and Unhealthy."

22. See White, "We're Kind of Devolving" for a discussion of evolution images and obesity.

23. Brenda R. Weber, "Stark Raving Fat: Celebrity, Cellulite, and the Sliding Scale of Sanity," *Feminism and Psychology* 22, no. 3 (2012): 346.

24. Kathleen LeBesco, *Revolting Bodies? The Struggle to Redefine Fat Identity* (Amherst: University of Massachusetts Press, 2003), 56.

25. Kathleen Rowe Karlyn, *The Unruly Woman: Gender and the Genres of Laughter* (Austin: University of Texas Press, 1995), 91.

26. Linda Mizejewski, *Pretty/Funny: Women Comedians and Body Politics* (Austin: University of Texas Press, 2014), 5.

27. Angela Stukator, "'It's Not Over until the Fat Lady Sings': Comedy, the Carnivalesque, and Body Politics," in *Bodies Out of Bounds: Fatness and Transgression*, ed. Jana Evans Braziel and Kathleen LeBesco (Berkeley: University of California Press, 2001), 199.

28. Ibid.

29. Anne Hole, "Performing Identity: Dawn French and the Funny Fat Female Body," *Feminist Media Studies* 3, no. 3 (2003): 315–328.

30. Michelle Dean, "Am I Doing Being a Woman Wrong?" *The Awl*, May 16, 2011, http://www.theawl.com/2011/05/bridesmaids-am-i-doing-being-a-woman-wrong.

31. This tendency to use McCarthy as the wacky catalyst for middle-class self-actualization also informs the 2016 movie *The Boss*, in which her character, a selfish and brash business mogul who loses everything thanks to an insider trading conviction, starts a new business venture with her former assistant Claire (Kristen Bell), helping Claire to leave her dead-end job and find romance along the way.

32. Stephen Gencarella Olbrys, "Disciplining the Carnivalesque: Chris Farley's Exotic Dance," *Communication and Critical/Cultural Studies* 3, no. 3 (2006): 240–259.

33. Jana Evans Braziel, "Sex and Fat Chicks: Deterritorializing the Fat Female Body," in *Bodies Out of Bounds: Fatness and Transgression*, ed. Jana Evans Braziel and Kathleen LeBesco (Berkeley: University of California Press, 2001), 231–254.

34. Jonah Weiner, Josh Eels, Julia Holmes, Gavin Edwards, Erika Berlin, Monica Herrera, Andy Greene, and Simon Vozick-Levinson, "Comedy's New Wave," *Rolling Stone*, September 15, 2011, 3–12.

35. Michelle Tauber, Oliver Jones, Elizabeth Leonard, and Paul Chi, "Melissa's Magic," *People*, July 15, 2013, 78.

36. Lori Berger, "Melissa McCarthy, Interviewed by Her Daughter, Viv, 3," *Redbook*, May 2011, 160.

37. Sonia Harmon, "Melissa McCarthy," *Ladies' Home Journal*, June 2011, 20.

38. Blaine Zuckerman, Lesley Messer, Charlotte Triggs, Oliver Jones, Monica Rizzo, Paul Chi, Vanessa Diaz, Catherine Kast, and Susan Young, "A Bridesmaid's Turn to Shine," *People*, September 19, 2011, 141.

39. Lily Rothman, "Two Funny for Words," *Time*, May 19, 2014, 60–61. See also Jennifer Garcia, Mary Green, Julie Jordan, Michelle Tauber, and Alynda Wheat, "Summer Movie Preview," *People*, May 26, 2014.

40. Keeps, "Funny Girl," 134–147.

41. Melissa McEwan, "Melissa McCarthy Deserves Better," *Shakesville*, December 6, 2011, http://www.shakesville.com/2011/12/melissa-mccarthy-deserves-better.html.

42. Quoted in Steven Gutierrez, "Mike and Molly's Weighty Controversy," *TV Guide*, November 8, 2010.

43. Newman, "Funny Girl," 84; Keeps, "Funny Girl," 134–147.

44. Michelle Tauber, Oliver Jones, Elizabeth Leonard, and Paul Chi, "Melissa's Magic," *People*, July 15, 2013, 78.

45. Valby, "The New Queen of Comedy."

46. Katty Kay and Claire Shipman, *The Confidence Code: The Science and Art of Self-Assurance—What Women Should Know* (New York: Harper Collins, 2014).

47. Kristina Monllos, "Ad of the Day: In Sequel to Viral Smash, Pantene Urges Women to Stop Apologizing," *AdWeek* online, June 18, 2014, http://www.adweek.com /news/advertising-branding/ad-day-sequel-viral-smash-pantene-urges-women-stop -apologizing-158410.

48. Jessica Valenti, "The Female 'Confidence Gap' Is a Sham," *The Guardian* on- line, April 23, 2014, http://www.theguardian.com/commentisfree/2014/apr/23/female -confidence-gap-katty-kay-claire-shipman.

49. Newman, "Funny Girl," 84. For other examples of McCarthy explaining this philosophy, see Karen Valby, "The Bridesmaid Who Steals the Movie," *Entertainment Weekly*, May 20, 2011; Mark Seliger, "Melissa McCarthy Gave the Bravest, Most Bat- shit, Most Balls-Out, and Hilarious Performance of the Year in Bridesmaids," *GQ*, August 2011, 88; and Andrew Goldman, "Melissa McCarthy Can Take a Joke," *New York Times Magazine*, October 2011, 18.

50. Weiner et al., "Comedy's New Wave."

51. Sady Doyle, "'Tammy': Melissa McCarthy Finally Gets Creative Control," *Salon*, July 2, 2014, http://www.salon.com/2014/07/02/tammy_melissa_mccarthy _finally_gets_creative_control/.

52. Ibid.

CHAPTER 2: GABOUREY SIDIBE

1. "Et cetera," *USA Today*, February 4, 2010, 10a.

2. Julie Jordan and Antoinette Y. Coulton, "Lupita Nyong'o Is PEOPLE's Most Beautiful," *People* online, April 23, 2014, http://www.people.com/people/package /article/0,,20360857_20809287,00.html.

3. The cases of Michael Brown, Eric Garner, and Trayvon Martin, among others, provide cogent examples.

4. Patricia Hill Collins, *Black Feminist Thought: Knowledge, Consciousness, and the Politics of Empowerment*, 2nd ed. (New York: Routledge, 2000).

5. Rebecca M. Puhl, Joerg Luedicke, and Chelsea A. Heuer, "The Stigmatizing Effect of Visual Media Portrayals of Obese Persons on Public Attitudes: Does Race or Gender Matter?" *Journal of Health Communication: International Perspectives* 18 (2013): 805–826.

6. Scott Stoneman, "Ending Fat-Stigma: *Precious*, Visual Culture, and Anti- Obesity in the 'Fat Movement,'" *Review of Education, Pedagogy, and Cultural Studies* 34, nos. 3–4 (2012): 200.

7. As Wray and Newitz explain in *White Trash*, the ascendance of "white trash" as a cultural category uses markers of taste (usually stereotypes about trailer parks and tacky fashion) to give a racial inflection to the overlapping of whiteness and poverty: by challenging cultural associations between whiteness and economic pros- perity, poor whites are constructed as not quite white. See Matt Wray and Annalee Newitz, eds., *White Trash: Race and Class in America* (New York: Routledge, 1997).

8. Ange-Marie Hancock, *The Politics of Disgust: The Public Identity of the Welfare Queen* (New York: New York University Press, 2004).

9. Catherine R. Squires, *The Post-Racial Mystique: Media and Race in the Twenty-First Century* (New York: New York University Press, 2014).

10. William L. Smith and Anthony L. Brown, "Beyond Post-Racial Narratives: Barack Obama and the (Re)shaping of Racial Memory in U.S. Schools and Society," *Race and Ethnicity Education* 17, no. 2 (2014): 163–164.

11. For an in-depth discussion of young black men and their aspirations concerning racial opportunity in the United States, see Jay MacLeod, *Ain't No Makin' It: Aspirations and Attainment in a Low-Income Neighborhood*, 3rd ed. (Boulder, CO: Westview, 2008).

12. Jasmine Nichole Cobb, "No We Can't! Postracialism and the Popular Appearance of a Rhetorical Fiction," *Communication Studies* 62, no. 4 (2011): 406–421. See also Smith and Brown, "Beyond Post-Racial Narratives."

13. Sarah Nilsen and Sarah E. Turner, eds., *The Colorblind Screen: Television in Post-Racial America* (New York: New York University Press, 2014).

14. Jason Rodriguez, "Color-Blind Ideology and the Cultural Appropriation of Hip-Hop," *Journal of Contemporary Ethnography* 35, no. 6 (2006): 645–668.

15. Squires, *The Post-Racial Mystique*, 6.

16. Ibid., 7.

17. Ibid., 6–7.

18. Eduardo Bonilla-Silva and Austin Ashe, "The End of Racism? Colorblind Racism and Popular Media," in *The Colorblind Screen: Television in Post-Racial America*, ed. Sarah Nilsen and Sarah E. Turner (New York: New York University Press, 2014), 57–79.

19. Stoneman, "Ending Fat-Stigma."

20. Armond White, "Pride and *Precious*," *New York Press*, November 4, 2009, http://www.nypress.com/article-20554-pride-precious.html.

21. Anthony Lane, "Making Peace," *New Yorker* online, November 9, 2009, http://www.newyorker.com/magazine/2009/11/09/making-peace.

22. David Edelstein, "When Push Comes to Shove," *New York* online, November 1, 2009, http://nymag.com/movies/reviews/61750/.

23. Jake Mooney, "The Audition that Left Them Speechless," *New York Times* online, December 9, 2007, http://www.nytimes.com/2007/12/09/nyregion/thecity/09 disp.html?pagewanted=print&_r=0.

24. Demetria Irwin, "Gabourey Sidibe Is Sweet but Not 'Precious,'" *New York Amsterdam News*, November 12–18, 2009, 18.

25. Paul Chi, "I Feel Like Cinderella," *People*, February 22, 2010, 77–78.

26. Tim Murphy, "Living the Life," *New York* online, September 25, 2009, http://nymag.com/movies/profiles/59419/.

27. Katti Gray, "Gabourey's Beautiful Gift," *Jet*, February 15, 2010, 44.

28. Jessica Winter, "Tough Over All," *O Magazine*, November 2009, 44. See also Ethan Alter, "Precious Gem," *Film Journal International* 112, no. 10 (October 2009): 12–16.

29. Dave Karger, "Oprah's New Passion," *Entertainment Weekly*, November 13, 2009, 48–51.

30. Irwin, "Gabourey Sidibe Is Sweet but Not 'Precious,'" 18.

31. Chi, "I Feel Like Cinderella."

32. Quoted in Donna Freydkin, "Chatty Gabby Sidibe Has Plenty to Talk About," *USA Today*, February 25, 2010, 6b.

33. Harriette Cole, "Making the Cover," *Ebony*, March 2010, 16.

34. Jada Yuan, "Because This Is a Town Where Gabourey Sidibe Can Be an 'It' Girl," *New York* online, December 12, 2010, http://nymag.com/news/articles/reasons toloveny/2010/70057/.

35. Quoted in Laura Brown, "Being Precious," *Harper's Bazaar*, February 2010, 168–171.

36. Freydkin, "Chatty Gabby Sidibe Has Plenty to Talk About."

37. Gabourey Sidibe, "Get Killer Confidence!" *Seventeen*, December 2011, 118.

38. Quoted in Brown, "Being Precious."

39. Chi, "I Feel Like Cinderella."

40. Murphy, "Living the Life."

41. Gray, "Gabourey's Beautiful Gift."

42. Chi, "I Feel Like Cinderella."

43. Mitzi Miller, "Gabourey Sidibe," *Essence*, March 2010, 132.

44. Regina Robertson, "Take Two," *Essence*, September 2010, 115.

45. Murphy, "Living the Life"; Irwin, "Gabourey Sidibe Is Sweet but Not 'Precious'"; Zorianna Kit, "And the Nominees Are . . . ," *Hollywood Reporter*, February 12, 2010, 6–12; "Best Actress," *Hollywood Reporter*, February 12, 2010, 9; Chi, "I Feel Like Cinderella."

46. Murphy, "Living the Life"; Brown, "Being Precious."

47. Freydkin, "Chatty Gabby Sidibe Has Plenty to Talk About."

48. Ibid.

49. Brown, "Being Precious."

50. Irwin, "Gabourey Sidibe Is Sweet but Not 'Precious.'"

51. Murphy, "Living the Life."

52. Erec Smith, "The Pragmatic Attitude in Fat Activism: Race and Rhetoric in the Fat Acceptance Movement," in *The Politics of Size: Perspectives from the Fat Acceptance Movement*, ed. Ragen Chastain (Santa Barbara, CA: ABC-CLIO, 2015), 151–162.

53. Ralina L. Joseph, "'Tyra Banks Is Fat': Reading (Post-)Racism and (Post-)Feminism in the New Millennium," *Critical Studies in Media Communication* 26, no. 3 (2009): 243.

54. See Jacqueline Bobo, *Black Women as Cultural Readers* (New York: Columbia University Press, 1995).

55. White, "Pride and *Precious*."

56. Felicia R. Lee, "To Blacks, Precious Is 'Demeaned' or 'Angelic,'" *New York Times* online, November 20, 2009, http://www.nytimes.com/2009/11/21/movies/21 precious.html?_r=0.

57. Lynn Hirschberg, "The Audacity of 'Precious,'" *New York Times Magazine* online, October 21, 2009, http://www.nytimes.com/2009/10/25/magazine/25precious-t .html?pagewanted=all.

58. Alter, "Precious Gem."

59. Mo'nique, "Gabourey Sidibe," *Interview* 39, no. 8 (October–November 2009): 90–91.

60. A. O. Scott, "Howls of a Life, Buried Deep Within," *New York Times*, November 5, 2009, http://www.nytimes.com/2009/11/06/movies/06precious.html; Claudia Puig, "'Precious' Is Painful, Poignant," *USA Today*, November 6, 2009, 3d.

61. Irwin, "Gabourey Sidibe Is Sweet but Not 'Precious.'"

62. Winter, "Tough Over All."

63. Ibid.

64. Puig, "'Precious' Is Painful, Poignant."

65. Karger, "Oprah's New Passion."

66. Clarence Waldron, "Lee Daniels: The Making of 'Precious,'" *Jet*, November 23, 2009, 24.

67. Scott, "Howls of a Life, Buried Deep Within."

68. Joyce King, "Lessons of 'Precious' Transcend Race," *USA Today*, December 18, 2009, 13a.

69. Hirschberg, "The Audacity of 'Precious.'"

70. Mo'nique, "Gabourey Sidibe."

71. Murphy, "Living the Life."

72. Kit, "And the Nominees Are . . ."

73. Chi, "I Feel Like Cinderella."

74. Karger, "Oprah's New Passion."

75. Alter, "Precious Gem."

76. Jeff Labrecque, "The Star of 'Precious' Goes Back to School with Laura Linney," *Entertainment Weekly*, December 18, 2009, 16.

77. Brown, "Being Precious."

78. Leslie Goffe, "Oscar Calling," *New African*, March 2010, 102.

79. Dave Karger, "Gabourey Sidibe," *Entertainment Weekly*, February 12, 2010, 43.

80. Murphy, "Living the Life."

81. Brown, "Being Precious."

CHAPTER 3: PETER DINKLAGE

Portions of this chapter previously appeared as "The Nonnormative Celebrity Body and the Meritocracy of the Star System: Constructing Peter Dinklage in Entertainment Journalism," *Journal of Communications Inquiry* 38, no. 3 (July 2014): 204–222, used by permission of Sage Publications.

1. Betty Adelson, *The Lives of Dwarfs: Their Journey from Public Curiosity toward Social Liberation* (New Brunswick, NJ: Rutgers University Press, 2005).

2. Emma Cueto, "Disney Special Needs Princess Petition Raises an Important Point about Inclusivity," *Bustle*, October 2014, http://www.bustle.com/articles/46573 -disney-special-needs-princess-petition-raises-an-important-point-about-inclusivity.

3. Robert F. Drake, "Welfare States and Disabled People," in *Handbook of Dis-*

ability Studies, ed. Gary L. Albrecht, Katherine D. Seelman, and Michael Bury (Thousand Oaks, CA: Sage, 2001), 412–429.

4. Marcia Rioux, "Disability, Citizenship and Rights in a Changing World," in *Disability Studies Today*, ed. Colin Barnes, Mike Oliver, and Len Barton (Cambridge, UK: Polity, 2002), 210–227.

5. Helena Hansen, Philippe Bourgois, and Ernest Drucker, "Pathologizing Poverty: New Forms of Diagnosis, Disability, and Structural Stigma under Welfare Reform," *Social Science and Medicine* 103 (February 2014): 76–83.

6. Kay Schriner, "A Disability Studies Perspective on Employment Issues and Policies for Disabled People: An International View," in *Handbook of Disability Studies*, 642–662. See also Paul Abberley, "Work, Disabled People, and European Social Theory," in *Disability Studies Today*, 120–138.

7. Rioux, "Disability, Citizenship and Rights in a Changing World."

8. Beth A. Haller, *Representing Disability in an Ableist World: Essays on Mass Media* (Louisville, KY: Avocado Press, 2010).

9. See Richard Dyer, *Stars* (London: BFI, 1979), for a discussion of stars and cultural contradictions.

10. Lisa Phillips, "Peter Dinklage," *Current Biography* 74, no. 4 (2013): 20–27.

11. Dan Kois, "Peter Dinklage Was Smart to Say No," *New York Times*, May 24, 2012.

12. Adelson, *The Lives of Dwarfs*, 358.

13. Luke Winslow, Lisa Perks, and Sharon Avital, "Limited Representation: A Homology of Discriminatory Media Portrayals of Little People and African Americans," paper presented at the National Communication Association Convention, Chicago, 2007.

14. Rosemarie Garland-Thomson, *Extraordinary Bodies: Figuring Physical Disability in American Culture and Literature* (New York: Columbia University Press, 1997), 6.

15. Betty Adelson, "Dwarfs: The Changing Lives of Archetypal 'Curiosities'—and Echoes of the Past," *Disability Studies Quarterly* 25, no. 3 (Summer 2005), http://dsq-sds.org/article/view/576/753.

16. Ian Tucker, "Up Front and on the Verge: Who? Peter Dinklage, What? Actor, They Say, 'This Guy Should Be the Next James Bond,' We Say, A Cultured Actor Whose Stature Is the Least of His Attributes," *The Observer*, March 21, 2004, 13.

17. Fiachra Gibbons, "Friday Review: 'Be Real—Call Me a Midget': At Long Last, a Film Has Dared to Portray a Dwarf as a Fully Rounded Human Being," *The Guardian*, March 19, 2004, 11.

18. Desson Howe, "Who Says Bigger Is Better? Peter Dinklage Fills a Tall Order in His New Movie," *Washington Post*, October 18, 2003, C1.

19. David Ansen, "What's the Big Deal?" *Newsweek* online, October 9, 2003, http://www.newsweek.com/whats-big-deal-138775.

20. Leslie Felperin, "Film: A Small Wonder: The Actor Dinklage and the Director Thomas McCarthy talk to Leslie Felperin," *The Independent*, March 26, 2004, Features, 11.

21. Liam Lacey, "The Little Movie that Could," *Globe and Mail*, October 9, 2003, R3.

22. Garry Maddox, "Star Turns Reveal the Secrets of Success in a Mad Mad World," *Sydney Morning Herald*, April 12, 2004, 14.

23. Fiachra Gibbons, "Fast Track to Success: Offbeat Venture Proves Film Festival Hit," *The Guardian*, September 20, 2003, 7.

24. Rick Groen, "It'll Melt your Cynical Heart," *Globe and Mail*, October 10, 2003, R3.

25. Cara Egan, "Comment and Analysis: Dwarfs Wear Black: At Just Over 4ft, Peter Dinklage Has Been Called the Sexiest Man Alive," *The Guardian*, March 25, 2004, 24.

26. Lacey, "The Little Movie that Could," R3.

27. Karen Durbin, "The New Season/Film: The Scene Stealers; Crib Sheet: Breakout Performers," *New York Times*, September 7, 2003, sec. 2, 49.

28. Dinitia Smith, "Dark, Handsome and Short: Star of a Sundance Hit Is Ready for an Encore," *New York Times*, October 2, 2003, 1E.

29. Felperin, "Film: A Small Wonder," 11.

30. See, for example, Mike Davies, "A Victory for the Little Man," *Birmingham Post*, March 23, 2004, 11.

31. Linda Barnard, "Size Doesn't Matter: Peter Dinklage Says He's Happy to Be at Vanguard of More Open-Minded Attitude to Diminutive Actors," *Toronto Star*, May 13, 2008, L6.

32. Peter Rubin, "Peter Dinklage Walks into a Bar . . . ," *GQ*, February 2004, 56.

33. Chris Norris, "Sexy Beast," *Rolling Stone*, June 9, 2011, 49.

34. Rubin, "Peter Dinklage Walks into a Bar," 58.

35. Howe, "Who Says Bigger Is Better?" C1.

36. Joyce Chen, "He's Going Ape: Dinklage Plays Orangutan Pirate in New 'Ice Age' Movie," *New York Daily News*, July 11, 2012, 39.

37. Tim Geary, "The World's Sexiest Dwarf," *Daily Telegraph*, March 19, 2004, 20.

38. Ibid.

39. Brian Hiatt, "Master of the Game," *Rolling Stone*, May 24, 2012, 44–49.

40. Rubin, "Peter Dinklage Walks into a Bar."

41. Hiatt, "Master of the Game."

42. Norris, "Sexy Beast," 48.

43. Hiatt, "Master of the Game."

44. Elizabeth Renzetti, "Like 'The Sopranos,' with Dragons: It's Riveting," *Globe and Mail*, March 31, 2012, R7.

45. Rachel Lehmann-Haupt, "The New Sexy," *Variety*, September 1, 2003, 28.

46. Roger Moore, "Why Peter Is an Agent of Change," *Daily Telegraph*, February 5, 2004, T3.

47. Gary Arnold, "Track Friendship in 'Station Agent'; Film Favorite in Sundance Debut," *Washington Times*, October 17, 2003, D1; see also Geary, "The World's Sexiest Dwarf," 20.

48. Demetrious Matheou, "Apocrypha Now," *Sunday Herald*, March 21, 2004, 13.

49. Petra Starke, "Award Winners Outside the Box," *South Australia Sunday Mail*, July 1, 2012, 15.

50. Louis Peitzman, "Is Peter Dinklage Hot?" *Buzzfeed*, March 13, 2013, http://www.buzzfeed.com/louispeitzman/is-peter-dinklage-hot.

51. Rubin, "Peter Dinklage Walks into a Bar."

52. Egan, "Comment and Analysis: Dwarfs Wear Black."

53. Paul K. Longmore, "Screening Stereotypes: Images of Disabled People in Television and Motion Pictures," in *Why I Burned My Book and Other Essays on Disability* (Philadelphia: Temple University Press, 2003). See also Sharon L. Snyder and David T. Mitchell, *Cultural Locations of Disability* (Chicago: University of Chicago Press, 2006).

54. Rachel Adams, *Sideshow U.S.A: Freaks and the American Cultural Imagination* (Chicago: University of Chicago Press, 2001).

55. Rosemarie Garland-Thomson, "The Politics of Staring: Visual Rhetorics of Disability in Popular Photography," in *Disability Studies: Enabling the Humanities*, ed. Sharon Snyder, Brenda Jo Brueggemann, and Rosemarie Garland-Thomson (New York, MLA: 2002), 56–57.

56. Dan Kennedy, "Will Little People, Big World Change Our Perceptions of Dwarfs?" *Slate*, March 24, 2006, http://www.slate.com/articles/arts/culturebox/2006/03/little_people_big_world.html.

57. Garland-Thompson, "The Politics of Staring," 63–65.

58. Lehmann-Haupt, "The New Sexy," 28. See also Emma Collins, "15 Reasons Peter Dinklage Redefines Sexy," *Hollywood Scoop*, June 6, 2014, http://www.hollyscoop.com/peter-dinklage/15-reasons-peter-dinklage-redefines-sexy.html.

59. Lehmann-Haupt, "The New Sexy," 28.

60. Hiatt, "Peter Dinklage Walks into a Bar."

61. Daniel Fierman, "Peter Dinklage," *Entertainment Weekly*, August 22–August 29, 2003, 61.

62. Rubin, "Peter Dinklage Walks into a Bar."

63. Ibid.

64. Norris, "Sexy Beast," 48.

65. Hiatt, "Master of the Game."

66. Lindy West, "Peter Dinklage: STUD," *GQ*, December 2011, 256.

67. Garland-Thomson, "The Politics of Staring," 57–58.

68. For a discussion of the visual politics of masculinity and disability, see chapter 1 on photography and disabled veterans in David Serlin, *Replaceable You: Engineering the Body in Postwar America* (Chicago: University of Chicago Press, 2004).

69. Garland-Thomson, "The Politics of Staring," 66.

70. Kom Kunyosying and Carter Soles, "Postmodern Geekdom as Simulated Ethnicity," *Jump Cut* 54 (2012), http://www.ejumpcut.org/archive/jc54.2012/Soles KunyoGeedom/.

71. Nico Lang, "How to Be a Girl in an Adam Sandler Movie," *Daily Dot*, July 27, 2015, http://www.dailydot.com/opinion/adam-sandler-pixels-sexism-michelle-monaghan/.

72. Rubin, "Peter Dinklage Walks into a Bar."

73. Marc Peyser, "Peter Dinklage," *Newsweek*, October 18, 2004, 81.

74. West, "Peter Dinklage: STUD," 256.

75. Rubin, "Peter Dinklage Walks into a Bar."

76. Hiatt, "Master of the Game."

77. Norris, "Sexy Beast."

78. Hiatt, "Master of the Game."

79. Liza Hamm, "Peter Dinklage," *People*, October 13, 2003, 117.

80. Mike Sager, "DiNK," *Esquire*, March 2014, 114–120.

81. Hiatt, "Master of the Game."

82. Ibid.

83. Angela McRobbie, "Post-Feminism and Popular Culture," *Feminist Media Studies* 4, no. 3 (2004): 255–264.

CHAPTER 4: DANNY TREJO

1. Eduardo Bonilla-Silva, "From Bi-Racial to Tri-Racial: Towards a New System of Racial Stratification in the U.S.A.," *Ethnic and Racial Studies* 27, no. 6 (2004): 931–950.

2. Scott Bowles, "The Illustrated Danny Trejo: Star's Life, and Tattoos, Are an Open Book," *USA Today*, September 3, 2010, 3d.

3. Gretchen Bakke, "Dead White Men: An Essay on the Changing Dynamics of Race in US Action Cinema," *Anthropological Quarterly* 83, no. 2 (2010): 407.

4. For a more detailed discussion of aging masculinities in action cinema, see Philippa Gates, "Acting His Age? The Resurrection of the 80s Action Heroes and Their Aging Stars," *Quarterly Review of Film and Video* 27 (2010): 276–289. See also Ellexis Boyle and Sean Brayton, "Ageing Masculinities and 'Muscle Work' in Hollywood Action Film: An Analysis of *The Expendables*," *Men and Masculinities* 15, no. 5 (2012): 468–485.

5. Tom Cohen, "Obama Administration to Stop Deporting Some Young Illegal Immigrants," CNN.com, June 16, 2012, http://www.cnn.com/2012/06/15/politics /immigration/.

6. Max Ehrenfreund, "Your Complete Guide to Obama's Immigration Executive Action," *Washington Post* online, November 20, 2014, http://www.washingtonpost .com/blogs/wonkblog/wp/2014/11/19/your-complete-guide-to-obamas-immigration -order/.

7. Jennifer Wingard, *Branded Bodies, Rhetoric, and the Neoliberal Nation State* (Lanham, MD: Lexington Books, 2013), 4–5.

8. Anna Brown, "The U.S. Hispanic Population Has Increased Sixfold since 1970," Pew Research Center, February 26, 2014, http://www.pewresearch.org/fact -tank/2014/02/26/the-u-s-hispanic-population-has-increased-sixfold-since-1970/.

9. Jens Manuel Krogstad and Mark Hugo Lopez, "Hispanic Nativity Shift," Pew Research Center, April 29, 2014, http://www.pewhispanic.org/2014/04/29/his panic-nativity-shift/.

10. "Census: Hispanics Pass Blacks as Largest U.S. Minority Group," FoxNews.

com, January 21, 2003, http://www.foxnews.com/story/2003/01/21/census-hispanics -pass-blacks-as-largest-us-minority-group/.

11. Krogstad and Lopez, "Hispanic Nativity Shift."

12. Hope Yen, "Census: White Population Will Lose Majority in U.S. by 2043," *Huffington Post*, January 12, 2012, http://www.huffingtonpost.com/2012/12/12/census -hispanics-and-black-unseat-whites-as-majority-in-united-states-population_n_228 6105.html.

13. Bonilla-Silva, "From Bi-Racial to Tri-Racial."

14. Charles Ramírez Berg, *Latino Images in Film: Stereotypes, Subversion, Resistance* (Austin: University of Texas Press, 2002); Chon A. Noriega, ed., *Chicanos and Film: Representation and Resistance* (Minneapolis: University of Minnesota Press, 1992); Clara E. Rodríguez, *Heroes, Lovers, and Others: The Story of Latinos in Hollywood* (Washington, DC: Smithsonian Books, 2004).

15. Ben Fritz, "Hollywood Takes Spanish Lessons as Latinos Stream to the Movies," *Wall Street Journal* online, August 9, 2013, http://www.wsj.com/articles/SB1 0001424127887324049504578545812929816462.

16. Anne Helen Petersen, "'Empire,' 'Jane the Virgin,' and the Nonwhite Family Melodrama," *Buzzfeed*, January 27, 2015, http://www.buzzfeed.com/annehelenpeters en/rogelio-my-brogelio#.gr3BDK1eB.

17. Mary C. Beltrán, *Latina/o Stars in U.S. Eyes: The Making and Meanings of Film and TV Stardom* (Urbana: University of Illinois Press, 2009).

18. Priscilla Peña Ovalle, *Dance and the Hollywood Latina: Race, Sex, and Stardom* (New Brunswick, NJ: Rutgers University Press, 2011).

19. For a detailed description of Trejo's early life, see Chris Nashawaty, "Acting on Convictions," *Entertainment Weekly*, April 26, 2002, 28; Amos Barshad, "Nothing Can Kill Danny Trejo," *Grantland*, October 9, 2013, http://grantland.com/features /the-life-career-machete-kills-star-danny-trejo/.

20. Bowles, "The Illustrated Danny Trejo."

21. Nashawaty, "Acting on Convictions."

22. For an overview of the exploitation film, see Randall Clark, *At a Theater or Drive-In near You: The History, Culture, and Politics of the American Exploitation Film* (New York: Garland, 1995).

23. Bowles, "The Illustrated Danny Trejo."

24. Marc Cabrera, "Guns, Sex and Bad Spanish Accents Coalesce into This Long Awaited Fiesta of Super-Razaness," *Monterey County Herald* (Monterey, CA), September 5, 2010.

25. Scott Bowles, "Overkill Just Numbs the Impact of 'Machete' and Its Pulpy Satire," *USA Today*, October 11, 2013, 2d.

26. Geoffrey MacNab, "Blunt Edges—and Not Much of a Point," *Independent Extra*, September 2, 2010, 16.

27. Dann Gire, "Outrageously Violent 'Machete' Doesn't Cut It as Genre Parody," *Chicago Daily Herald*, October 20, 2013, 22.

28. Sean P. Means, "For Rodriguez, 'Machete' Is the Franchise the Audience Built," *Salt Lake City Tribune*, October 10, 2013.

29. Bowles, "Overkill Just Numbs the Impact of 'Machete' and Its Pulpy Satire."

30. Rick Romancito, "Film Clips," *Taos News*, September 9, 2010, Z-37.

31. Susan Jeffords, *Hard Bodies: Hollywood Masculinity in the Reagan Era* (New Brunswick, NJ: Rutgers University Press, 1994).

32. Yvonne Tasker, *Spectacular Bodies: Gender, Genre, and the Action Cinema* (London: Routledge, 1993).

33. Mary C. Beltrán, "The New Hollywood Racelessness: Only the Fast, Furious, (and Multicultural) Will Survive," *Cinema Journal* 44, no. 2 (2005): 54.

34. Jay Fernandez, Borys Kit, and Gregg Kilday, "Mexploitation," *Hollywood Reporter*, August 27, 2010.

35. Matthew Odam and Charles Ealy, "Commission Must Decide if 'Machete' Qualifies for Funds," *Austin American-Statesman*, August 28, 2010, A1.

36. Sean Brayton, "Razing Arizona: Migrant Labour and the 'Mexican Avenger' of *Machete*," *International Journal of Media and Cultural Politics* 7, no. 3 (2011): 277.

37. See Matt Wray and Annalee Newitz, eds., *White Trash: Race and Class in America* (New York: Routledge, 1997).

38. Not surprisingly, Trejo has also found roles in popular television dramas wallowing in the degradation of white masculinity. He had a small role as an informant against the Mexican drug cartels in *Breaking Bad*, which followed an average, middle-aged white man as he slowly transformed into a methamphetamine kingpin in New Mexico. And he took on a recurring role on *Sons of Anarchy*, which centered on the melodrama of white motorcycle gangs in California. Both shows are part of a wave of highly acclaimed cable television dramas largely focused on white masculinity and the corruption of white male power (for example, *The Sopranos*, *Mad Men*, *Boardwalk Empire*, and *House of Cards*, to name a few). While Trejo's roles on TV did not position him as the violent antidote to the corruption of white culture, his casting certainly reflects the meanings attached to his persona: his presence helps articulate the dangers and violence of a world in which white men desperately try to cling to power.

39. Richard Dyer, *White: Essays on Race and Culture* (New York: Routledge, 1997).

40. "Celebrating Pacoima," *Daily News of Los Angeles*, December 2, 2012, A3. See also Lisa M. Sodders, "Parading through Pacoima," *Daily News of Los Angeles*, December 12, 2004, N3.

41. Susan Abram, "New Type of Graffiti Brings a Coat of Revitalization," *Daily News of Los Angeles*, June 11, 2012, A1.

42. "Danny Trejo Opening Taco Shop in L.A.," *Hollywood Reporter*, March 24, 2015.

43. Nashawaty, "Acting on Convictions," 28.

44. For a discussion of moral polarity and the action cinema's melodramatic logic, see Russell Meeuf, "Collateral Damage: Terrorism, Melodrama, and the Action Film on the Eve of 9/11," *Jump Cut* 48 (2006), http://www.ejumpcut.org/archive/jc 48.2006/CollatDamage/.

CHAPTER 5: BETTY WHITE

1. Lesley Goldberg, Philiana Ng, Stacey Wilson, and Leslie Bruce, "Don't Call It a Comeback for White," *Hollywood Reporter*, weekend edition, July 9, 2010, 10–11.

2. "Betty White Honored with 2009 Screen Actors Guild Lifetime Achievement," *Screen Actors Guild Awards*, September 15, 2009, http://www.sagawards.org /media-pr/press-releases/betty-white-honored-2009-screen-actors-guild-lifetime -achievement-award.

3. Angela McRobbie, "Post Feminism and Popular Culture," *Feminist Media Studies* 4, no. 3 (2004): 255–264. As McRobbie and other critics of postfeminist culture explain, however, this vision of gender ignores the many women for whom this vision of playful, girlish consumption is impossible thanks to stifled economic opportunities. Postfeminist pop culture focuses on the romantic and personal dramas of affluent white career women (exemplified by a television show such as *Sex and the City*) or else includes a color-blind vision of women of color removed from the socioeconomic realities of race and poverty (such as the movie *How Stella Got Her Groove Back* or the TV program *Grey's Anatomy*). Moreover, by insisting that the political work of feminism has become outdated, postfeminism willfully ignores the continuing structural inequalities facing women today, from policies maintaining the wage gap to the gutting of welfare systems to the lack of strong family leave policies in the United States. Instead, the postfeminist worldview imagines a world where individual choices (and individual consumption) can transform a woman's identity and opportunities, especially if she chooses to look pretty and find true love (typically of the heterosexual variety).

4. Suzanne Ferriss and Mallory Young, "Introduction: Chick Flicks and Chick Culture," in *Chick Flicks: Contemporary Women at the Movies*, ed. Suzanne Ferriss and Mallory Young (New York: Routledge, 2008), 4. For a more detailed examination of the politics of postfeminism, see Yvonne Tasker and Diane Negra, eds., *Interrogating Postfeminism: Gender and the Politics of Popular Culture* (Durham, NC: Duke University Press, 2007).

5. McRobbie, "Post Feminism and Popular Culture."

6. Deborah Jermyn, "Introduction—'Get a Life, Ladies. Your Old One Is Not Coming Back': Ageing, Ageism, and the Lifespan of a Female Celebrity," *Celebrity Studies* 3, no. 1 (March 2012): 2.

7. Kathleen Rowe Karlyn, *Unruly Girls, Unrepentant Mothers: Redefining Feminism on Screen* (Austin: University of Texas Press, 2011).

8. Kyle Buchanan, "Leading Men Age, but Their Love Interests Don't," *Vulture*, April 18, 2013, http://www.vulture.com/2013/04/leading-men-age-but-their-love -interests-dont.html.

9. Sharon Waxman, "Maggie Gyllenhaal on Hollywood Ageism: I Was Told 37 Is 'Too Old' for a 55-Year-Old Love Interest," *The Wrap*, May 20, 2015, http://www.the wrap.com/maggie-gyllenhaal-on-hollywood-ageism-i-was-told-37-is-too-old-for-a -55-year-old-love-interest/.

10. Peter G. Peterson, *Gray Dawn: How the Coming Age Wave Will Transform America—and the World* (New York: Crown, 1999).

11. Laurence J. Kotlikoff and Scott Burns, *The Coming Generational Storm: What You Need to Know about America's Economic Future* (Cambridge, MA: MIT Press, 2005); Laurence J. Kotlikoff and Scott Burns, *The Clash of Generations: Saving Ourselves, Our Kids, and Our Economy* (Cambridge, MA: MIT Press, 2012).

12. Robert B. Hudson, "The Transformed Political World of Older Boomers," *Journal of Gerontological Social Work* 56, no. 2 (2013): 85–89.

13. Muriel Gillick, *The Denial of Aging: Perpetual Youth, Eternal Life, and Other Dangerous Fantasies* (Cambridge, MA: Harvard University Press, 2006), 3–4.

14. Stephen Katz and Barbara Marshall, "New Sex for Old: Lifestyle, Consumerism, and the Ethics of Aging Well," *Journal of Aging Studies* 17, no. 1 (2003): 5.

15. Gillick, *The Denial of Aging*, 5–8.

16. Ibid., 3.

17. Su Holmes and Deborah Jermyn, "Here, There and Nowhere: Ageing, Gender and Celebrity Studies," in *Women, Celebrity and Cultures of Ageing: Freeze Frame*, ed. Deborah Jermyn and Su Holmes (New York: Palgrave Macmillan, 2015).

18. Hollie McKay, "Oscars 2014: Kim Novak, John Travolta Ridiculed for 'Frozen' Appearances," FoxNews.com, March 3, 2014, http://www.foxnews.com/entertainment /2014/03/03/kim-novak-trying-too-hard-to-stay-young/.

19. Philippa Gates, "Acting His Age? The Resurrection of the 80s Action Heroes and Their Aging Stars," *Quarterly Review of Film and Video* 27 (2010): 276–289.

20. Ellexis Boyle and Sean Brayton, "Ageing Masculinities and 'Muscle Work' in Hollywood Action Film: An Analysis of *The Expendables*," *Men and Masculinities* 15, no. 5 (2012): 468–485. See also Chris Holmlund's chapter on the aging Clint Eastwood in *Impossible Bodies: Femininity and Masculinity at the Movies* (New York: Routledge, 2001).

21. Sadie Wearing, "Subjects of Rejuvenation: Aging in Postfeminist Culture," in *Interrogating Postfeminism: Gender and the Politics of Popular Culture*, ed. Yvonne Tasker and Diane Negra (Durham, NC: Duke University Press, 2007), 277–310.

22. Jermyn, "Introduction," 2.

23. Deborah Jermyn, "'Glorious, Glamorous, and That Old Standby, Amorous': The Late Blossoming of Diane Keaton's Romantic Comedy Career," *Celebrity Studies* 3, no. 1 (2012): 40.

24. Ibid., 43.

25. Also see Margaret Tally, "Hollywood, Female Sexuality, and the 'Older Bird' Chick Flick," in *Chick Flicks: Contemporary Women at the Movies*, ed. Suzanne Ferriss and Mallory Young (New York: Routledge, 2008), 119–131.

26. Kathleen Rowe Karlyn, "Comedy, Melodrama, and Gender: Theorizing the Genres of Laughter," in *Screening Genders*, ed. Krin Gabbard and William Luhr (New Brunswick, NJ: Rutgers University Press, 2008), 155–167.

27. Sean Dowling, "Be Careful When Searching for Britney Spears and Betty White," MSN.com, September 29, 2015, http://www.msn.com/en-us/video/viral/be -careful-when-searching-for-britney-spears-and-betty-white-online/vi-AAeVpvN.

28. Katharina Niemeyer, "Introduction: Media and Nostalgia," in *Media and Nostalgia: Yearning for the Past, Present, and Future*, ed. Katharina Niemeyer (New York: Palgrave Macmillan, 2014), 2.

29. Anne Helen Petersen, Rachel Wilkerson Miller, Julie Gerstein, and Jessica Probus, "We Have Reached Peak Granny," *Buzzfeed*, May 29, 2015, http://www.buzz feed.com/annehelenpetersen/peak-granny#.yr4LwbpoL.

30. Jennifer Szulman, "'Golden Girls'-Inspired Underwear Make 'Granny Panties' Popular Again," *New York Daily News* online, November 25, 2015, http://www .nydailynews.com/entertainment/tv/golden-girls-inspired-granny-panties-sale-article -1.2446493.

31. Katz and Marshall, "New Sex for Old," 12.

32. Ibid., 6.

33. Rob Stein, "Advisers to FDA Recommend Agency Approve Drug to Boost Female Libido," NPR.com, June 4, 2015, http://www.npr.org/sections/health-shots /2015/06/04/411260331/advisers-to-fda-consider-controversial-drug-to-boost-female -libido.

34. Katz and Marshall, "New Sex for Old," 9–10.

CHAPTER 6: CONCLUSION

1. To situate this increase in trans bodies in popular culture within the longer history of trans identity in the United States, see Joanne Meyerowitz, *How Sex Changed: A History of Transsexuality in the United States* (Cambridge, MA: Harvard University Press, 2002).

2. John Phillips, *Transgender on Screen* (New York: Palgrave Macmillan, 2006).

3. E. Jessica Groothis, "The Look, Interrupted: How Cinema Looks at Trans Women's Bodies," *The Transadvocate*, July 20, 2015, http://www.transadvocate.com /the-look-interrupted-how-cinema-looks-at-trans-womens-bodies_n_15301.htm ?utm_content=buffer878ab&utm_medium=social&utm_source=facebook.com &utm_campaign=buffer.

4. Ibid.

5. Emily Skidmore, "Constructing the 'Good Transsexual': Christine Jorgensen, Whiteness, and Heteronormativity in the Mid-Twentieth-Century Press," *Feminist Studies* 37, no. 2 (2011): 270–300.

6. Zach Seemayer, "Drake Bell Apologizes for 'Insensitive' Caitlyn Jenner Tweets," ET online, June 5, 2015, http://www.etonline.com/news/165704_drake_bell _apologizes_for_insensitive_caitlyn_jenner_tweets/.

7. Maane Khatchatourian, "Director Peter Berg Slams Caitlyn Jenner's ESPYs Award," *Variety* online, July 16, 2015, http://variety.com/2015/film/news/peter-berg -slams-caitlyn-jenner-espys-award-1201541529/.

8. Elinor Burkett, "What Makes a Woman?" *New York Times* online, June 6, 2015, http://www.nytimes.com/2015/06/07/opinion/sunday/what-makes-a-woman .html?fb_ref=Default&_r=2.

9. Dana Beyer, "What Makes a Woman? A Trans Woman Responds to a Mid-20th Century Era Feminist," *Huffington Post*, June 8, 2015, http://www.huffingtonpost .com/dana-beyer/what-makes-a-woman-a-tran_b_7533324.html.

10. Ann Friedman, "How Do You Know You're a Woman?" *The Cut*, June 12, 2015, http://nymag.com/thecut/2015/06/how-do-you-know-youre-a-woman.html.

11. Thomas Page McBee, "Trans, but Not Like You Think," *Salon*, August 6, 2012, http://www.salon.com/2012/08/07/trans_but_not_like_you_think/.

12. Kai Cheng Thom, "Not Born This Way: On Transitioning as a Transwoman Who Has Never Felt 'Trapped in the Wrong Body,'" *XOJane*, July 9, 2015, http://www.xojane.com/issues/im-a-transwoman-who-never-felt-trapped-in-the-wrong-body?utm_source=FBPAGE&utm_medium=post&utm_campaign=Issues.

13. Bobby Noble, "'My Own Set of Keys': Meditations on Transgender, Scholarship, Belonging," *Feminist Studies* 37, no. 2 (2011): 254–269.

14. Benny LeMaster, "Discontents of Being and Becoming Fabulous on *RuPaul's Drag U*: Queer Criticism in Neoliberal Times," *Women's Studies in Communication* 38, no. 2 (2015): 167–186. See also Brenda Weber, *Makeover TV: Selfhood, Citizenship, and Celebrity* (Durham, NC: Duke University Press, 2009).

15. Lisa Duggan, "The New Homonormativity: The Sexual Politics of Neoliberalism," in *Materializing Democracy: Toward a Revitalized Cultural Politics*, ed. Russ Castronovo and Dana D. Nelson (Durham, NC: Duke University Press, 2002), 179.

16. For another discussion of the way "homonormative liberalism" has come to define citizenship and inclusion for transgender individuals in media rhetoric, especially as it intersects with race and religion, see the analysis of geography and sex-reassignment surgery in Elizabeth Bucar and Anne Enke, "Unlikely Sex Change Capitols of the World: Trinidad, United States, and Tehran, Iran, as Twin Yard Sticks of Homonormative Liberalism," *Feminist Studies* 37, no. 2 (2011): 301–328.

17. Kevin D. Williamson, "Laverne Cox Is Not a Woman," *National Review* online, May 30, 2014, http://www.nationalreview.com/379188/laverne-cox-not-woman.

18. See Katy Steinmetz, "Laverne Cox Talks to TIME about the Transgender Movement," *Time* online, May 30, 2014, http://time.com/132769/transgender-orange-is-the-new-black-laverne-cox-interview/.

19. Matthew Breen, "Laverne Cox: The Making of an Icon," *Advocate*, August/September 2014, 52–57.

20. Steinmetz, "Laverne Cox Talks to TIME."

21. Michelle Higgins, "A Woman in Full," *Flare*, Summer 2015, 73–74.

22. Tessa Berenson, "Laverne Cox Says Transgender People Need More than Just Media Visibility," *Time* online, April 25, 2015, http://time.com/3835554/laverne-cox-time-people-party-transgender/.

23. Ibid.

24. Laverne Cox, "Threat or Threatened?" *Advocate*, August 2013, 54.

25. Breen, "Laverne Cox: The Making of an Icon."

26. Rebecca Mead, "Office Hours," *New Yorker*, October 27, 2014, 21.

27. Mac McClelland, "Caged Heat," *Rolling Stone*, June 18, 2015, 42–47.

28. Hugh Ryan, "TV's Transformative Moment," *Newsweek Global*, July 17, 2013, 1.

29. Ibid.

30. Melissa Maerz, "Lady Liberated," *Entertainment Weekly*, June 19, 2015, 24–29.

31. Elio Iannacci, "A Revolutionary Moment," *Maclean's*, June 16, 2014, 64–65.

32. Maerz, "Lady Liberated."

33. "It's Show Time," *Marie Claire*, November 2014, 100.

34. Sara Vilkomerson, "GLAM SLAM," *InStyle*, November 2014, 308–311.

35. Emma Teitel, "From Bruce to Caitlyn, with Love," *Maclean's*, June 15, 2015, 10.

36. Maya Rhodan, "Laverne Cox Urges Fans to See More than Caitlyn Jenner's Outer Beauty," *Time* online, June 2, 2015, http://time.com/3904750/laverne-cox-caitlyn-jenner/.

37. Brenda Weber, *Makeover TV: Selfhood, Citizenship, and Celebrity* (Durham, NC: Duke University Press, 2009).

38. Laverne Cox, "Laverne Cox," *Seventeen*, May 2015, 97.

39. Wendy Brown, *Regulating Aversion: Tolerance in the Age of Identity and Empire* (Princeton, NJ: Princeton University Press, 2006).

40. Isaac West, *Transforming Citizenships: Transgender Articulations of the Law* (New York: New York University Press, 2013).

41. Richard Dyer, *Heavenly Bodies: Film Stars and Society* (London: Routledge, 1986).

Selected Bibliography

Abberley, Paul. "Work, Disabled People, and European Social Theory." In *Disability Studies Today*, edited by Colin Barnes, Mike Oliver, and Len Barton, 120–138. Cambridge, UK: Polity, 2002.

Adams, Rachel. *Sideshow U.S.A: Freaks and the American Cultural Imagination*. Chicago: University of Chicago Press, 2001.

Adelson, Betty. "Dwarfs: The Changing Lives of Archetypal 'Curiosities'—and Echoes of the Past." *Disability Studies Quarterly* 25, no. 3 (2005). http://dsq-sds.org/article/view/576/753.

———. *The Lives of Dwarfs: Their Journey from Public Curiosity toward Social Liberation*. New Brunswick, NJ: Rutgers University Press, 2005.

Ahmed, Sarah. *Strange Encounters: Embodied Others in Post-Coloniality*. New York: Routledge, 2000.

Bakke, Gretchen. "Dead White Men: An Essay on the Changing Dynamics of Race in US Action Cinema." *Anthropological Quarterly* 83, no. 2 (2010): 400–428.

Beltrán, Mary C. *Latina/o Stars in U.S. Eyes: The Making and Meanings of Film and TV Stardom*. Urbana: University of Illinois Press, 2009.

———. "The New Hollywood Racelessness: Only the Fast, Furious, (and Multiracial) Will Survive." *Cinema Journal* 44, no. 2 (2005): 50–67.

Bobo, Jacqueline. *Black Women as Cultural Readers*. New York: Columbia University Press, 1995.

Boero, Natalie. "All the News That's Fat to Print: The American 'Obesity Epidemic' and the Media." *Qualitative Sociology* 30, no. 1 (March 2007): 41–60.

———. *Killer Fat: Media, Medicine, and Morals in the American Obesity Epidemic*. New Brunswick, NJ: Rutgers University Press, 2012.

Bonilla-Silva, Eduardo. "From Bi-Racial to Tri-Racial: Towards a New System of Racial Stratification in the U.S.A." *Ethnic and Racial Studies* 27, no. 6 (2004): 931–950.

Bonilla-Silva, Eduardo, and Austin Ashe. "The End of Racism? Colorblind Racism and Popular Media." In *The Colorblind Screen: Television in Post-Racial America*, edited by Sarah Nilsen and Sarah E. Turner, 57–79. New York: New York University Press, 2014.

Boyle, Ellexis, and Sean Brayton. "Ageing Masculinities and 'Muscle work' in Hollywood Action Film: An Analysis of *The Expendables*." *Men and Masculinities* 15, no. 5 (2012): 468–485.

Brayton, Sean. "Razing Arizona: Migrant Labour and the 'Mexican Avenger' of *Machete*." *International Journal of Media and Cultural Politics* 7, no. 3 (2011): 275–292.

Braziel, Jana Evans. "Sex and Fat Chicks: Deterritorializing the Fat Female Body." In *Bodies Out of Bounds: Fatness and Transgression*, edited by Jana Evans Braziel and Kathleen LeBesco, 231–254. Berkeley: University of California Press, 2001.

Brown, Wendy. *Regulating Aversion: Tolerance in the Age of Identity and Empire*. Princeton, NJ: Princeton University Press, 2006.

Bucar, Elizabeth, and Anne Enke. "Unlikely Sex Change Capitols of the World: Trinidad, United States, and Tehran, Iran, as Twin Yard Sticks of Homonormative Liberalism." *Feminist Studies* 37, no. 2 (2011): 301–328.

Cashmore, Ellis. *Beyond Black: Celebrity and Race in Obama's America*. New York: Bloomsbury Academic, 2012.

Chin, Gilbert, and Elizabeth Culotta. "The Science of Inequality: What the Numbers Tell Us." *Science* 23 (May 2014): 818–821. Available online at http://www.sciencemag.org/content/344/6186/818.

Clark, Randall. *At a Theater or Drive-In near You: The History, Culture, and Politics of the American Exploitation Film*. New York: Garland, 1995.

Cobb, Jasmine Nichole. "No We Can't! Postracialism and the Popular Appearance of a Rhetorical Fiction." *Communication Studies* 62, no. 4 (2011): 406–421.

Collins, Patricia Hill. *Black Feminist Thought: Knowledge, Consciousness, and the Politics of Empowerment*. 2nd ed. New York: Routledge, 2000.

Curry, Ramona. *Too Much of a Good Thing: Mae West as Cultural Icon*. Minneapolis: University of Minnesota Press, 1996.

Dagbovie, Sike Alaine. "Star-Light, Star-Bright, Star Damn Near White: Mixed-Race Superstars." *Journal of Popular Culture* 40, no. 2 (2007): 217–237.

Drake, Robert F. "Welfare States and Disabled People." In *Handbook of Disability Studies*, edited by Gary L. Albrecht, Katherine D. Seelman, and Michael Bury, 412–429. Thousand Oaks, CA: Sage, 2001.

Duggan, Lisa. "The New Homonormativity: The Sexual Politics of Neoliberalism." In *Materializing Democracy: Toward a Revitalized Cultural Politics*, edited by Russ Castronovo and Dana D. Nelson, 175–194. Durham, NC: Duke University Press, 2002.

———. *Twilight of Equality? Neoliberalism, Cultural Politics, and the Attack on Democracy*. Boston: Beacon, 2003.

Dyer, Richard. *Heavenly Bodies: Film Stars and Society*. London: Routledge, 1986/2003.

———. *Stars*. London: British Film Institute, 1979.

———. *White: Essays on Race and Culture*. New York: Routledge, 1997.

Ferriss, Suzanne, and Mallory Young. "Introduction: Chick Flicks and Chick Culture." In *Chick Flicks: Contemporary Women at the Movies*, edited by Suzanne Ferriss and Mallory Young, 1–25. New York: Routledge, 2008.

Gamson, Joshua. *Claims to Fame: Celebrity in Contemporary America*. Berkeley: University of California Press, 1994.

Garland-Thomson, Rosemarie. *Extraordinary Bodies: Figuring Physical Disability in American Culture and Literature*. New York: Columbia University Press, 1997.

———. "The Politics of Staring: Visual Rhetorics of Disability in Popular Photography." In *Disability Studies: Enabling the Humanities*, edited by Sharon Snyder, Brenda Jo Brueggemann, and Rosemarie Garland-Thomson, 56–75. New York: MLA, 2002.

Gates, Philippa. "Acting His Age? The Resurrection of the 80s Action Heroes and Their Aging Stars." *Quarterly Review of Film and Video* 27 (2010): 276–289.

Gillick, Muriel. *The Denial of Aging: Perpetual Youth, Eternal Life, and Other Dangerous Fantasies*. Cambridge, MA: Harvard University Press, 2006.

Giroux, Henry. *Against the Terror of Neoliberalism: Politics beyond the Age of Greed*. New York: Routledge, 2008.

———. "Neoliberalism, Corporate Culture, and the Promise of Higher Education: The University as a Democratic Public Sphere." *Harvard Educational Review* 72, no. 4 (2002): 425–463.

Groothis, E. Jessica. "The Look, Interrupted: How Cinema Looks at Trans Women's Bodies." *The Transadvocate*, July 20, 2015. http://www.transadvocate.com/the-look-interrupted-how-cinema-looks-at-trans-womens-bodies_n_15301.htm?utm_content=buffer878ab&utm_medium=social&utm_source=facebook.com&utm_campaign=buffer.

Haller, Beth A. *Representing Disability in an Ableist World: Essays on Mass Media*. Louisville, KY: Avocado, 2010.

Hancock, Ange-Marie. *The Politics of Disgust: The Public Identity of the Welfare Queen*. New York: New York University Press, 2004.

Hansen, Helena, Philippe Bourgois, and Ernest Drucker. "Pathologizing Poverty: New Forms of Diagnosis, Disability, and Structural Stigma under Welfare Reform." *Social Science and Medicine* 103 (February 2014): 76–83.

Heuer, Chelsea A., Kimberly J. McClure, and Rebecca M. Puhl. "Obesity Stigma in Online News: A Visual Content Analysis." *Journal of Health Communication* 16, no. 9 (2011): 976–987.

Hole, Anne. "Performing Identity: Dawn French and the Funny Fat Female Body." *Feminist Media Studies* 3, no. 3 (2003): 315–328.

Holmes, Su, and Deborah Jermyn. "Here, There and Nowhere: Ageing, Gender and Celebrity Studies." In *Women, Celebrity and Cultures of Ageing: Freeze Frame*, edited by Deborah Jermyn and Su Holmes, 11–24. New York: Palgrave Macmillan, 2015.

Holmlund, Chris. *Impossible Bodies: Femininity and Masculinity at the Movies*. New York: Routledge, 2001.

Hudson, Robert B. "The Transformed Political World of Older Boomers." *Journal of Gerontological Social Work* 56, no. 2 (2013): 85–89.

Jeffords, Susan. *Hard Bodies: Hollywood Masculinity in the Reagan Era*. New Brunswick, NJ: Rutgers University Press, 1994.

Jermyn, Deborah. "'Glorious, Glamorous, and That Old Standby, Amorous': The

Late Blossoming of Diane Keaton's Romantic Comedy Career." *Celebrity Studies* 3, no. 1 (2012): 37–51.

———. "Introduction—'Get a Life, Ladies. Your Old One Is Not Coming Back': Ageing, Ageism, and the Lifespan of a Female Celebrity." *Celebrity Studies* 3, no. 1 (2012): 1–12.

Joseph, Ralina L. "'Tyra Banks Is Fat': Reading (Post-)Racism and (Post-)Feminism in the New Millennium." *Critical Studies in Media Communication* 26, no. 3 (2009): 237–254.

Karlyn, Kathleen Rowe. "Comedy, Melodrama, and Gender: Theorizing the Genres of Laughter." In *Screening Genders*, edited by Krin Gabbard and William Luhr, 155–167. New Brunswick, NJ: Rutgers University Press, 2008.

———. *Unruly Girls, Unrepentant Mothers: Redefining Feminism on Screen*. Austin: University of Texas Press, 2011.

———. *The Unruly Woman: Gender and the Genres of Laughter*. Austin: University of Texas Press, 1995.

Katz, Stephen, and Barbara Marshall. "New Sex for Old: Lifestyle, Consumerism, and the Ethics of Aging Well." *Journal of Aging Studies* 17, no. 1 (2003): 3–16.

Kotlikoff, Laurence J., and Scott Burns. *The Clash of Generations: Saving Ourselves, Our Kids, and Our Economy*. Cambridge, MA: MIT Press, 2014.

———. *The Coming Generational Storm: What You Need to Know about America's Economic Future*. Cambridge, MA: MIT Press, 2005.

Kunyosying, Kom, and Carter Soles. "Postmodern Geekdom as Simulated Ethnicity." *Jump Cut* 54 (2012). http://www.ejumpcut.org/archive/jc54.2012/Soles KunyoGeedom/.

LeBesco, Kathleen. *Revolting Bodies? The Struggle to Redefine Fat Identity*. Amherst: University of Massachusetts Press, 2003.

LeMaster, Benny. "Discontents of Being and Becoming Fabulous on *RuPaul's Drag U*: Queer Criticism in Neoliberal Times." *Women's Studies in Communication* 38, no. 2 (2015): 167–186.

Littler, Jo. "Celebrity and Meritocracy." *Soundings* 26 (2004): 118–130.

Longmore, Paul K. "Screening Stereotypes: Images of Disabled People in Television and Motion Pictures." Chap. 7 in *Why I Burned My Book and Other Essays on Disability*. Philadelphia: Temple University Press, 2003.

Luther, Catherine A., Carolyn Ringer Lepre, and Naeemah Clark. *Diversity in U.S. Mass Media*. Malden, MA: Wiley-Blackwell, 2012.

Lyons, Pat. "Prescription for Harm: Diet Industry Influence, Public Health Policy, and the 'Obesity Epidemic.'" In *The Fat Studies Reader*, edited by Esther Rothblum and Sondra Solovay, 75–87. New York: New York University Press, 2009.

MacLeod, Jay. *Ain't No Makin' It: Aspirations and Attainment in a Low-Income Neighborhood*. 3rd ed. Boulder, CO: Westview, 2008.

Marshall, P. David. *Celebrity and Power: Fame in Contemporary Culture*. Minneapolis: University of Minnesota Press, 1997.

———. "The Promotion and Presentation of the Self: Celebrity as Marker of Presentational Media." *Celebrity Studies* 1, no. 1 (2010): 35–48.

McRobbie, Angela. "Post-Feminism and Popular Culture." *Feminist Media Studies* 4, no. 3 (2004): 255–264.

McRuer, Robert. *Crip Theory: Cultural Signs of Queerness and Disability*. New York: New York University Press, 2006.

Meeuf, Russell. "Collateral Damage: Terrorism, Melodrama, and the Action Film on the Eve of 9/11." *Jump Cut* 48 (2006). http://www.ejumpcut.org/archive/jc48.2006 /CollatDamage/.

Meyerowitz, Joanne. *How Sex Changed: A History of Transsexuality in the United States*. Cambridge, MA: Harvard University Press, 2002.

Miller, Toby. *Cultural Citizenship: Cosmopolitanism, Consumerism and Television in a Neoliberal Age*. Philadelphia: Temple University Press, 2006.

Mizejewski, Linda. *Pretty/Funny: Women Comedians and Body Politics*. Austin: University of Texas Press, 2014.

Niemeyer, Katharina. "Introduction: Media and Nostalgia." In *Media and Nostalgia: Yearning for the Past, Present, and Future*, edited by Katharina Niemeyer, 1–23. New York: Palgrave Macmillan, 2014.

Nilsen, Sarah, and Sarah E. Turner, eds. *The Colorblind Screen: Television in Post-Racial America*. New York: New York University Press, 2014.

Noble, Bobby. "'My Own Set of Keys': Meditations on Transgender, Scholarship, Belonging." *Feminist Studies* 37, no. 2 (2011): 254–269.

Noriega, Chon A., ed. *Chicanos and Film: Representation and Resistance*. Minneapolis: University of Minnesota Press, 1992.

Olbrys, Stephen Gencarella. "Disciplining the Carnivalesque: Chris Farley's Exotic Dance." *Communication and Critical/Cultural Studies* 3, no. 3 (2006): 240–259.

Ovalle, Priscilla Peña. *Dance and the Hollywood Latina: Race, Sex, and Stardom*. New Brunswick, NJ: Rutgers University Press, 2011.

Petersen, Anne Helen. "'Empire,' 'Jane the Virgin,' and the Nonwhite Family Melodrama." *Buzzfeed*, January 27, 2015. http://www.buzzfeed.com/annehelenpetersen /rogelio-my-brogelio#.gr3BDK1eB

———. *Scandals of Classic Hollywood: Sex, Deviance, and Drama from the Golden Age of American Cinema*. New York: Plume, 2014.

Peterson, Peter G. *Gray Dawn*. New York: Crown, 1999.

Phillips, John. *Transgender on Screen*. New York: Palgrave Macmillan, 2006.

Povinelli, Elizabeth A. *Economies of Abandonment: Social Belonging and Endurance in Late Liberalism*. Durham, NC: Duke University Press, 2011.

Puhl, Rebecca M., Joerg Luedicke, and Chelsea A. Heuer. "The Stigmatizing Effect of Visual Media Portrayals of Obese Persons on Public Attitudes: Does Race or Gender Matter?" *Journal of Health Communication: International Perspectives* 18 (2013): 805–826.

Puhl, Rebecca M., Jamie Lee Peterson, Jenny A. DePierre, and Joerg Luedicke. "Headless, Hungry, and Unhealthy: A Video Content Analysis of Obese Persons Portrayed in Online News." *Journal of Health Communication* 18, no. 6 (2013): 686–702.

Raisborough, Jayne. *Lifestyle Media and the Formation of the Self*. New York: Palgrave Macmillan, 2011.

Ramírez Berg, Charles. *Latino Images in Film: Stereotypes, Subversion, Resistance.* Austin: University of Texas Press, 2002.

Rioux, Marcia. "Disability, Citizenship and Rights in a Changing World." In *Disability Studies Today*, edited by Colin Barnes, Mike Oliver, and Len Barton, 210–227. Cambridge, UK: Polity, 2002.

Rodríguez, Clara E. *Heroes, Lovers, and Others: The Story of Latinos in Hollywood.* Washington, DC: Smithsonian Books, 2004.

Rodriguez, Jason. "Color-Blind Ideology and the Cultural Appropriation of Hip-Hop." *Journal of Contemporary Ethnography* 35, no. 6 (2006): 645–668.

Rojek, Chris. *Celebrity.* London: Reaktion Books, 2001.

Ronson, Jon. *So You've Been Publicly Shamed.* New York: Penguin, 2015.

Schriner, Kay. "A Disability Studies Perspective on Employment Issues and Polices for Disabled People: An International View." In *Handbook of Disability Studies*, edited by Gary L. Albrecht, Katherine D. Seelman, and Michael Bury, 642–662. Thousand Oaks, CA: Sage 2001.

Sender, Katherine, and Margaret Sullivan. "Epidemics of Will, Failures of Self-Esteem: Responding to Fat Bodies in *The Biggest Loser* and *What Not to Wear*." *Continuum: Journal of Media and Cultural Studies* 22, no. 4 (2008): 573–584.

Serlin, David. *Replaceable You: Engineering the Body in Postwar America.* Chicago: University of Chicago Press, 2004.

Skerski, Jamie. "From Prime-Time to Daytime: The Domestication of Ellen DeGeneres." *Communication and Critical/Cultural Studies* 4, no. 4 (2007): 363–381.

Skidmore, Emily. "Constructing the 'Good Transsexual': Christine Jorgensen, Whiteness, and Heteronormativity in the Mid-Twentieth-Century Press." *Feminist Studies* 37, no. 2 (2011): 270–300.

Smith, Erec. "The Pragmatic Attitude in Fat Activism: Race and Rhetoric in the Fat Acceptance Movement." In *The Politics of Size: Perspectives from the Fat Acceptance Movement*, edited by Ragen Chastain, 151–162. Santa Barbara, CA: ABC-CLIO, 2015.

Smith, William L., and Anthony L. Brown. "Beyond Post-Racial Narratives: Barack Obama and the (Re)shaping of Racial Memory in U.S. Schools and Society." *Race and Ethnicity Education* 17, no. 2 (2014): 153–175.

Smythe, Suzanne. "The Good Mother: A Critical Discourse Analysis of Literacy Advice to Mothers in the 20th Century." PhD diss., University of British Columbia, 2006.

Snyder, Sharon L., and David T. Mitchell. *Cultural Locations of Disability.* Chicago: University of Chicago Press, 2006.

Squires, Catherine. *The Post-Racial Mystique: Media and Race in the Twenty-First Century.* New York: New York University Press, 2014.

Sternheimer, Karen. *Celebrity Culture and the American Dream: Stardom and Social Mobility.* New York: Routledge, 2011.

Stevenson, Nick. *Cultural Citizenship: Cosmopolitan Questions.* Berkshire, UK: Open University Press, 2003.

Stoloff, Sam. "Normalizing Stars: Roscoe 'Fatty' Arbuckle and Hollywood Consolidation." In *American Silent Film: Discovering Marginalized Voices*, edited by Gregg Bachman and Thomas J. Slater, 148–175. Carbondale: Southern Illinois University Press, 2002.

Stoneman, Scott. "Ending Fat-Stigma: *Precious*, Visual Culture, and Anti-Obesity in the 'Fat Movement.'" *Review of Education, Pedagogy, and Cultural Studies* 34, nos. 3–4 (2012): 197–207.

Stukator, Angela. "'It's Not Over until the Fat Lady Sings': Comedy, the Carnivalesque, and Body Politics." In *Bodies Out of Bounds: Fatness and Transgression*, edited by Jana Evans Braziel and Kathleen LeBesco, 197–213. Berkeley: University of California Press, 2001.

Tally, Margaret. "Hollywood, Female Sexuality, and the 'Older Bird' Chick Flick." In *Chick Flicks: Contemporary Women at the Movies*, edited by Suzanne Ferriss and Mallory Young, 119–131. New York: Routledge, 2008.

Tasker, Yvonne. *Spectacular Bodies: Gender, Genre, and the Action Cinema*. London: Routledge, 1993.

Tasker, Yvonne, and Diane Negra, eds. *Interrogating Postfeminism: Gender and the Politics of Popular Culture*. Durham, NC: Duke University Press, 2007.

Turner, Graeme. *Understanding Celebrity*. Los Angeles: Sage, 2004.

Wearing, Sadie. "Subjects of Rejuvenation: Aging in Postfeminist Culture." In *Interrogating Postfeminism: Gender and the Politics of Popular Culture*, edited by Yvonne Tasker and Diane Negra, 277–310. Durham, NC: Duke University Press, 2007.

Weber, Brenda R. *Makeover TV: Selfhood, Citizenship, and Celebrity*. Durham, NC: Duke University Press, 2009.

———. "Stark Raving Fat: Celebrity, Cellulite, and the Sliding Scale of Sanity." *Feminism and Psychology* 22, no. 3 (2012): 344–359.

West, Isaac. *Transforming Citizenships: Transgender Articulations of the Law*. New York: New York University Press, 2013.

White, Francis Ray. "'We're Kind of Devolving': Visual Tropes of Evolution in Obesity Discourse." *Critical Public Health* 23, no. 3 (2013): 320–330.

Wilson, Clint C. II, Félix Gutiérrez, and Lena M. Chao. *Racism, Sexism, and the Media: The Rise of Class Communication in Multicultural America*. Thousand Oaks, CA: Sage, 2003.

Wingard, Jennifer. *Branded Bodies, Rhetoric, and the Neoliberal Nation-State*. Lanham, MD: Lexington Books, 2013.

Winslow, Luke, Lisa Perks, and Sharon Avital. "Limited Representation: A Homology of Discriminatory Media Portrayals of Little People and African Americans." Paper presented at the National Communication Association Convention, Chicago, 2007.

Wray, Matt, and Annalee Newitz, eds. *White Trash: Race and Class in America*. New York: Routledge, 1997.

Index

Page numbers in italics refer to figures.